WORLD WAR III
AND THE DESTINY
OF AMERICA

WORLD WAR III

AND THE DESTINY
OF AMERICA

by
Charles R. Taylor

Sceptre Books

A Division of Royal Publishers

Nashville

Third printing

Library of Congress Cataloging in Publication Data

Taylor, Charles.
    World War III and the Destiny of America.

    1. Bible—Prophecies—World War III. I. Title.
BS649.W67T38   236   79-21069
ISBN 0-8407-5681-X

ACKNOWLEDGMENT

Dr. Lydia R. Strother, A.B., M.A., Ph.D, gave graciously of her time in reading the manuscript and in lending her suggestions. She has been a university professor in modern languages and literature. Her husband, Mr. Claude L. Strother, assisted by providing scientific information. He has worked at various government and industrial defense laboratories and was responsible for design and evaluation of advance and electronic countermeasure systems for the Atlas, Terrier, CORVUS, ARM-1, and Polaris missiles.

It was in the book *Prepare for Armageddon*, by the Strothers, that I found some of the specific scientific data utilized in this book.

CONTENTS

INTRODUCTION

Abundant documentary evidence is given in this book as to the potential fulfillment of a great many Bible prophecies, as well as for the fulfillment of details contained in two visions. Scientific, geographic, and historical data are presented that extensively clarify the description and meanings of these fulfillments.

In writing this book, I have not written as a seer nor as a prophet. I have gathered together and correlated prophecies written by God-inspired men over a period of nearly four thousand years. My entire life has been devoted to Bible study, and since 1932, that study has centered on the acquisition of an understanding of Bible prophecy—especially as it relates to this present generation which I believe is the last generation of the church age. This generation is to see the destinies of all nations brought into focus and established.

This book has also been written to clarify what I believe is "the destiny of America." It is an effort to eliminate false teachings and ideas, not by refuting them, but by presenting such a preponderance of truth as to make the acceptance of such errors and false teachings intolerable.

Only One Possible Answer

Many people have much knowledge concerning the Bible, but in the final analysis knowledge without understanding is folly (see Prov. 15:14).

In writing this book, I have chosen to use two basic translations of the Bible: the Authorized King James Version and the

New Scofield Reference Bible published by Oxford University Press in 1967. The King James Version was translated from the original Hebrew, Aramaic, and Greek languages directly into the English language by over fifty eminent scholars working at four major universities. It is not, therefore, the work of one man who could not have that amount of combined scholastic ability. The Oxford edition of the King James Version replaced some of the archaic terms used in the earlier edition. When any other version or translation has been utilized, the identity of that version or translation has been noted in the text of this book.

For verification purposes, cross-references have been used. The Bible says, "by the mouth of two or three witnesses let every word be established" (Deut. 17:6; 19:15; Matt. 18:16; 2 Cor. 13:1; 1 Tim. 5:19; Heb. 10:28; 1 John 5:7-9).

There are many references in the Bible pertaining to a great battle by fire between the superpower nations and their respective allies. This war is called a battle between "kingdoms of nations" (Isa. 13:4).

Production of the first atomic bomb brought these prophecies into focus and into the realm of possibility. Now we can understand how these prophecies can be fulfilled—in a *thermonuclear* World War III. It would be very frightening were it not for the promises of deliverance and continuation of life after "the day" of the holocaust (see Ezek. 39:8; Isa. 18:6,7).

Bible prophecies concerning the nuclear war are explained in this book. The order of events leading up to that war is described from the Bible and is shown from documented news of today. Scientific data are included to verify the full potential of the events depicted.

How to escape and what to do also is declared. Read carefully—the life you save may be your own.

May this writing be a blessing to *you*.

Charles Taylor
Pasadena, Calif.
Summer, 1979

Section I

NO ESCAPE: THE UNITED STATES AND WORLD WAR III

1

EARTH AND "THE BOMB"

Planet Earth can withstand only one all-out thermonuclear war.

When will it be?

The battle of Armageddon will see all the armies of the world gathered together against Jerusalem. But since the ultimate destruction of those armies will be by the power of the resurrected Christ when He returns to this earth (Rev. 19:11–20:4), therefore, World War III—the nuclear war, the great battle by fire described throughout the Scriptures—must come before the battle of Armageddon.

It is to be that battle which ultimately shall escalate from the present Middle East Crisis. Many Bible prophecies declare this to be fact.

Possessors of "The Bomb"

Many nations now possess the capacity to produce nuclear weapons, but only two nations, the United States (U.S.) and the Union of Soviet Socialist Republics (U.S.S.R.), possess the horrendous super bombs, missiles, missile-carrying nuclear submarines, and the strategic air forces adequate to deliver them any place on earth with such devastating effects as those described in the Bible.

Nuclear warheads now deployed on missiles by these countries have the capacity to produce holocausts of fire that can kill

Anti-Missile Defense Escalation

millions of people; and those who survive such blasts might wish they were dead, for heat destruction, plus X-ray, beta, and gamma-ray disfigurement, will be indescribably terrible.

Areas That Will Be Hit

The precise and specific targets which will be hit in the holocaust of nuclear fire are known by God alone. Each country has ICBMs aimed at exact targets at all times. Only the touch of a button stands between you and eternity at every moment.

The prophecies of the Bible do record, however, many specific areas and countries that are "marked for judgment." These areas include Russia and its satellite nations, the Arab world with special emphasis on Egypt, and "the mountains of Israel" which would include the Syrian-Lebanese mountains that were a part of Israel during the reign of King David and of Solomon (when Israel was at the height of its ancient kingdom one thousand years before the birth of Jesus). Also, in the process of that battle by fire which I refer to as "World War III," the revived Roman Empire area of Western Europe and its great overseas ally, the United States, will be greatly devastated by bombardment from without and by tyranny and insurrection from within.

The Precision of the Word of God

Over 2,500 years ago, the prophets put in writing the exact alignment of the nations at the time of the end; not the end of the world, but the end of this present age which precedes the personal return of Christ. That Second Coming will be to establish peace and righteousness on earth in place of the present chaotic wickedness and wretchedness.

It is all recorded in the Bible which now has been translated in one form or another, either by the printed page or by recording, into well over three thousand different languages so that all may know the power and love of God. The prophecies of

holocaust + loss of life by fire, WAR etc.

the Bible are exact. Hundreds of them have been fulfilled in minute detail. Some are being fulfilled *now*.

The Bomb

(October 16, 1977, *Los Angeles Times*) United Nations (UPI)— Strategic nuclear warheads in the United States and Soviet Union ready to be unleashed at the push of a button and destroy mankind now total 12,000, and "their combined explosive power is believed to be equivalent to 1.3 million Hiroshima-size bombs," a recent U.S. report on the arms race estimated.

In addition, there are about four times as many smaller tactical weapons in the arsenals of the two super-powers amounting to 50,000 more Hiroshima atom bombs. . . .

The arms race costs about $350 billion annually at present prices. . . .

"Since World War II," the report said, "direct costs of the arms race have exceeded $6 trillion."

Russia and the Arabs

Isaiah and Ezekiel proclaimed in ancient times that "in the latter days," the Soviet Union would be "the stay of (supplier of)" the Arabs and the "guard unto" the Arab nations. Are these prophecies coming to pass? Here is documentary evidence that God's Word is being exactly fulfilled:

(May 29, 1978, *U.S. News & World Report*) Richard M. Nixon's May, 1972, talks with Soviet leaders in Moscow set the stage for detente—a policy aimed at avoiding military conflict between the superpowers. Americans thought detente also meant neither nation would try to take advantage of the other in troubled parts of the world.

What the record shows:

1972. Soviets sent 55 million dollars in arms to Africa, 970 million to the Mideast. Egypt was the major recipient.

1973. Arms worth 2.655 billion dollars were consigned by Russia to the Mideast to replace Arab losses in the 1973 war with Israel. Syria received much of this aid.

1974. U.S.S.R. arms shipments to Africa went up to 235 million dollars while aid to Mideast dropped to 1.785 billion. Contracts were signed for a billion in sales to Libya.

1975. Africa received 600 million dollars worth of arms. Soviet shipments to Arab nations—850 million dollars.

1976. Soviet arms shipments to Africa—1.07 billion. Mideast—830 million. Also signed: a billion dollar arms agreement with Iraq to include MiG-21s and 23s. Libya received jet fighters and bombers.

1977–78. The Soviets poured an estimated billion dollars worth of arms into Ethiopia.

In addition, Moscow since 1972 has paid all expenses of thousands of African and Arab pilots, gunners and technicians that were trained in the Soviet Union.

Yes, I would say that the Soviets have been and are the suppliers of the Arab nations "in the latter days."

Egypt's Destiny

Bible prophecy warns Egypt of ties with Russia. Isaiah 19:13,14 state: ". . . they have also seduced Egypt, even they that are the stay of the tribes thereof. . . . they have caused Egypt to err."

Egypt will see terrible defeat in the coming conflict. Daniel 11:42 proclaims: "He [the antichrist king of the Tribulation period] shall stretch forth his hand upon the countries: and the land of Egypt shall not escape."

Isaiah 19:20 specifies: ". . . they shall cry unto the LORD because of the oppressors. . . ."

Salvation for Egypt

Judgment is coming on Egypt, for this is a specific Bible prophecy. More detail on this will be given in later chapters. However, I must state here that Egypt's fall is not to be fatal nor forever. Two Bible promises to Egypt need to be explained at this point to illustrate more completely God's mercy and grace.

When Egypt strikes Israel in the attack that will trigger World War III, because of the fear that Russia's intervention will help the Arabs win the war, the military might of Western Europe under a new military king (the Antichrist) and also the strategic power of the United States will be brought into action to defend Israel. Furthermore, God's power will be felt, for it is written in Isaiah 19:16,17: "In that day shall Egypt be like unto women: and it shall be afraid and fear because of the shaking of the hand of the Lord of hosts, which He shaketh over it. And the land of Judah shall be a terror unto Egypt. . . ."

Isaiah goes on to prophesy that the people of Egypt, coming under the cruel dominion of the antichrist king, shall "cry unto the Lord because of the oppressors" (v. 20) and shall erect an altar to the Lord in the midst of the land. The Bible promise is that ". . . he shall send them a saviour, and a great one, and he shall deliver them" (v. 20). This will have its fulfillment when Jesus returns as Messiah-Saviour and King of kings at the end of the seven-year Tribulation period. The people of Egypt will acknowledge Him as Lord and Redeemer, and God will honor them, for it is prophesied in Isaiah 19:25: ". . . Blessed be Egypt, my people, and Assyria the work of my hands, and Israel mine inheritance."

Egypt *will* be redeemed, but not until after having endured severe judgment for having started the horrendous World War III.

Note

A proper guideline for the study of Bible prophecy is needed to avoid half-truths and misconceptions. Although there are some very sound books on Bible prophecy available, unfortunately, there are also multitudes of false proclamations which have been printed.

"A text, without the context, becomes a pretext." When

isolated statements are used—or misused when isolated—it is then that false doctrines and/or teachings come forth. There is neither error nor contradiction in the original text of the inspired Word of God, the Bible. Just as in the field of mathematics, where it has been stated, "Figures don't lie, but liars figure," the same is true in relation to the study of Bible prophecy. The Scriptures change not, but false interpreters can change the wording to cause it to seem to mean that which it was never intended to portray. Foreseeing this, God set forth a divine directive for the proper use of His Word. Both in the Levitical law, often referred to as the Law of Moses, and also in the pattern for New Testament church procedure, God has directed: ". . . In the mouth of two or three witnesses shall every word be established" (Deut. 19:15; Matt. 18:16; and 2 Cor. 13:1).

In the light of these admonitions let us examine the Bible prophecy portions with the explanatory context materials included, compare these portions with parallel Bible prophecy texts, and arrive at the clarified truth of the prophetic patterns which are set forth in the eternal Word of the eternal God.

Reliability of Bible Truths

Inasmuch as it is written that God cannot lie (Num. 23:19; Heb. 6:18) and that His Word abideth forever (1 Pet. 1:25; Matt. 5:18), we can rely fully upon the unchangeable Word of the living God. It can and will, therefore, when thus properly utilized, proclaim and prophesy that which is the truth.

This is the reason that I have compiled so extensive a combination and coordination of Bible prophecies.

2

BIBLE RECORDED PROPHECIES ABOUT WORLD WAR III

"Open thy doors, O Lebanon, that the fire may devour thy cedars." Thus reads the first verse of the eleventh chapter of Zechariah. The balance of that chapter is a proclamation of judgments against the false leaders (shepherds) of Israel, and also gives God's promise of protection of, and of His special provision for, "the flock of the slaughter" (the faithful ones of the end-time).

Isaiah

Isaiah, writing almost two hundred years before Zechariah (approx. 800 B.C.), described the end-time events in these words:

> The noise of a multitude in the mountains, like as of a great people; a tumultuous noise of the kingdoms of nations gathered together: the LORD of hosts mustereth the host of the battle. They come from a far country . . . even the LORD, and the weapons of his indignation, to destroy the whole land (Isa. 13:4,5).

The portrayal is of many kingdoms and nations being brought together for a great battle in the Israeli and Lebanese mountains (the mountains of Lebanon were a part of Israel in the golden era of the great kings of Israel over one thousand years before the birth of Jesus of Nazareth). Note, especially, that the "host" is referred to as coming "from a far country," and that it is a gathering of "the kingdoms of nations" rather than of all nations. Also, they are mustered unto the mountains of Israel—not to the valley of Megiddo.

These things being so, the battle which is referred to in this instance, therefore, is not, and cannot be, the battle of Armageddon. Alignments of nations headed up under the superpower "kingdoms of nations" are to clash in the great battle by fire portrayed here.

> And they shall be afraid: pangs and sorrows shall take hold of them . . . they shall be amazed one at another; their faces shall be as flames (Isa. 13:8).

As to the Lord's hand in the battle, it has been proclaimed as a specific type of battle to take place at a specific location. Note also:

> Howl ye; for the day of the LORD is at hand; it shall come as a destruction from the Almighty (Isa. 13:6).

This particular battle is portrayed as being a form of judgment upon specific nations. Documentations in this book will identify those nations.

Joel

The Hebrew prophet Joel, a contemporary of Isaiah, also wrote of this same specific judgment:

> Alas for the day! for the day of the LORD is at hand, and as a destruction from the Almighty shall it come (Joel 1:15).

This prophet also was given to see the future time when God would bring a judgment involving a "battle by fire."

Joel 1:19 describes the beginning of the "time of Jacob's

trouble" referred to by Jeremiah and described in Daniel 12:1 as
". . . a time of trouble, such as never was since there was a
nation even to that same time" as follows:

> O LORD, to thee will I cry: for the fire bath devoured the pastures
> of the wilderness, and the flame hath burned all the trees of the field.
> The beasts of the field cry also unto thee: for the rivers of water are
> dried up, and the fire hath devoured the pastures of the wilderness
> (Joel 1:19,20).

The Time of Trouble—
Starting with "A Day of Judgment"

The second chapter of Joel opens with the established
manner of the use of a trumpet to call attention to a special
proclamation:

> Blow ye the trumpet in Zion, and sound an alarm in my holy
> mountain (Joel 2:1).

This is to be a special proclamation in the holy Mount Zion in
Jerusalem pertaining to a matter concerning the entire nation
of Israel. Note the proclamation:

> Let all the inhabitants of the land tremble; for the day of the LORD
> cometh . . . (Joel 2:1).

Definition of "The Day of the Lord"

"The Day of The Lord," when used in this context, refers to
the day wherein God shall begin to deal specifically with "the
inhabitants of the land" of Israel. It is the beginning of the
seventieth prophetic "week" of years referred to in Daniel 9;
and as to the nations, it is the beginning of the Tribulation
period—a span of nearly seven years at the close of the age of
grace wherein God will pour out His wrath upon the people of
the nations of the world for their rejection of Himself and of His

22

Son, Jesus Christ. It will be a time of great tribulation, of fearful judgments, and of woe.

Jesus, when He was upon the earth, declared:

> For then shall be great tribulation such as was not since the beginning of the world to this time, no, nor ever shall be. And except those days should be shortened, there shall no flesh be saved: but for the elect's sake those days shall be shortened (Matt. 24:21,22).

The specific order of events of the entire "day of the Lord" will be given in the closing chapters of this book. May it suffice to state here that the reference is to a total period of approximately seven years of duration, and that the beginning day of God's severe judgments often is referred to as "The Day" or as "A Day." We do have, therefore, a perfect harmony in the continuity of the prophecy of Joel.

"The Day of the Lord Is at Hand"

As recorded in Joel 1:15, Joel had declared: ". . . the day of the LORD is at hand, and as a destruction from the Almighty shall it come." He continues his prophecy as follows:

> . . . for the day of the LORD cometh, for it is nigh at hand, A day of darkness and of gloominess, a day of clouds and of thick darkness, as the morning spread upon the mountains [As the light of the morning is seen first upon the mountaintop and gradually spreads on down unto the valley below: so is this "day" likened unto the beginning of "the day of the Lord."]; a great people and a strong; there hath not been ever the like, neither shall be any more after it, even to the years of many generations [The immensity of the destructive elements of the battle about to be described is noted, for it will be "many generations" before there can again be such "a great people and a strong" upon the face of the earth.].
>
> A fire devoureth before them, and behind them a flame burneth [In nuclear warfare, as described in more detail in the next chapter pertaining unto scientific data, many die from the initial flash-blast

and many more die from the fires that are created thereby; therefore "fire devoureth before . . . and after"]; the land is as the garden of Eden before them, and behind them a desolate wilderness; yea, and nothing shall escape them (Joel 2:1–3).

How specifically true this is known to be in this present age of nuclear warfare capability. Bible prophecy is precise, it is recorded in advance and unalterable, and it is true.

Horses in the Nuclear Age

The appearance of them is as the appearance of horses; and as horsemen, so shall they run (Joel 2:4).

This reference is not as foolish as it might sound on the surface. And it has a verifying cross-reference in Ezekiel 38, wherein it is prophesied that "the chief prince of Meshech and Tubal" (Moscow and Tobolsk—Russia and Siberia, the U.S.S.R.) shall come against Israel ". . . in the latter years." Ezekiel also foresaw air power, though he lived in the days of chariot-fighting, for he wrote in Ezekiel 38:9 "Thou shalt ascend and come like . . . a cloud to cover the land"; then he declared:

And thou shalt come from thy place out of the north parts, thou, and many people with thee, all of them riding upon horses, a great . . . and a mighty army (Ezek. 38:15).

Stalin's Horses

"The Russian Bear Prowls Forth To His Doom" was the title of the article by Dr. Louis S. Bauman (then Pastor of the First Brethren Church of Washington, D.C.), which appeared on page eleven of the August, 1950, *The King's Business* magazine.

Who is it that owns a full one half of all the horseflesh on the face of the earth today? Russia! The agents of Stalin, before World War II, scoured the earth for all the horses fit for battle, bought them, and sent them to Russia. Other nations may put their trust in gasoline for mobile purposes if they wish to, but the wily old northern bear scents the possibility of bombs breaking up the oil fields of the earth to such an extent that the great gas-propelled war machines will be stalled in their tracks—out of gas! If that day comes, the nation that has the horses will rule the earth—so reason the Communist chieftans.

Horses still are the fastest and surest means of transport of men, light and heavy artillery, field equipment, etc. over mountainous terrain. In spite of the vast number of Russian tanks, land transport over the Caucasus Mountains to the mountains of Lebanon could be, and very well may be, greatly expedited by the use of horses; and in the event, as suggested by Dr. Bauman, that the Russians decide to go that way (and Bible prophecy indicates that they will), horse cavalry could be vital. And Russia has the horses!

Joel's Portrayal of Missiles and Rockets

Continuing in the words of the prophet Joel, who lived over eight hundred years before Christ, note his God-inspired description of what could only portray missiles, jets, etc.:

Like the noise of chariots on the tops of the mountains shall they leap, like the noise of a flame of fire that devoureth the stubble . . . (Joel 2:5).

Like the noise of a flame that devours stubble, such as a prairie fire's roar: what a description! How else but by divine inspiration could Joel know how to write such a deliberate statement so many years prior to the existence of combustion and jet motors? Likewise, how else but by divine inspiration could he foresee to write the following?

Before their face the peoples shall be much pained: all faces shall gather blackness (Joel 2:6).

25

Pain and blackness can denote much fear, or terror; but the Hebrew word used here in the original is not *phobos*, denoting fear, or terror; but it is *parur* which is a word denoting blackness caused by flame.

Israel Shall "Cry Unto the Lord"

The chronology of Joel's end–time prophecy actually starts with Joel 1:13, which portrays the people of Israel as being back in the Promised Land of Palestine, but not having the Temple wherein they can offer their sacrifices and burnt offerings. Note the wording of that preliminary verse:

> Gird yourselves, and lament, ye priests; howl, ye ministers of the altar; come, lie all night in sackcloth, ye ministers of my God. [Orthodox Jews have returned today from over one hundred different nations of the world. They look forward to the reestablishment of the altar sacrifices in Jerusalem. Although they are a minority among all the people who have migrated back to Israel, they are a very real God-fearing remnant therein.]; for the meat offering and the drink offering is withholden from the house of your God (Joel 1:13).

The Jewish people of Israel today have synagogues but do not have a tabernacle or temple. Consequently they cannot offer the temple sacrifices, and we have a precise fulfillment of Joel's declaration: "the meat offering and the drink offering is withholden from the house of your God."

In like manner, we see the fulfillment of the next verse:

> Sanctify ye a fast, call a solemn assembly, gather the elders and all the inhabitants of the land into the house of the LORD, your God, and cry unto the LORD (Joel 1:14).

Deliverance Promised

Ultimately, Israel will have full deliverance, but it will not come until after the wicked ones and the wicked ways are

26

purged out of her. The promise of that deliverance is found throughout the Scriptures, and in Joel's prophecy it reads:

> So shall ye know that I am the LORD your God dwelling in Zion, my holy mountain: then shall Jerusalem be holy, and there shall no strangers pass through her any more (Joel 3:17).

Judgment to Come Before Deliverance

As previously stated in this writing, Joel declares the judgment to come:

> Alas for the day! for the day of the LORD is at hand, and as a destruction from the Almighty shall it come (Joel 1:15).

Many Inhabitants of the Earth to Be Burned

Israel is the focal point of the coming judgments in that it will be the trigger of the coming "battle by fire" referred to herein as World War III. Israel is in the center of all Bible prophecy. It shall go through its "time of Jacob's trouble," but the whole world will face severe judgment. Note the words of the prophet Isaiah:

> The earth mourneth and fadeth away, the world languisheth and fadeth away, the haughty people of the earth do languish. The earth also is defiled under the inhabitants thereof; because they have transgressed the laws, changed the ordinance, broken the everlasting covenant.
> Therefore hath the curse devoured the earth, and they that dwell therein are desolate: therefore the inhabitants of the earth are burned, and few men left (Isa. 24:4-6).

"The Lord, and the Weapons of His Indignation"

Isaiah 13 is a great key to the manner of the battle to be fought.

The first sixteen verses of that chapter look unto "the time of the end" wherein God speaks of the "burden of Babylon." The conquest of ancient Babylon by the Medes is foretold in verses 17 to 22; but the first portion of this chapter looks far beyond to this present age and time as the context shows. Babylon was a city on the plains of Shinar. The prophecy of the first portion of this chapter has to do with many nations. Note the truth of this as we consider the following verses from Isaiah 13:

> And I will punish the world for their evil . . . and I will cause the arrogancy of the proud to cease, and will lay low the haughtiness of the terrible (Isa. 13:11).

> They come from a far country, from the end of heaven, even the LORD, and the weapons of his indignation . . . (Isa. 13:5).

> The noise of a multitude in the mountains . . . a tumultuous noise of the kingdoms of nations gathered together. The LORD of hosts mustereth the host of the battle (Isa. 13:4).

That the gathering is unto a great battle, there is no question. Likewise, note that it is "the Lord of hosts" that "mustereth" (calls together) "the host."

Specific cross-references in regard to this same battle are recorded in many places.

> . . . it shall be in the latter days, and I will bring thee against my land . . . (Ezek. 38:16).

Such statements have to do with the "gathering" of "the kingdoms of nations," which would indicate alignment of nations under the leadership of those known today as "superpowers." It is notable also that they are to come "from the end of heaven"—or rather, in language of today, from the opposite sides of the earth.

That it is the Lord who causes it all to come to pass also is verified. For example, Ezekiel 38 begins:

> Thus saith the LORD God . . .

"The Weapons of His Indignation" — Other Nations!

The Bible gives us a specific example of the fact that the use of the terminology, "the weapons of his indignation," has been utilized to mean the setting of one power against another national power in judgment, or "indignation."

Jeremiah, another prophet of the Lord God, proclaimed:

> I have laid a snare for thee, and thou art also taken, O Babylon, and thou wast not aware: thou art found, and also caught, because thou hast striven against the LORD.
>
> The LORD hath opened his armory, and hath brought forth the weapons of his indignation: for this is the work of the LORD GOD of hosts in the land of the Chaldeans [Babylonians] (Jer. 50:24, 25).

Illustration: Babylon Conquered by the Medes

The identity of the "weapon" chosen in this instance is given as follows:

> Make bright the arrows; gather the shields: The LORD hath raised up the spirit of the kings of the Medes: for his device is against Babylon, to destroy it, because it is the vengeance of the LORD (Jer. 51:11).

Historical records show that Babylon was conquered by the Medes in 539 B.C. This takes on even added significance when it is noted that Jeremiah began his public ministry in the thirteenth year of King Josiah in Jerusalem, which would place that date at 626 B.C. That is almost one hundred years before the conquest of Babylon!

Biblically and historically, the prophet Daniel recorded the incident in Daniel:

> In that night was Belshazzar the king of the Chaldeans slain. And Darius the Median took the kingdom . . . (Dan. 5:30,31).

This marked the end of the Babylonian Empire, fulfilling Bible prophecy.

Babylon had been used in similar manner to fulfill God's directive, for we find in Ezekiel:

> I shall put my sword into the hand of the king of Babylon, and he shall stretch it out upon the land of Egypt (Ezek. 30:25).

In fulfillment, Egypt was the furthermost portion of the Babylonian conquest and empire.

"The Weapons of His Indignation" — World War III

The prophet Isaiah was the first to record the magnitude of what we now refer to as World War III:

> The earth also is defiled under the inhabitants thereof: because they have transgressed the laws . . . therefore, the inhabitants of the earth are burned, and few men left (Isa. 24:5,6).

In order to get more quickly into the specifics of the events that have to do with the soon-coming battle by fire which we now call World War III, note the following information from Ezekiel 38 and 39. The text of those two chapters reveals that "in the latter years" the leader of the U.S.S.R. as we know it today will, together with the satellite Warsaw Pact nations of Eastern Europe and the full alignment of the Arab nations from West Pakistan to Turkey to Morocco, "come against" the land of Israel. The text reveals also that the major confrontation will begin "on the mountains of Israel," which would be, historically, the Lebanese and Anti-Lebanese (Syrian area) Mountains, including Mount Hermon, where much of the Arab guerrilla fighting already has taken place. In the days of King David and Solomon, these mountains were referred to as "the mountains of Israel" for they were a part of the nation of Israel when it was in the height of its ancient kingdom, one thousand years before Christ.

A portion of the prophecy which Ezekiel recorded is as follows:

> And it shall come to pass . . . when Gog [the Biblical term used for the end-time leader of the mighty Russian military forces] shall come against the land of Israel, saith the LORD GOD, that my fury will come up in my face. For in my jealousy and in the fire of my wrath have I spoken, Surely in that day there shall be a great shaking in the land of Israel . . . (Ezek. 38:18,19).

God Calls Forth His "Weapons"

When Russia dares to enter the Middle East conflict "like a whirlwind," as stated in Daniel 11:40, the judgment of the Lord God will begin. Ezekiel records:

> . . . I will call for a sword against him throughout all my mountains, saith the LORD GOD. . . And I will plead against him with pestilence and with blood; and I will rain upon him, and upon his bands, and upon the many people that are with him, an overflowing rain, and great hailstones, fire and brimstone (Ezek. 38:21,22).

> And I will turn thee back, and leave but the sixth part of thee, and will cause thee to come up from the north parts, and will bring thee upon the mountains of Israel . . . Thou shalt fall upon the mountains of Israel . . . (Ezek. 39:2–4).

> And I will send a fire on Magog [the land of Russia], and among them that dwell carelessly in the isles [the coastlands of Western Europe and the U.S.A.]: and they shall know that I am the LORD.

> So will I make my holy name known in the midst of my people Israel . . . (Ezek. 39:6,7).

By way of brief commentary at this point: God declares that ". . . I will call for a sword against him . . . ," according to Ezekiel 38:21. This denotes the use of manmade weapons against Russia and against those nations aligned therewith.

"The sword of his indignation" against the Russian Confederacy will be, in this case, the military leader who shall be given full authority over the Western European Union which is the military arm of the European Economic Community, better known as the Common Market. Bible prophecy in Daniel 9:26 specifically declares that ". . . the people of the prince that shall come shall destroy the city and the sanctuary . . ." and Jerusalem and its temple (sanctuary) were destroyed by the Romans in A.D. 70. The actual boundary line between Eastern and Western Europe today is the ancient Roman wall of stone which still is in existence as the southern boundary of Czechoslovakia with Austria and with West Germany, and on west, it is the southern boundary of East Germany and West Germany. Another old Roman Empire wall separates England and Scotland, and we may see Scotland secede from England after it becomes a province of the European community following the official establishment of that confederation on January 1, 1980 (the European Community is electing its first Common Market Parliament in special elections June 7, 8, and 9 of 1979, effective January 1, 1980.)

The other nations that were a part of the old Roman Empire, but are not yet in the Common Market, are Greece, Spain, Portugal, and Austria. Greece signed the Common Market treaty in Athens on May 28, 1979, and the Greek parliament ratified it within a few days. As soon as the agreement is ratified by the parliaments of each of the other nine member states, Greece will be the tenth official member. All of the Common Market states reportedly are in favor of ratification, and Greece is scheduled to take part economically as of January 1, 1981.

(May 29, 1979, *Los Angeles Herald Examiner*) Athens, Greece—Greece became the 10th member of the European Common Market yesterday, culminating 22 years of efforts by Premier Caramanlis to join his country economically with Europe.

A host of officials representing nine EEC members, including French President Valery Giscard d'Estaing, were on hand for glittering signing ceremonies in Athens' neo-classical Zappeion Congress Hall. . . .

Greece's active membership is scheduled to start Jan. 1, 1981, after the 10 member parliaments ratify the agreement.

Spain now has adopted its "democratic" constitution, making it eligible to join the European community. Portugal is a member of NATO and also has applied for Common Market membership, as has Austria.

Daniel 7:24 specifically declares that there are to be ten nations that will "give their power and strength unto the beast [the end–time beast–king, the Antichrist]," and that he is to come on the international scene after there are ten nations in coalition, for he is to come up "after them." When they accept him (and his country) and make him their leader or "king" it is declared that he will put down (subdue) three of the original ten, replacing them with three nations or kings of his own choosing, dividing the land "for gain" in fulfillment of Daniel 11:39. The eleventh king is to be the key figure in the great Bible drama of the end–time Tribulation period, for he shall be revealed in his time as being the devil's Antichrist. The prime candidate for that dubious distinction at this time appears to be the king of Spain, Juan Carlos I. Watch this man! Another could arise, for he is not to be revealed as to identity until right after the great event called "the Rapture of the church," but no known person in Europe today has the training and the potential that comes anywhere near that of Juan Carlos I.

Confrontation: the U.S. vs. the U.S.S.R.

With the United States in full commitment to the Western European nations via the Atlantic Alliance and also its complete commitment to Israel by way of unilateral agreement and presidential proclamations; and with the full commitment of the U.S.S.R. to the Arab nations which in turn are committed to one another and dedicated to the present war with Israel (and most of them to the destruction of Israel), the confrontation of the only two real super-powers in the world today is being held back from military and strategic arms conflict only by the restraining power of God. Tensions mount daily. It is no longer a question as to whether there will be a World War III—it is only, when shall it come?

The Bible Description of World War III

Ezekiel states:

> And I will send a fire on Magog [the land of Russia], and among them that dwell carelessly in the isles [the "isles" of the Mediterranean Sea and the Atlantic Ocean] (Ezek. 39:6).

In the coming conflict, when Russia's leader thinks "an evil thought" as stated in Ezekiel 38:10 and strikes at Israel "like a whirlwind" in accordance with the specific prophecy recorded in Daniel 11:40, that dreaded all–out push-button war computerized by milli–second phase–array radar and all the sophisticated satellite communications systems will cause "all hell to break loose," for the Russians know full well that any such action would call for all-out war with the U.S. and the Allied powers. The Kremlin is not so foolish that it will move in strength against Israel without first doing its utmost to knock out all opposition by a furious first–strike offensive against America and the NATO or W.E.U. bases.

The scenario of the action to take place will be in the closing chapters of this book, as has been previously stated. But let us take one more look at the Bible prophecies in special relation to the elements to be in evidence in the process of, or as a direct result of, World War III.

The related prophecy previously quoted from Ezekiel states:

> And I will plead against him with pestilence and with blood; and I will rain upon him, and upon his bands, and upon the many people

34

that are with him, an overflowing rain, and great hailstones, fire, and brimstone (Ezek. 38:22).

The book of Revelation is the last book in the Bible. It carries some vast and amazing details of divine prophecy. These details are given, for the most part, in topical order rather than in chronological order, and they are best understood when its prophecies are compared with parallel passages from other portions of the total Bible account.

In all Scripture, the most detailed account of the specifics of World War III are found in the eighth chapter of the book of Revelation. The portrayal was dictated to the apostle John, as evidenced by his opening statement in the first two verses of that book:

> The Revelation of Jesus Christ, which God gave unto him, to show unto his servants things which must shortly come to pass; and he sent and signified it by his angel unto his servant, John: Who bare record of the word of God, and of the testimony of Jesus Christ, and of all things that he saw (Rev. 1:1,2).

Description of World War III as Revealed From Heaven

Seven great judgments to come upon the earth are each heralded by the sounding of seven trumpets by angels who are portrayed as standing before God in heaven. It is the four trumpet judgments proclaimed in chapter 8 which describe the devastation to be wrought during and as a result of World War III.

Three other trumpet judgments follow and are described in Revelation 9 and 11. These last three trumpet judgments, however, are specifically portrayed as "woes" to come upon the earth. The separation is definite even as the text reveals. The last three are to be divine judgments far beyond the capacity of mankind to imagine, let alone to produce.

But the first four trumpet judgments are a very real description of thermonuclear warfare and are totally within the scope of man's ability to produce today.

Note that the exact extent of the devastation is clearly prophesied here. Only by divine inspiration could such specific figures be given and then be caused to occur nearly nineteen hundred years later, for the Revelation was written in A.D. 95. The prophecy will be quoted here, and the potential for its exact fulfillment will be shown in the pages that follow. Take note of these prophetic statements:

And I saw the seven angels which stood before God; and to them were given seven trumpets (Rev. 8:2).

And the seven angels which had the seven trumpets prepared themselves to sound (Rev. 8:6).

The first angel sounded, and there followed hail and fire mingled with blood, and they were cast upon the earth: and the third part of trees was burnt up, and all green grass was burnt up (Rev. 8:7).

And the second angel sounded, and, as it were a great mountain burning with fire was cast into the sea: and the third part of the sea became blood; and the third part of the creatures which were in the sea, and had life, died; and the third part of the ships were destroyed (Rev. 8:8,9).

And the third angel sounded, and there fell a great star from heaven, burning as it were a lamp, and it fell upon the third part of the rivers, and upon the fountains of waters, And the name of the star is called Wormwood; and the third part of the waters became wormwood; and many men died of the waters, because they were made bitter (Rev. 8:10,11).

And the fourth angel sounded, and the third part of the sun was smitten, and the third part of the moon, and the third part of the stars, so as the third part of them was darkened, and the day shone not for the third part of it, and the night likewise (Rev. 8:12).

3

SCIENTIFIC DATA THAT VERIFY BIBLE PROPHECIES

Verification of Bible prophecy requires the statement of more than one prophet of God.

Deuteronomy 19:15 and Matthew 18:16 both state that in the mouth of two or more witnesses "every word may be established."

Chapter Two of this book closed with the description of a specific war wherein nuclear warfare was used. Before defining this scriptural description with scientific data, let us follow the scriptural pattern and verify it with another Bible prophecy.

Ezekiel recorded both the alignment of the nations involved in this war and a description of the nature of the battle procedures. This is quite remarkable in that he lived over five hundred years before Christ was born, and his written record is therefore over 2,500 years old. His report is summarized in Ezekiel 38:22:

> And I will plead against him [Gog, the prophesied end-time leader of the Russian coalition of nations described in Ezekiel 38:2 and 39:1] with pestilence and with blood; and I will rain upon him, and upon his bands, and upon the many people that are with him, an overflowing rain, and great hailstones, fire, and brimstone.

Ultra-Fundamentalist Viewpoint

Some ultrafundamentalist Bible scholars insist that inasmuch as the Ezekiel terminology specifies that "I" will rain . . . , the battle must be in the form of divine intervention apart from any act of man. Not discounting the possibility of this, and most certainly not discounting God's capability to do so, let us, nevertheless, consider two previously mentioned Bible declarations:

> . . . a day of clouds and of thick darkness, as the morning spread upon the mountains: a great people and a strong; there hath not been ever the like, neither shall be any more after it, even to the years of many generations. A fire devoureth before them; and behind them a flame burneth: the land is as the garden of Eden before them, and behind them a desolate wilderness; yea, and nothing shall escape them (Joel 2:2,3).

Isaiah likewise recorded a significant prophecy concerning *people* and *flames*:

> The noise of a multitude in the mountains, like as of a great people; a tumultuous noise of the kingdoms of nations gathered together: The Lord of hosts mustereth the host of the battle. They come from a far country, from the [opposite] end of heaven, even the Lord, and the weapons of his indignation, to destroy the whole land. Howl ye; for the day of the Lord is at hand; it shall come as a destruction from the Almighty . . . , they shall be amazed one at another; their faces shall be as flames (Isa. 13:4–8).
>
> Their children also shall be dashed to pieces before their eyes; their houses shall be spoiled, and their wives ravished (Isa. 13:16).

This type of action would not be done by God nor by any angelic "Heavenly host"; it is an action that can only be attributed to man's inhumanity to man.

Fundamental and Scientific Descriptions and Definitions

Examining the most obvious definitions first, and then the more astounding ones which describe World War III as outlined in the Bible, let us first consider the elements referred to in the Revelation 8:7–12 passage and then look at those factors mentioned in Ezekiel 38. Following are some very noteworthy scientific facts relative to the warfare elements mentioned:

(1) The Definition: "Hailstones"

Reports of the hydrogen bomb tests by the United States in the Marshall Islands indicate that not only is there a very intense fireball and destructive beta and gamma rays, there are also great hailstones. Large dents in the armor plating of the surface ships were noted. At first this seemed a mystery, but films and other data compiled indicated that the tremendous air turbulence caused by the blasts resulted in the formation of very large hailstones. It was determined that these huge hailstones were the cause of the dents—even in the armor plating of these ships.

This scientific data verifies Bible prophecies. As to further information pertaining to the formation of unusual hailstones, note the documentation concerning the movements of extreme cold fronts referred to under the heading: (6) The Definition: "Overflowing Rain."

Scientific findings prove again and again the accuracy of Bible prophecy.

(2) The Definition: "Fire"

It is impossible to describe the immensity of heat produced in an H-bomb explosion.

On August 6, 1945, the first atomic bomb was dropped on Hiroshima, Japan. The second, a plutonium material bomb, was dropped on Nagasaki on August 9, 1945. At Hiroshima the heat blast alone caused the greatest number of deaths. This is no small wonder when you consider the force and intensity of that blast; the temperature at the center reached, momentarily, an officially estimated sixty million degrees centigrade (127,200,000 F), three times hotter than the center of the sun, and ten thousand times the temperature of the sun's surface!

President Harry Truman at that time stated: "The force from which the sun draws its power has been loosed against those who brought war to the Far East."

Quoting from a compilation of data accumulated since 1935, Dr. Donald Barnhouse, in *Eternity* magazine, stated that "the immense energy of the sun is derived from the fusion of light hydrogen atoms into heavier helium atoms," and that "the sun is an enormous hydrogen bomb."

Mankind, in copying that process, is actually reproducing small "suns." One gram of matter converted into energy by that type of process generates twenty-five million kilowatt-hours of energy, or the explosive equivalent of twenty thousand tons of TNT.

Effects of the "Primitive" Hiroshima Bomb

The Hiroshima bomb, though utilizing more matter due to its primitiveness, was still classified as a "nominal" twenty kiloton explosion. It obliterated only a four-square mile area, yet its blast was so intense that 50,000 people were killed, 55,000 more were wounded, and 200,000 were left homeless. A subsequent report from the scientists at Kyushu Imperial University classified the effects of the bomb on the human body under three headings: (1) instant death; (2) symptoms like those of dysentery followed by death; (3) throat ulcers, bleeding gums, falling hair, and eventual death.

Japanese newsmen reporting the Nagasaki bomb effects stated that persons were paralyzed ten miles from the explosion center, and others with only minute wounds eventually died. Such is the terror of nuclear warfare.

From Kiloton to Megaton Bombs

In 1963 the Russians exploded a fifty-seven-megaton bomb over Siberia. Instead of the "nominal" explosive power of twenty thousand tons of TNT, that bomb had the explosive power of fifty-seven million tons of TNT, and there is no limit to the explosive capability other than the practicality of producing such monsters of destruction.

(March 26, 1953, *New York Times*) Washington—President Eisenhower has decided to let the American people see a motion picture of what its most terrifying weapon, the hydrogen bomb, can do . . . The motion picture depicts "Operation Ivy," the test of a hydrogen weapon in the Pacific in November, 1952.

In the climax of the blast a whole island disappeared, transmuted into deadly vapor and ash. Since then, however, this explosion has been dwarfed by the even larger thermonuclear blast of March 1, 1953. The latest blast surprised even the controlling scientists, according to President Eisenhower. Its effect flared beyond the control boundaries and the "fallout" of radioactive ash burned Americans, natives of Pacific islands and Japanese fishermen many miles away. . . .

Exceptional Adequacy of Delivery Systems

(November 19, 1967, *Los Angeles Times*) The Soviet Union's new missiles carry devices that can foil *any* anti-missile defense, Marshal Nikolai Krykov, chief of Soviet strategic rocket forces said at a Moscow ceremony . . . today [italics mine].

(November 7, 1967, *Los Angeles Times*) . . . Unlike conventional inter-continental missiles, which follow an up-and-down ballistic trajectory reaching a peak altitude of 800 miles, the orbital missile is fired like a satellite into a low orbit perhaps 100 miles high. There is no way of determining what the fractional orbital ballistic system's (FOBS) target is until retro-rockets are fired to bring it down to earth, some three minutes before impact.

Now there is the MIRV-type warhead which multiplies the complexity of the danger inasmuch as each FOBS can carry multiple-reentry pods of rockets, multiplying the target capacity of each FOBS fired.

(December 7, 1969, Copley News Service, from "The Eaker Report") Our [Russian] scientists and engineers developed our SS-9

41

missile, and we now have deployed nearly 400 of them. They have 40-megaton warheads, more than four times the power of U.S. ICBMs. Our [Russian] tests prove that one SS-9 with multiple warheads can destroy a squadron of their ICBMs despite their hardened silos.

Fortunately, we know the exact location of their ICBMs. . . .

(January 15, 1975, *Los Angeles Times*) Washington—The Soviet Union has begun deployment of its newest generation of heavy missiles capable of carrying multiple warheads to separate targets, Secretary of Defense James R. Schlesinger said Tuesday. . . . The United States has confirmed evidence of the SS-18 missile armed with MIRVs.

(February 22, 1978, *The Register*, Orange Co., Calif.) Washington (AP)—The Russians have started deploying their fourth advanced land-based missile capable of hitting the United States, U.S. intelligence sources said.

The SS-16 is the lightest of the four new types of Soviet intercontinental ballistic missiles placed in firing position since late 1974. They are replacing older and less accurate weapons.

Scientific Report on "Destruction by Fire"

The following documentations are excerpt quotations from *Prepare for Armageddon,** a highly technical book published in 1969 by Dr. Lydia Strother and Claude L. Strother, both highly qualified research diagnosticians. Strother designed advanced guidance and electronic counter-measure systems in numerous U.S. government projects. (Reprint is with their permission.)

Blast Effects of a Twenty Megaton Bomb

For an illustration of the order of destruction that can be caused, a 20 megaton thermonuclear warhead impacting on the ground for a surface burst will be assumed. A surface burst does not provide the greatest blast area damage, but it does produce the maximum size crater—in which shelters, of course, do not survive. Up to a point,

*Published by Lee Press, Cardiff-by-the-Sea, Calif., pp. 107–14.

as the altitude of the explosion is increased over the target site, the destruction radius increases: at the same time the amount of fallout decreases proportionately. . . .

The damage radius for both blast and heat effects is estimated in Figure 1. The effects at the radii shown should be considered only as typical; variations in the range of the heat effects, as a function of the weather, would result. That is, on a hazy day the range of the lethal heat front would be reduced considerably. The "fireball" radius would be 2-3 miles; the thermal radiation produced would last several seconds. It is significant to note that 20 to 30 percent of the fatal casualties at Hiroshima and Nagasaki were produced from the initial flash burns, as distinct from flame burns. . . .

In addition to the heat effects, there is, produced simultaneously with the explosion, an intense radiation which is lethal to the same approximate range as for the heat and blast. (This is different from the fallout radiation which will be discussed subsequently.) This radiation consists of neutrons, X-rays and gamma rays; the latter having greater range and more capability for penetrating buildings, etc. The speed of propagation of the X-rays is the same as that of light, 186,000 miles per second.

The shock front, or blast, is propagated more slowly and will take a few seconds to reach the outermost limits shown in the figure.

At the center of the explosion will be a crater some 600 feet deep. This crater would slope upward for a one-half mile radius to a 150 foot high wall of earth and debris which had been pushed up and out from the center of the crater. Thus, in the one-mile diameter crater, shelter survival would not have been possible, unless the shelter had been 1,000 feet or more underground—which is generally not practical.

In addition to the blast, heat, radiation and cratering effects, there may very well result what is called a fire storm. The intense heat ignited by a single nuclear explosion might be expected to start countless small fires from buildings, stored fuel, trash, etc. If these numerous small fires tended to form a common flue-effect, sending a single large column of hot gases upward and consuming all available oxygen in the base fire, this would constitute a fire-storm. As to whether such an effect would be produced, in many instances, can only be speculation, because of the obvious unavailability of data. . . .

Although it would be relatively easy to provide shielding against

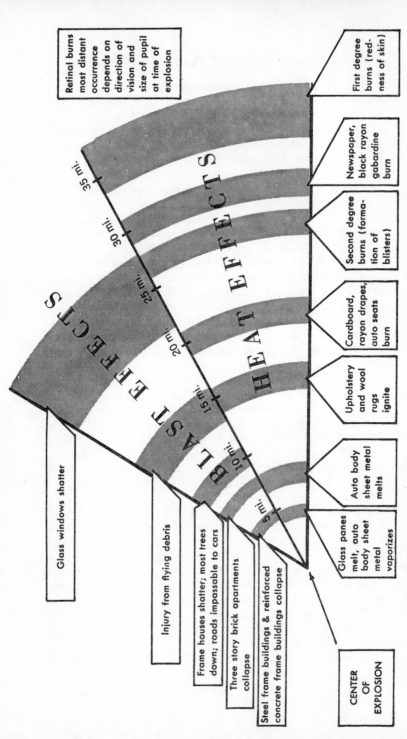

Blast and Heat Effects of a Twenty Megaton Surface Explosion On a Clear Day

HEAT EFFECTS

Retinal burns most distant occurrence depends on direction of vision and size of pupil at time of explosion

First degree burns (redness of skin)

Newspaper, black rayon gabardine burn

Second degree burns (formation of blisters)

Cardboard, rayon drapes, auto seats burn

Upholstery and wool rugs ignite

Auto body sheet metal melts

Glass panes melt, auto body sheet metal vaporizes

BLAST EFFECTS

Glass windows shatter

Injury from flying debris

Frame houses shatter; most trees down; roads impassable to cars

Three story brick apartments collapse

Steel frame buildings & reinforced concrete frame buildings collapse

CENTER OF EXPLOSION

5 mi. 10 mi. 15 mi. 20 mi. 25 mi. 30 mi. 35 mi.

the heat and radiation inside buildings, the blast would simply destroy these structures. Note that in Figure 1 building destruction is shown up to 10-11 miles. The blast effect is generally spoken of in terms of pounds per square inch, or psi. Frequently the blast is referred to as an overpressure of so many psi. This blast, or overpressure, in psi corresponds to wind velocity in miles per hour.

psi	wind velocity
2	70 miles per hour
5	160 miles per hour
10	290 miles per hour
20	470 miles per hour

The following table and discussion pertaining thereto provides an indication of the range in damage area which would be caused by lower yield weapons.

weapon yield in megatons	lethal radius (5 psi) in miles	lethal area; square miles inside 5 psi
½	3.45	37.5
1	4.32	58.6
2	5.41	93.
5	7.4	172.
10	9.3	272.
20	11.8	438.

For example, the metropolitan area of San Diego, California, is 275.7 square miles. The lethal area covered by a 10 megaton air burst is 272 square miles. So 10 megatons would be a good first guess for civil defense planning for San Diego.

Potential Targets in the United States

Reprinted in *Prepare for Armageddon* (pp. 110–14) is a listing of likely target cities in the United States as compiled by Thomas Martin and Donald Latham in their exceptional work, *Strategy for Survival*. That listing is given, in a condensed form, in the following pages. The listing does not include reference to naval bases. Martin and Latham do provide a separate tabulation of naval base target areas, which may be obtained by referring to Appendix 10 in their book.

Targets in the United States
(Key)

1. SAC bomber base.
2. SAC missile base.
3. ADC base.
4. AF support base.

5. Population, 50 largest cities.
6. Population over 200,000
7. Population over 50,000.

City	Target Category	Possible Attack Level Megatons	City	Target Category	Possible Attack Level Megatons
ALABAMA			Oxnard	3	2
Birmingham	5	10	Pomona	7	2
Huntsville	7	1	Riverside-		
Mobile	4,6	10	San		
Montgomery	4,7	1	Bernardino	3,6	5-7
Tuscaloosa	7	0.5	Sacramento	1,3	7-12
ALASKA			San Diego	5	10
Anchorage	4	2	San Francisco	5	30-40
Fairbanks	4	1-2	San Jose	6	6
ARIZONA			San Rafael	3	2-5
Phoenix	4,5	10	Santa Barbara	7	0.5
Tucson	1,2,3,6	185	Victorville	3	2
ARKANSAS			COLORADO		
Blytheville	1	5	Colorado		
Fort Smith	7	0.5	Springs	4,7	20-40
Little Rock	1,2,7	185	Denver	1,2,5	95
CALIFORNIA			Pueblo	7	0.5
Bakersfield	7	1	CONNECTICUT		
Fairfield	1	5	Bridgeport	6	10
Fresno	6	2	Hartford	6	5
Lompoc	1,2	5-25	New Haven	6	5
Long Beach	5	1	Norwalk	7	1
Los Angeles	5	50-100	Stamford	7	5
Marysville	1,2	50	Waterbury	7	2
Merced	1,3	5	DELAWARE		
Oakland	5	2	Dover	3,4	2
Ontario-			Wilmington	6	5
Pomona	7	2			

SCIENTIFIC DATA THAT VERIFY BIBLE PROPHECIES

City	Target Category	Possible Attack Level Megatons	City	Target Category	Possible Attack Level Megatons
DISTRICT OF COLUMBIA			Gary	7	2
			Hammond	7	0.5
Washington	3,4,5	8-15	Indianapolis	6	5
FLORIDA			Peru	1,3	5
Ft. Lauderdale			South Bend	6	2
Hollywood	6	5	Terre Haute	7	1
Homestead	1	5	IOWA		
Jacksonville	6	5	Cedar Rapids	7	1
Miami	5	10	Des Moines	6	5
Orlando	1,6	5-7	Sioux City	7	2
Panama City	3	2	KANSAS		
Pensacola	4,7	1	Salina	1,2	65
St. Petersburg	6	4	Topeka	1,2,7	10-14
Tampa	1,4,5	5-10	Wichita	1,2,4,6	185
Valparaiso	1,4	5	KENTUCKY		
West Palm Bch.	7	5	Lexington	7	0.5
GEORGIA			Louisville	5	5
Albany	1,7	5	LONG ISLAND		
Atlanta	4,5	20	Westhampton		
Columbus	7	4	Beach	3	2
Macon	1,4	5-6	LOUISIANA		
Marietta	3	2	Alexandria	4	2
Savannah	1,7	5-7	Baton Rouge	7	2
HAWAII			Lake Charles	1,4,7	5
Honolulu	4,5	5	New Orleans	5	10
IDAHO			Shreveport	1,6	5-7
Mtn. Home	1,2	50	MAINE		
ILLINOIS			Bangor	1,3	5
Aurora	7	0.3 to 0.5	Limestone	1,3	5
Belleville	4	1-2	Portland	7	2
Chicago	5	30-60	MARYLAND		
Davenport-			Baltimore	5	20
Rock Island-			Camp Springs	3,4	2
Moline	6	5	MASSACHUSETTS		
Decatur	7	0.5	Boston	5	20-50
Joliet	7	1	Brockton	7	1
Peoria	7	2	Chicopee	1,3	2
Rock Island	6	5	Falmouth	3,4	2
Springfield	7	1	Holyoke	1,3	5-7
INDIANA			Lowell	7	0.5
East Chicago	7	0.1	Pittsfield	7	1
Evansville	7	1	Springfield	1,3,6	5-7
Fort Wayne	7	1	Worcester	6	2

City	Target Category	Possible Attack Level Megatons	City	Target Category	Possible Attack Level Megatons
MICHIGAN			NEW MEXICO		
Ann Arbor	7	0.5	Albuquerque	4,6	2
Bay City	6	0.5	Clovis	4	2
Detroit	5	10	Roswell	1,2,3	65
Flint	6	2	NEW YORK		
Grand Rapids	6	5	Albany	6	1
Kalamazoo	7	1	Buffalo	5	10
Lansing	7	1	Newburgh	3,4	2
Kinross	1,3	5	New York	5	100
Marquette	1,3	5	Niagara Falls	3,7	2-4
Oscoda	1,3	5	Plattsburg	1,2	65
Saginaw	7	0.5	Rochester	5	5
MINNESOTA			Rome-Utica	1,2	5-10
Duluth-Superior	3,7	5-7	Syracuse	3,4,6	2
Minneapolis	5	40	Troy	7	0.5
Saint Paul	5	2	NORTH CAROLINA		
MISSISSIPPI			Asheville	7	1
Columbus	1		Charlotte	6	2
Jackson	7		Goldsboro	1,2	5
MISSOURI			Greensboro	7	2
Kansas City	3,4,5		Raleigh	7	1
Saint Louis	5		Winston-Salem	7	1
Sedalia	1,2		NORTH DAKOTA		
Springfield	7		Grand Forks	1,3	5
Warrensburg	1,2	505-1505	Minot	1,2,3	505-1505
MONTANA			OHIO		
Billings	7	0.2	Akron	5	5
Glasgow	1,3	5	Canton	6	2
Great Falls	1,2,7	505-1502	Cincinnati	5	20
NEBRASKA			Cleveland	5	40
Lincoln	1,2,7	65	Columbus	1,5	5-15
Omaha	1,2,4,5	50	Dayton	1,3,5	5-10
NEVADA			Hamilton	7	2
Las Vegas	4,7	2-3	Shelby	4	1
Reno	4,7	0.25	Toledo	5	5
NEW HAMPSHIRE			Warren-Youngstown	6	5
Manchester	7	1	OKLAHOMA		
Portsmouth	1	5	Altus	1,2	65
NEW JERSEY			Burns Flat	1	5
Atlantic City	7	2	Elk City	1	5
Jersey City	6	0.25	Lawton	7	0.25
Newark	6	0.50	Oklahoma City	4,5	20
Trenton	6	2	Tulsa	6	2
Wrightstown	3,4	2			

City	Target Category	Possible Attack Level Megatons	City	Target Category	Possible Attack Level Megatons
OREGON			Del Rio	4	1-2
Eugene	7	1	El Paso	1,6	5-10
Klamath Falls	3	2	Fort Worth	1,5	20-25
Portland	3,5	20-22	Galveston-		
PENNSYLVANIA			Texas City	7	10
Allentown-			Houston	5	20
Bethlehem	6	4	Laredo	4,7	0.2
Erie	7	2	Lubbock	4,7	2
Harrisburg	6	1	Port Arthur	7	2
Middletown	4	2	San Antonio	4,5	10
Philadelphia	5	30	Waco	4,7	2
Pittsburgh	5	20	Wichita Falls	1,7	5
Reading	7	1	**UTAH**		
Scranton	6	4	Ogden	4,7	2
Youngstown	6	5	Salt Lake City	6	5
RHODE ISLAND			**VIRGINIA**		
Pawtucket-			Hampton	3,6	10-12
Providence	6	6-9	Newport News	3,6	10-12
SOUTH CAROLINA			Norfolk	3,5	10-12
Charleston	3,4,7	3.5-4.5	Richmond	6	5
Columbia	7	2	**WASHINGTON**		
Greenville	3,4,7	2	Everett	3	2
Myrtle Beach	4	2	Moses Lake	1,2,3	50
Sumter	4	2	Seattle	5	10
SOUTH DAKOTA			Spokane	1,2,3,6	12-17
Rapid City	1	50	Tacoma	3,4,6	5-7
TENNESSEE			**WEST VIRGINIA**		
Chattanooga	6	5	Charleston	7	2
Knoxville	7	2	Wheeling	7	0.5
Memphis	5	10	**WISCONSIN**		
Nashville	6	4	Green Bay	7	1
TEXAS			Madison	3,4,7	2
Abilene	1,2	65	Milwaukee	5	20
Amarillo	1,7	2	**WYOMING**		
Austin	7	5	Cheyenne	1,2	19
Dallas	5	40			

(3) The Definition: "Brimstone"

"Brimstone" is described in *Smith's Bible Dictionary* as "Sulphur. Found on the shores of the Dead Sea."

Genesis 19:24 reads, "Then the LORD rained upon Sodom and Gomorrah brimstone and fire from the LORD out of heaven" [because of the extreme corruptness of these cities].

Because of the use of the word *brimstone* in relation to the act of God in the destruction of Sodom and Gomorrah, it's possible that modern napalm and incendiary bombs are a fulfillment of "brimstone." Definitions in dictionaries, however, indicate that these items are both commonly made from petroleum products. Inasmuch as brimstone is specifically defined as sulphur (sulfur), my research turned to further descriptions of sulfur and sulfur by-products. Sulfur is yellow; sulfur dichloride is described as being "a dark brown or reddish liquid that resembles sulfur chloride"; and sulfur chloride is described as "a heavy non-flammable gas of pungent suffocating odor." One other factor: "Sulfurizing is necessary in the preparation of most kinds of dried fruit." Unrelated as this may seem to the subject at hand, my mind went back to 1967 and a detailed description in my files of the nature of Russian-produced nerve gas which was used in Yemen; and, it also tied in another of the Bible prophecy factors—blood—which is to be evident as part of the total warfare in the battle which is about to take place.

"Hail, Fire, Brimstone—and Blood"

Documented news accounts verified deaths in Yemen caused by "blood emerging from mouth and nose, but without any mark on the skin" and also a very few (less than five percent) who survived, but who "have difficulty breathing, and cough continuously." Note the dispatches:

(January 13, 1967, *Los Angeles Times*) Washington—The United States is secretly engaged in a flourishing chemical and biological warfare weapons program which has already stockpiled a far-reaching offensive capability, Science magazine reported Thursday. . . . The program, according to the article, is centered at Ft. Detrick, Md., in a $75 million laboratory which has a scientific staff of 598 persons, including 120 Ph.Ds, 34 veterinarians and 14 medical doctors. "Only about 15 percent of their findings are published through conventional scientific channels," the magazine said.

(May 31, 1967, *Los Angeles Times*) Washington (AP)—The House Appropriations Committee has received secret testimony that the Soviets are ahead of the United States in development of germ and chemical warfare weapons. The testimony was given by Lt. Gen. Austin W. Betts, Army chief of research and development. . . .

(June 2, 1967, *Los Angeles Times*) Bonn (UPI)—The West German cabinet decided Thursday to sell about 20,000 gas masks to Israel. State Secretary Karl Guenther von Hase . . . said the Israeli request to buy the masks was made "days ago."

(June 15, 1967, *Los Angeles Times*) . . . it has long been well-established that poison gas was being used on occasion by the Egyptians in the Yemen. . . . Furthermore, the Egyptians have not been satisfied with the most terrible of the World War I gases. Although mustard gas has been used regularly by them, they have also employed the far more cruel and deadly *nerve gas*, presumably supplied to them by the Soviets. This is, in fact, the first use of nerve gas in combat. . . .

The Egyptians began launching more frequent gas attacks, including *nerve gas attacks*, at Bua and other objectives in the Yemen after June 4. . . .

Just what this means is now causing some concern in Washington [italics mine].

(4) The Definition: "Blood"

Details of Nerve Gas Description, Use, and Effects

Columnist Drew Pearson and Near East correspondent Joe Alex Morris, Jr., both wrote detailed documentary reports which were published in the *Los Angeles Times* (January 6 and 12, 1967). By utilizing excerpts from these articles and in view of the aforementioned information concerning the definition of "sulfur," we arrive at the following description and analysis:

Nine Ilyushin bombers escorted by two MIG fighters appeared over Kitaf at 7:30 a.m. on Jan. 5 (1967). They dropped two marker bombs. . . . Nine Ilyushin 28s then dropped the gas, three aircraft at a time, three bombs per aircraft upwind of the village of Ketaf (Kitaf).

The bombs made a crater three feet deep and six feet wide and released the gas in a grey-green cloud which drifted with the wind over the village of Ketaf. All but 5 percent of the people within two kilometres downwind of the bombs and impact point have died or, in the opinion of the International Red Cross mission sent to the spot, are likely to die . . . 120 men, women and children died within half an hour, as well as goats, sheep, donkeys and chickens. More died later, and inhabitants put the total at 200.

According to this report the gas had no external effect on the skin or eyes, but the victims suffered headaches, difficulty in breathing, coughing of *blood* and nose bleeding and died within 10 to 30 minutes [italics mine].

Another part of the reports reads:

All the animals in the area also perished, and crops and vegetation turned brown. Until the following morning a grey-green cloud of gas hung low over the village. Those unfortunate enough to breathe it compared its smell to yeast or fresh fruit. Most of the victims were dead within 10 to 50 minutes of the attack. *They died with blood emerging* from mouth and nose, but without any mark on their skin. Affected survivors . . . have difficulty breathing and cough continuously [italics mine].

Evidences of "Brimstone" in Nerve Gas

With the above documented detail in mind, note again the description of sulfur, which is "brimstone." Webster's dictionary describes sulfur as yellow, and sulfur dichloride as "a brown or reddish liquid." When the three colors are mixed, the net result is indeed, a grey-green color.

Sulfur chloride is described as "a heavy gas." The grey-green nerve gas "hung low over the village" until the following morning. Sulfur chloride is also described as having a "pungent suffocating odor." Pungent means: "1. Causing a sharp sensation, as of the taste, smell, or feelings; pricking; biting; acrid. 2. Sharply painful, penetrating, poignant. 3. Caustic; stinging; biting."

Comparative Table of Sulfur Products and Nerve Gas.

	NERVE GAS REPORTS
1. *Sulfur: Brimstone* "*A heavy gas.*"	1. Drifted, but "*hung low over the village.*"
2. "*Pungent*" (see above dictionary description).	2. Survivors "*have difficulty breathing and cough continuously.*"
3. *Color: yellow; "a brown or reddish liquid.*"	3. Even without other unknown ingredients, the combined grey-green color persisted; and, in Mr. Morris' report, is a statement as follows: "*The gas exploded in a liquid cloud which was described variously as green or red.*"
4. "Sulfurizing is essential in the preparation of most dried *fruit.*"	4. "Those unfortunate enough to breathe it compared the smell to yeast or fresh *fruit.*"

After correlating the above information and facts, I can only conclude that the preponderance of the evidence listed makes the presence of brimstone most likely, and in fact, virtually essential in nerve gas to produce the many corroborating results. In addition, we find that the effects produced by the above-described nerve gas fit the prophecy recorded in Ezekiel 38:22 wherein it is stated that the judgments would include pestilence, blood, and brimstone. This is also verified and cross-referenced with the judgments recorded in Revelation 8:7 which proclaim that there followed hail and fire mingled with blood.

The verbal inspiration of the Bible remains resplendent in its every detail.

Two other factors yet remain to be defined to complete the list of "ingredients" listed by Ezekiel and also in Revelation as being a part of the judgments to come at or in relation to World War III. They are "pestilence" and "overflowing rain."

(5) The Definition: "Pestilence"

The current availability of "pestilence" in warfare weapons is well known. Both the U.S. and the U.S.S.R. have stockpiles of such elements in their strategic warfare arsenals. A further quotation from the *Science* magazine article will give an idea of the "pestilence" factor. (*Science* is the official publication of the American Association for the Advancement of Science, an organization of more than ten thousand members from nearly all fields.)

(January 13, 1967, *Los Angeles Times*) Washington—The United States is secretly engaged in a flourishing chemical and biological warfare weapons program. . .

"Only about 15 percent of their findings are published through conventional specific channels," the magazine said. "The rest become a part of secret literature managed by the Department of Defense and available to other government agencies and contractors on a "need to know" basis.

"On the basis of the few scientific papers made public on the subject of chemical and biological weapons," the article said, "potential agents include: anthrax, dysentary plague, Rocky Mountain fever, encephalitis, yellow fever, botulism and several others."

There is no question as to the present scientific capability to fulfill the Bible-prophesied factor—"pestilence."

U.S. Orders Germ Agents Destroyed

(December 18, 1970, Copley News Service) Washington (AP)— The Pentagon announced today plans to destroy all germ warfare stockpiles under conditions of "absolute safety and security."

The offensive biological agents and toxin stockpiles, manufactured originally for use against humans and crops, will be destroyed at their current locations in Pine Bluff, Ark., the Rocky Mountain Arsenal, Denver, Colo., Ft. Detrick, Md., and Beale Air Force Base, Calif. . . . The destruction of the germ warfare stockpiles . . . is due to begin early next year and be completed in about a year's time. . . .

Lt. Col. Gerald G. Watson of Kilgore, Tex., the project officer in charge of the destruction program, told a briefing: "We think the identity of the agents and the amount in the stockpile should remain security information." He said the disposal operation will cost $12,169,000.

"The factors of absolute safety and security were more important to us than cost or time," Watson said. . . .

Under Nixon's directive issued Nov. 25, 1969, the United States renounced the use of lethal biological agents and weapons "and all other methods of biological warfare."

At the same time he directed the disposal of "existing stocks of bacteriological weapons."

Commentary: Significance of Germ Weapons' Destruction

Since the U.S. Government has fully documented evidence on hand that "the Soviets are ahead of the United States in development of germ and chemical warfare weapons," it would seem, on the surface, foolhardy for the United States to destroy the biological weapons that we do have. Consider, however, the "absolute safety and security" which is involved.

In the event of an all-out nuclear first-strike by Russia, which is fully anticipated by this country (and is also prophesied in the Bible), such a devastating attack could conceivably release these very deadly bacteriological elements upon the population of this country.

The location of germ warfare stockpiles in the United States is no secret. The news item just quoted specified these locations. This makes the danger even greater.

Russia, on the other hand, evidently counting on the effectiveness of such a major thrust, has seen no need to gain even the propaganda advantage of announcing any disposal of its known stockpiles of bacteriological agents. This could be a great error on their part.

In the Bible, God's proclamation recorded in Ezekiel 39:2 specifies concerning the army of the chief prince of Moscow and Tobolsk, "I will turn thee back, and leave but the sixth part of thee. . . ."

Part of the destruction of five-sixths of Russia's armies could be by means of shock-released bacteriological supplies upon its own forces. This can only be a matter of speculation at this point, of course, but when you come to Sections VI and VII of this writing, and the progression of events is portrayed, you will see great potential for just such an occurrence.

(6) The Definition: "Overflowing Rain"

Weather phenomena following thermonuclear explosions are many and of wide range. One of the most concise but authentic statements on this topic is a quotation from *The Hell Bomb*, a booklet by Franklin Hall. On page 18 of that writing is the following documentation:

> On Friday, January 26, 1951, the weather bureau predicted a cold wave for the northeastern states, due to a high pressure area centering in Canada. On January 27 an atomic explosion took place near Las Vegas. As it passed over Wisconsin, temperatures between 24 and 53 degrees below zero were reported. All over the nation, temperatures tumbled, often to new record lows. . . .
>
> On January 28, another explosion at Las Vegas caused an inrush of a high pressure area from the Arctic circle, bringing freezing rain and sleet as far as the Gulf of Mexico. On February 1st, the greatest of the blasts was set off, and by nightfall, the entire nation was blanketed by the worst storm in many years, with a death toll of 270 persons. The damage to crops was enormous.

These great influxes of cold air were produced by nuclear blasts which were underground. Imagine the far greater inrush of Arctic air fronts that would be produced by the simultaneous explosion of many surface and high altitude blasts, such as would occur in the case of an all-out thermonuclear attack!

This also would be a secondary reason, or cause, for "great hailstones."

Scientific Data Summary

By combining the inspired Scripture accounts of the soon-to-come World War III, as given in summary in Ezekiel 38:22 and in Revelation 8:7, a listing of the elements to be present in that warfare was found to be (1) hail; (2) fire; (3) brimstone; (4) blood; (5) pestilence; and (6) overflowing rain. There remain yet seven other warfare factors to consider in the over-all context of the prophecies recorded in Ezekiel, chapters 38 and 39, and in Revelation 8.

In noting the balance of the Revelation 8 prophecy we find that three of the factors are but very evident results of the effects of an all-out thermonuclear exchange.

(7) The Definition: "Mountain of Fire Cast Into the Sea"

Considering that this prophecy was recorded in A.D. 95, the upheavals and the destructive powers "cast into the sea" would indeed have seemed "as a great mountain of fire." One third of the oceans (sea) was visualized as turning to blood as vast numbers of rockets and satellites with multi-megaton warheads (and both are now deployed) were seen ". . . cast into the sea: and the third part of the sea became blood; and the third part of the creatures which were in the sea, and had life, died; and the third part of the ships were destroyed" (Rev. 8:8,9).

Inasmuch as a great portion of the nuclear striking power of both the United States and the U.S.S.R. is presently deployed in Polaris or Poseidon-type nuclear submarines, and also that the strategic front lines of fighter bomber class planes are on American aircraft carriers from the Mediterranean Sea to the Pacific Ocean, it takes no stretch of the imagination to foresee that one third of the "seas" will indeed become "blood" when a sufficient number of nuclear bombs are exploded therein to "destroy" these vessels so as to cancel out their retaliatory striking power. Such is the widespread deployment of these thousands of ships and submarines that actual and factual fulfillment of the statement "the third part of the sea became blood" is most likely to occur as the blood of the men on these ships blends with the blood of the millions upon millions of the sea creatures which will bleed and die as a result of the shock waves plus the radiation effects from the nuclear bombardment.

Not a Meteor

Some think this must be a totally divine act of God, such as the manifestations of a meteor or "falling star." It will be, to be sure, a divine judgment, for it is prophesied in the Bible; but it will be, even as the other factors described in this writing, the result of the use of "the weapons of his indignation." He will bring forth from his arsenal of the nations those who shall fight one against the other—in this instance the super-powers of this present generation: the United States and its allies in Western Europe and the U.S.S.R. with its satellite colleagues.

There is no way possible, with the widespread use of the seas today, that one third of the ships could be gathered together into any single area so that they might be destroyed by any meteor or any other "mountain cast into the sea."

There simply was no other way in which the scribe of the Book of Revelation could describe the devastation in a manner that the people of his day would believe or understand. We most certainly can understand it today.

(8) The Definition: "Burning"—Radioactive Fallout

Revelation 8:10 and 11 read as follows:

> And the third angel sounded, and there fell a great star from heaven, burning [continuously] as it were a lamp, and it fell upon the third part of the rivers, and upon the fountains of waters; and the name of the star is called Wormwood; and the third part of the waters became wormwood; and many men died of the waters, because they were made bitter.

John had no way of knowing when he penned this prophecy that such death-dealing potential could ever be in the arsenals of men. He wrote as commanded, and by faith in the knowledge of the resurrected Christ who dictated it. (See Rev. 1:1, 17–19.)

Radioactive clouds "from heaven" drifting over the lakes, rivers, ponds, and springs, which are "fountains of waters" for drinking purposes (before they became so polluted), would

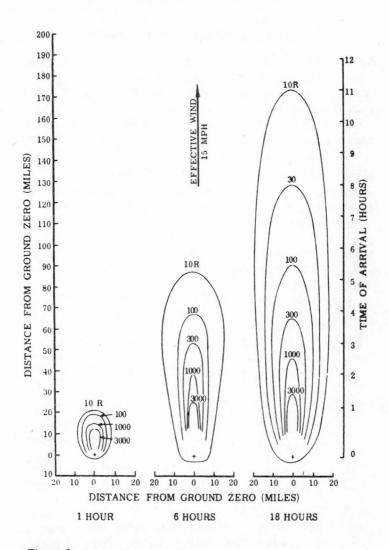

Figure 2.
TOTAL-DOSE CONTOURS FROM EARLY FALLOUT AT 1, 6, and 18 HOURS AFTER SURFACE BURST WITH 1-MEGATON FISSION YIELD (15 MILES PER HOUR EFFECTIVE WIND SPEED). [9]

most certainly fulfill this prophecy to the letter; and I cannot at present think of any other factor that would. God knew well in advance the type of destructive and harmful devices mankind would produce.

This is, in fact, more supporting evidence for the divine inspiration of the Bible.

Scientific Data Concerning Radioactive Fallout

Quoting from the highly authoritative book, *Prepare for Armageddon,* on pages 117–119 are found these specific details regarding fallout distance patterns:

Radioactive dust begins to settle down in the vicinity of the explosion in a few minutes and continues to be deposited downwind hours and days later. . . .

The gamma radiation from the fallout is measured in roetgens; again the lethal danger point is in the order of 300 roetgens, with some added fraction for a continued rather than an instant exposure. The intensity of the fallout radiation will continue to decrease every hour after the explosion . . . by a factor of 10 in several hours. This decay is continuous, so that the following decrease in intensity occurs:

Time (hr)	Decay	Radiation Intensity
1	—	1,000 R/hr. (per hour)
7	1/10	100 R/hr. (per hour)
7x7=49 (2 days)	1/100	10 R/hr. (per hour)
7x7x7=343 (2 wks.)	1/1,000	1 R/hr. (per hour)

The local or early fallout in the vicinity of the nuclear explosion is largely deposited within 24 hours. This fallout will be carried downwind at the prevailing wind rate. Figure 2 shows the fallout pattern for a surface burst of a one megaton weapon with typical wind conditions. (Ground zero refers to the point on the ground directly under the bomb at the time of the explosion. The term is also used in the case of a surface burst.) Naturally, with higher yield weapons, the intensity and range of the "local" fallout will increase markedly.

(9) The Definition: "Darkness"—Atomic Clouds

In *Prepare for Armageddon* we find the following:

> The radioactive particles, while still in the atmosphere, along with massive *clouds* of dust and other minute particles of debris would tend to darken the sky, as during a storm. This darkness would be especially pronounced if the attack were launched in a time of year when the forests are dry. Very likely huge forest fires would be started, and no effort for control would be possible in areas where the fallout was intense enough to confine everyone to shelters . . . [italics mine].

The statement quoted above is virtually an exact prognosis of the following Bible prophecy:

> And the fourth angel sounded, and the third part of the sun was smitten, and the third part of the moon, and the third part of the stars; so that the third part of them was darkened, and the day shone not for the third part of it, and the night likewise (Rev. 8:12).

Another Bible prophecy is thus verified by scientific research.

Scientific Proof

Each of the nine "definitions" of elements and factors documented in this chapter relate to the tremendously powerful instruments of destruction which man's modern scientific research and development have led him to devise. I believe this all relates to the accurately prophesied "Battle by Fire" which only an all-knowing and all-wise God could cause His human instruments for righteousness to record and preserve over centuries of time—from the writings of Isaiah and Joel of the 8th century B.C. on through the writings of Zechariah, Ezekiel, and Daniel of the 5th century B.C. and on to the words of Christ and His scribe, John, in A.D. 95. Fact-conscious, intelligent, and scientific people of today can know that these factors and developments cannot have "just happened," because there is documentable proof that it is all occurring according to such an exact plan that it would be absolutely impossible for any man or group of men to have devised it. Who, for instance, in the chariot racing days of 2,700 years ago could have even remotely imagined atomic fission or "brimstone" nerve gas that can kill in minutes without leaving any visible trace of outward body contact?

The Apex and Acme of Truth

The apostle Peter recorded in 2 Peter 1:21, "prophecy came not in old time by the will of man: but holy men of God spake as they were moved by the Holy Ghost." With such profound evidence before us, how can biblical prophecies be explained as to their content except we admit that there is no other answer than absolute divine inspiration? In all fairness to "cause and effect" and by way of proven "laboratory findings," such as have been given and shall be still further documented in this book, we have proof positive that there is a living God who does concern Himself with the affairs of mankind. This great, omnipotent and all-wise God, by divine foreknowledge of the "thoughts and intents of the heart" of man, has set forth an eternal plan, into which God in love has offered to man the all-inclusive "whosoever will may come," whereby every person may make up his or her own mind and choose whether or not to believe in this living and eternal God.

4

SOUND THE ALARM

The potential for the fulfillment of each of the great prophecies of the Bible concerning a tremendous "battle by fire" has been set before us.

Every prophecy shall be fulfilled, and the world will, indeed, see "Men's hearts failing them for fear, and for looking after those things which are [soon] coming on the earth: for the [hydrogen] powers of heaven shall be shaken" (Luke 21:26).

Well did Harry Truman speak when he said in 1945, "The source from which the sun draws its power has been loosed. . . ." Mankind, in producing atomic, and now hydrogen bombs, is actually reproducing small "suns." Just one gram of matter converted into energy looses the explosive equivalent of twenty thousand tons of TNT; and one fusion process hydrogen bomb can equal the explosive power of from one to two hundred million tons of TNT!

As of this writing, each of the opposing factions in the Middle East crisis area is backed with the assurance of the "protection" of one or the other of the two great super-powers, the United States and the U.S.S.R. Each of these great powers possesses thousands of multi-megaton, bomb-tipped missiles constantly aimed at the populace as well as at the military targets of the other.

"Ban the Bomb" Mania

It is no wonder that the youth of today, who have been taught by atheistic or deistic professors that there is no

God who cares for them, find themselves frustrated. They have had every spiritual foundation removed, every moral fiber shattered, and every hope destroyed. They see only dust and ashes and are told by skilfully trained mob leaders that it is all the fault of "the establishment," everything is wrong, and any means is justified to tear down what has destroyed their dreams.

Some cry "Ban the Bomb" for very subversive reasons for they are following after the Communist infiltrators who are endeavoring to destroy our American way of life. They have been sold a bill of goods and want America to destroy its weapons and source of nuclear deterrence so that the enemy can assert itself against us—even if this means devastation to accomplish the chaos from which (these duped ones are told) will rise an Aquarian Utopia.

Many others, however, cry "Ban the Bomb" because they are dreadfully afraid (and rightly so) of the vast destructive powers that will be unleashed if the stockpiles of potential holocaust materials continue to mount. They have no hope. O where is that elusive factor called peace? They have tried the liberalism of sex, pot, and perversion only to find disillusionment, sorrow, and distress. Many have ended up insane or mentally destroyed for life, while multiplied thousands of other students from Sweden, France, England, and America have committed suicide, unable to stand the stress of the irresponsible forces about them. "The Bomb" is like a sword of Damocles above them, and they see no escape. It is no wonder that in all of this Freudian psycho-society they join any popular front movement to try to find a way out.

There Is a Way

The greatest teacher who ever walked on the face of this earth declared:

> I say unto you, My friends, Be not afraid of them that kill the body, and after that have no more that they can do. But I will forwarn you whom ye shall fear: Fear him which after he hath killed

hath power to cast into hell; yea, I say unto you, Fear Him. Are not five sparrows sold for two farthings [one-half cent], and not one of them is forgotten before God? But even the very hairs of your head are all numbered. Fear not, therefore: ye are of more value than many sparrows. Also, I say unto you, whosoever shall confess me before men, him shall the Son of Man [Jesus] also confess before the angels of God; But he that denieth me before men shall be denied before the angels of God (Luke 12:4–9).

Confess

To confess Jesus in the manner described by Him in the inspired Scriptures is to confess that you need Him. You cannot save yourself. It is written that "All have sinned, and come short of the glory of God . . ." (Rom. 3:23) and, ". . . There is none righteous, no, not one" (Rom. 3:10). But praise God that it is also written: "The wages of sin is death; but the gift of God is eternal life through Jesus Christ our Lord" (Rom. 6:23).

Jesus, the Son of God, lived the perfect life which neither you nor I could possibly live; and then, in His perfection, He sacrificed His very life blood when He died on the cross of Calvary. He paid the price for your sin, and for mine, when He died in agony on that cruel tree. Now, having ransomed us and paid the price for all of our sin, He offers to us eternal life with Him, with God, and with the holy angels of all the unlimited expanse of heaven. We only need to recognize His supreme sacrifice, humble ourselves enough to acknowledge our need, and accept that free gift which He offers. It is written, ". . . Believe on the Lord Jesus Christ, and thou shalt be saved . . ." (Acts 16:31); and also, "Therefore being justified by faith, we have peace with God through our Lord Jesus Christ" (Rom. 5:1).

Remember the Warning

The prophet Isaiah warned, ". . . the haughty [proud] people of the earth do languish . . . they have transgressed, . . . Therefore, the inhabitants of the earth are burned, and few men left" (Isa. 24:4–6).

Here Is The Answer

Even if many Christians have already been taken to heaven, and even if many other men have already been burned by nuclear warfare by the time you read this message, *you can still be saved for all eternity.* The answer—*the only* answer—is to ask God to forgive your sin now. He promises that He will do so, for it is also written in the Bible that ". . . whosoever shall call upon the name of the Lord shall be saved" (Rom. 10:13).

Romans 10:9 and 10 say:

> If thou shalt confess with thy mouth the Lord Jesus, and shalt believe in thine heart that God hath raised him from the dead, thou shalt be saved: For with the heart man believeth unto righteousness [His righteousness, given unto you in exchange for your confession of your need of His salvation]; and with the mouth confession is made unto salvation [salvation from the wages of sin, which is both physical and spiritual death in eternal separation from God].

According to Revelation 1:1, it was the resurrected and living Jesus Christ who revealed to His servant John "the revelation of things which must shortly come to pass" including the great thermonuclear war. All seems in readiness. Mankind has the bombs and the strategic forces with which to deliver them. Only God is holding this all back so that whosoever will may trust in Christ now and be saved from such terror. He will not or cannot wait much longer to fulfill a vast number of Bible prophecies that pertain to this generation.

Christ has promised to acknowledge each individual in heaven who acknowledges Him on this earth. Give witness, therefore, to your faith in Him. If you have previously accepted His salvation and seek to declare it, or if you believe this presentation of the greatest offer ever made—salvation from the wages and punishment of sin by means of acknowledging His payment in full for you on the cross of Calvary—space is provided below for you to acknowledge this with your signature.

5

WILL AMERICA BE DESTROYED?

America will be greatly affected by World War III, but it will not be destroyed according to the Bible.

That the United States will be involved in World War III can be shown in several ways. Three will be considered here: knowledge, reason, and the basic element of faith in the divine inspiration of the Bible.

Knowledge

The United States is fully committed directly (and indirectly through NATO) to protect Israel against attack. Israel is surrounded by aggressive Arab forces, and Russia's involvement in the Mid-east is a matter of record. Virtually any newspaper will verify these facts.

Reason

Common knowledge of the news of the day gives us an insight, well-expressed by reports from Washington D.C.:

(March 22, 1970, *Los Angeles Times*) Washington—"If Russia disturbs the balance of power in the Middle East, the United States will move to assure Israel's security," President Nixon said Saturday.

(May 2, 1978, *Jerusalem Post*) Washington—President Jimmy Carter yesterday told Prime Minister Menachem Begin that the

U.S. will "never waiver" in its "absolute commitment to Israel's security," even though "we may, from time to time, have a transient difference with the leaders of Israel."

At a White House reception marking Israel's 30th anniversary of independence, the president declared that "the establishment of the nation of Israel was a fulfillment of Biblical prophecy," and he thanked God that Israel is strong today. . . .

Carter said he was proud that the U.S. was the first country to recognize Israel in 1948 and that the U.S. has since remained deeply committed to Israel's security.

"*I can say, without reservation, as the President of the United States of America, that we will continue to do so, not just for 30 years, but forever,*" Carter said (italics mine).

Knowledge and Bible Prophecy

Specific Bible prophecies have been quoted in previous chapters which declare that *one third of the earth* will experience thermonuclear attack. Now it is time to ask, "which one third?"

Numerous Bible prophecies declare specific areas that will be "judged." Prophecies recorded in Isaiah, Ezekiel, Daniel and Revelation proclaim that the warfare which we have referred to as World War III will ultimately escalate from the Middle East crisis over the Promised Land, the territory of Israel. The nations which are to be involved in this all-out war, according to the Bible, are found in four prerecorded categories:

1. The land of Israel.

2. The Arab regions described in Ezekiel 38:5 as "Persia, Ethiopia and Libya." This would include all Arab States from Pakistan to Morocco, except the Arabian Peninsula which was never conquered by Persia and was not a part of the "Ethiopia" nor "Libya" of Bible times.

3. The U.S.S.R. and the satellite nations referred to in Ezekiel 38:3 and 6. Meshech and Tubal were two of the sons of Japheth the son of Noah. They migrated northward after the

flood and settled in the areas of Moscow and Tobolsk, the present capitals of Russia and Siberia which constitute the U.S.S.R. Their brother Gomer went north and west and became the forefather of the Eastern European nations, his territory extending to the Germany of today. Gomer's sons included Togarmah whose family separated. "Togarmah of the north quarters" (see Ezek. 38:6) consists of that which was Estonia, Latvia, and Lithuania before they were absorbed by Russia. The other portion of Togarmah's family settled in Turkey and Asia Minor, ultimately becoming a part of the Persian Empire.

4. The ten-nation coalition of countries of Western Europe which will "befriend" Israel (referred to in Dan. 11:40–43 and 9:26, 27 and alluded to in Dan. 2:42–44 and in Rev. 17:12,13) plus the United States which also has befriended Israel and is fully committed to its protection today. (Note: Due to its falling into vile wickedness in these "last days," America is destined to be "cut . . . with pruning hooks" and to see its productive branches "cut down"; but it will survive its severe and woeful judgment and will continue as "a nation" during the millennial reign of Christ, for this is a definite portion of its destiny according to the prophet Isaiah.)

Tabulation of Nations Involved in World War III

Utilizing the above biblical prophecy, I tabulated the sum of the areas of the countries mentioned. The amazing statistics of this tabulation are reported below.

Total Land Area by Continents

Using one of the finest and largest atlases known today, the *Life Pictorial Atlas of the World*,* the total land area by continent was first determined.

*By the editors of *Life* and Rand McNally (New York: Time Inc., 1961), p. 22.

Continent	Total Land Area in Square Miles
Africa	11,635,000
Antarctica	5,100,000
Asia	17,035,000
Australia	2,974,581
Europe	3,850,000
North America	9,435,000
South America	6,860,000
Total land mass	56,889,581

(Note: Round figures are used in the totals. This is necessary because of the fluctuations of volcanic islands and the total impossibility of obtaining exact measurement of multiplied thousands of islands in the world.)

One Third of the World

Inasmuch as Bible prophecies in Revelation 8 depict that one third of the trees will be burned up, one third of the rivers and fountains of waters will be poisoned, and one third of the sky darkened—as well as one third of the ships and creatures of the sea destroyed—to arrive at a figure, *one third of the total land mass*, which automatically would include one third of the rivers, springs, etc., the determination was reached as follows: 56,889,581 divided by 3 equals 18,963,194 square miles.

Specific Land Areas to be Involved in World War III

According to the prophecy recorded in Daniel 11:40, World War III will start with a concerted thrust against the land of Israel by "the king of the south," identified in Isaiah 19 as being the mightiest of the Arab League nations, Egypt (including its Arab partners). The war will immediately expand by the entering of "the king of the north" (the Arabs' mighty ally, the U.S.S.R.). This "Chief prince of Moscow and Tobolsk" will have with him, in fulfilment of Ezekiel 38:6, the satellite nations of the Warsaw Pact area referred to as Gomer and all his bands and "Togarmah of the north quarters, and many people with thee" (v. 6). Egypt and the entire Arab League coalition is embraced by the ancient areas referred to in Ezekiel 38:5 as "Persia, Ethiopia and Libya." All of the nations in these regions will be involved.

In the four verses just preceding the key verse 40 of Daniel 11, "the king" of the "time of the end" is described. Called "the beast" in Revelation 13 and 17, this is the one to whom the ten leaders (kings) of the Western European area of the old Roman Empire will "give their power and strength" in fulfillment of the prophecy recorded in Revelation 17:13. Having been given full authority and power by these European nations, the king shall ". . . enter also into the glorious land [Israel], . . ." according to Daniel 11:41. He shall do so ostensibly to protect Israel from "the king of the north" and "the king of the south." By this move we see clearly that Western Europe is to be in the conflict.

By way of the Atlantic Alliance, NATO, unilateral action, or in self defense, the United States will take part in the fray to assist in the defeat of the "mighty army" of the Russian military colossus. The all-out thermonuclear exchange will be the quick and very devastating result!

In summary, the alignment of the nations scheduled to be involved in World War III, by their groups, is as follows:

Category of Alignment	Area in Square Miles
The object of the conflict, the land of Israel (as of 1949)	7,990
The Persian Empire area at the time of the prophecy (500 B.C.)	1,850,010
The other Arab areas by ancient titles (Ethiopia and Libya)	3,487,943
The lands of Meshech and Tubal (Moscow and Tobolsk: U.S.S.R.)	8,650,140
The land area of Warsaw Pact nations ("Gomer and his bands . . .")	381,934
The Ten Nation Empire area of Western Europe (Roman region)	763,412
The area of the U.S. (specified by description in prophecy) . .	3,675,630
Area allowance for ancient Persian part of West Pakistan . .	146,135
Exactly	18,963,194

For the benefit of skeptics as to the precision of these land area figures compared to specific Bible prophecies written over twenty-five hundred years ago, the following is the full tabulation by category and country:

Land Area Chart of Countries Listed in the Bible as Participants in World War III
(Area figures quoted are from *Life Pictorial Atlas of the World*, by Life and Rand McNally.)

Category and Country	Land Area in Sq. Mi.
1. Israel (prior to 1967)	7,990
2. The Arab nations (according to Bible listings) (Source: *Hammond Historical Atlas* [Maplewood, N.J.: Hammond, Inc., 1960], p. H-5)	
Afghanistan	250,900
Cyprus	3,572
Egypt	386,100
Iraq	171,554
Iran	629,180
Jordan	37,291
Lebanon	4,014
Syria	71,291
Turkey	296,108
	1,850,010
"Ethiopa" and "Libya" (ancient)	
Ethiopia	457,147
Somalia	246,137
Sudan	967,248
Algeria	919,352
Libya	679,358
Morocco	170,382
Tunisia	48,319
	3,487,943
3. Land of Meshech and Tubal (grandsons of Noah) U.S.S.R., including Baltic States (Togarmah of No. Qtrs.)	
	8,650,140

Plus the satellite nations
Gomer, etc.

Bulgaria	43,036
Czechoslavakia	49,353
East Germany	41,634
Hungary	35,909
Poland	120,327
Rumania	91,675
	381,934

4. Ten-nation empire (Western Europe of the
Old Roman Empire)

Austria	32,365
Belgium	11,775
England	50,890
France	212,766
West Germany	95,885
Italy	116,273
Luxemberg	998
The Netherlands	12,526
Portugal	35,589
Spain	194,345
	763,412

Plus the United States	3,675,630

5. Allowance for Persian part of Pakistan	146,135

Total Land Area	18,963,194

Which One Third of the World?
Summary Statement

The chart, which was utilized to determine the above totals, listed the land areas by continents, and the total was 56,889,581 square miles. This figure, divided by three, gave the net land area which Bible prophecy declared was to be affected in the coming devastation. The net area was found to be 18,963,194 square miles.

The tabulation chart was devised by this writer from specific Bible references which refer to land areas that according to Bible prophecies are where the war is to occur. Even though coordination was anticipated because of my awareness of the accuracy of Bible declarations, you cannot, nevertheless, imagine the heart-leap of joy when the two figures were compared and found to be so extremely close that only a very minute adjustment was needed to make them exactly equal. A recheck of the historical map showed that the Persian Empire included only a portion of Pakistan—an adjustment was not only allowable but turned out to be even more biblically correct and accurate. How wondrous is God's Word! What a marvellously divine God we have in which to trust!

In the overall picture, there is also latitude for certain variations, because, for instance, it would not be necessary for one third of the Sahara Desert sections of the Arab world to be burned up by nuclear explosions. Other fringe areas, however, such as Cuba, parts of Greenland, and other small regions used by either the United States or the U.S.S.R. for military bases or logistics, would most likely come under attack in an all-out confrontation, and these would compensate for any such variations.

Amazing Accuracy

In the light of the facts just presented, where land areas listed by the Hebrew prophets over five hundred years before the birth of Jesus coincide precisely with figures recorded by John when he wrote the Book of Revelation in A.D. 95, there can be no possible answer but absolute divine inspiration of those Scripture texts. Let us review the summaries:

The sum of all of the areas of the countries to be affected . . . 18,963,194 sq. mi.

74

The result of dividing the total land area of the world by three . . . 18,963,194 sq. mi.

Who is there who will be so naive or foolish as to try to "explain away" such precision of two completely different sets of mathematical figures? Any effort to do so would be utter folly. Here is undeniable proof of the precise accuracy of Bible prophecy. There is no other explanation possible.

The U.S.A.

I have stipulated that the United States constitutes a part of the one third of the world to be involved in devastation and judgment, and I have listed it as such on the "Category of Alignment" chart as being "specified by description in prophecy." Can that be verified?

President Predicts 'Heartland' Growth

New Waterway Dedicated as Key to Revival

BY DON IRWIN
Times Staff Writer

PATH—Shaded area on map traces McClellan-Kerr Arkansas Navigation Project's path.
(AP) Wirephoto map

CATOOSA, Okla.—President Nixon dipped into the American heartland Saturday to dedicate the 436-mile McClellan-Kerr Arkansas Navigation Project linking landlocked Oklahoma and Arkansas with the Gulf of Mexico.

The President foresaw benefits for the nation as a whole in the $1.2 billion project, the costliest waterway development in U.S. history.

It will mean "a whole new era of growth" for the "new maritime states" it serves, Mr. Nixon told a friendly crowd of about 25,000. The Democratic governors of the two states and a bipartisan congressional delegation were gathered on raw earth beside the upstream terminus of the project that has made the once-impassable Arkansas River a navigable link with the Mississippi and the Gulf.

Foresees Waterway Extension

Mr. Nixon foresaw a day when the waterway would be extended upstream from Catoosa—15 miles from downtown Tulsa—to Kansas and Colorado. He predicted that the inexpensive waterborne transportation it affords would extend nationwide benefits.

"This great region, so ready for development, can provide part of the answer to the increasingly acute problem of congestion and uncontrolled growth in America's largest metropolitan areas," Mr. Nixon said.

Many Americans who have left rural homes in the Midwestern country he likes to call "the heartland" to seek higher incomes in cities really want to return, the President said.

"I say let the people who want to live in the heartland of America have jobs, have opportunity, and not be drawn away—and that's what this project means," Mr. Nixon said to applause.

6

THE BIBLE'S DESCRIPTION OF THE UNITED STATES

There is one chapter of the Bible which gives so graphic a picture of this nation, and which also contains so pertinent a proclamation concerning this country, that it must, and can only, apply to America. I do not believe there is any other country to which Isaiah 18 could apply in *all* of its descriptive detail.

Note with me now the detail of that description and also the exactness of the application of the proclaimed destiny of *the nation* described in this prophetic chapter.

The Message of Isaiah 18

"Woe . . ." is the first word of the chapter. It is a positive warning to someone—the nation that fits the description which follows.

"Woe to the land shadowing with wings . . ." (v. 1). The emblem of the United States is a bald eagle with extended "shadowing" wings. This in itself is but an indication, for other nations, including Mexico, Ecuador, and Zambia, have birds with open wings as emblems.

"Which is beyond the rivers of Ethiopia: That sendeth ambassadors by the sea . . ." (vv. 1,2). Since all Bible geography is referred to in its relation to the Promised Land of Israel

(Palestine), this is depicting a message of "woe" to a far country which is "beyond . . . Ethiopia" and which is overseas from the land of Israel. This factor alone eliminates all nations of Europe, Asia, and Africa, for any of these could be reached by way of land routes from the land of Israel. "The nation," therefore, to whom this message is addressed is to be a "land shadowing with wings" which is beyond the land routes and which "sendeth ambassadors by the sea."

America is in the new world—overseas from Israel. Thus the identity narrows down to a transoceanic area such as America; and the United States has been notably a free country sending *many ambassadors* to virtually every country in the world, ever seeking to negotiate and to communicate officially through the ambassadors of our State Department. This is another confirmation.

Further Narrowing of Identity

The message of Isaiah 18 is one of "Woe" and of "Go," as stipulated in verses one and two. The specific message is ". . . Go, ye swift messengers . . ." (v. 2). The reference to the sending of ambassadors by the sea ". . . in vessels of bulrushes upon the waters . . . ," such as in the bulrush-type boats of the lake areas of the Nile River, would indicate that a speedy vessel would be required. The bulrush boats, which were duplicated by Norwegian explorer Thor Heyerdahl who along with other scientists floated across the Atlantic Ocean in "Ra II," could hardly be referred to as "swift." These are to be "swift messengers," and please note that they are sent "to a nation," not a continental area. *This is a specific message to one specific nation.*

"A Nation . . ."

". . . to a nation scattered and peeled . . . ," reads Isaiah 18:2. More recent translations specify "outspread and polished" or "broad and highly developed." This, although not exclusively descriptive of America, is agreeable with its identity. The United States is one of the broadest, and it is certainly the most highly developed country on the face of the earth.

"Go . . . to a nation . . . broad and highly developed, to a *people* . . . (v. 2, italics mine). Although consisting of many ethnic groups and of fifty separate states united into a nation, the United States also is truly a people. Further specific proof of this may be found in the Preamble to the Constitution of the United States which reads: *"We, the people of the United States,* in order to form a more perfect *union"* (italics mine).

George Washington is reported to have had a vision of the progress and the destiny of the United States during the stay at Valley Forge in the winter of 1777. In that vision the messenger was depicted as a bright angel on whose brow rested a crown of light on which was traced the word, "Union." It is noteworthy that the word "Union" was not used in any part of the Declaration of Independence of 1776, but that it *was* in the Preamble to the Constitution which was written in 1787 after the vision.

More Specific Identity

The special message of Isaiah 18 is directed to ". . . a people terrible from their beginning hitherto . . ." (v. 2). From the time of the signing of the Declaration of Independence in 1776 until the present date, the United States has never lost a declared war. It proclaimed its independence from England and then defeated that country in the Revolutionary War. One of its early flags bore the ensign "Don't Tread On Me," and this nation never has been subject to any other nation from that day to this. It is, indeed, "a nation terrible [tenacious] from its beginning hitherto."

"Meted Out and Trodden Down"

". . . a nation meted out and trodden down . . ." (v. 2). No other nation on earth is so completely surveyed and "meted out" as is the United States. Most of America has its county lines, quarter sections, and one-mile roads. Every acre is accounted for in the government archives. The United States consists of 3,071 counties and 59 county equivalents for a total of 3,130. It has a fifty-state land area of 3,615,211 square miles traversed by 3,838,146 lineal miles of roadways, as of December 31, 1975. According to the Federal Highway Commission, traffic on those roadways in 1975 consisted of 106,712,551 automobiles, 462,144 buses, and 25,775,715 trucks for a total of 132,950,410 registered vehicles. And you can add to that, if you wish, 1,500,000 freight and passenger cars on 199,215 miles of railroad tracks traversing the country. Most assuredly it can be said that this land is traversed and "trodden down." In addition we can see here a direct fulfillment of Daniel 12:4 which proclaims that in the time of the end ". . . many shall run to and fro. . . ." If you don't think so, just try walking across one of our freeways or expressways!

"Whose Land the Rivers Have Spoiled"

Whereas many nations have only one or two major rivers, the United States has a vast number of rivers. According to the Interstate Commerce Commission, the ton mileage carried on America's inland waterways in 1976 was 352 *billion* tons, and this does not include export shipping. With the opening of the Arkansas River Basin Waterway in 1970, wheat and other cargo from the Great Plains now can travel on river barges from within one mile of Tulsa, Oklahoma, directly to the ocean ports and thence to any seaport in the world. Yes, this nation is, indeed, ". . . a nation . . . whose land the rivers have spoiled [traversed]!" (v. 2).

(And for any who prefer the ultra-literal viewpoint, just consider the magnitude of the ecology reports currently available as to the "spoiling" of the rivers and waterways by many forms of pollution.)

Identity by National Strength and Prestige

Isaiah 18:3 proclaims: "All ye inhabitants of the world, and dwellers on the earth, see ye, when he [this nation] lifteth up an ensign on the mountains [Note: And we have even placed an 'ensign' plaque on the moon!]; and when he bloweth a trumpet, hear ye."

As of today, the United States is the strongest and most highly developed nation on earth, having an annual Gross National Product rating of almost $2 trillion per annum. No other nation comes near such a total. All nations listen when "Uncle Sam" *speaks*. Surely, this also is a mark of distinctive identity. Need there be any further documentation? No other nation on earth so completely matches every descriptive detail given in this amazing prophecy. The message proclaimed in Isaiah 18 is, therefore, a message to this particular land and to this particular people—to *this nation:* the United States of America.

7

GOD'S MESSAGE TO THIS LAND: A JUDGMENT

Isaiah 18:4 reads: "For so the LORD said unto me, I will take my rest, and I will consider in my dwelling place . . . ." (Isaiah, it must be remembered, lived in the eighth century B.C., two thousand years before the discovery of America.)

God is portrayed here as stating that He is about to sit down and take a close look at this particular nation. The first word of this chapter is "woe." This denotes a deep consideration for judgment; ". . . like a clear heat upon herbs, and like a cloud of dew in the heat of harvest" (v. 4). Both of these metaphors imply severe damage. Herbs require moisture rather than the injurious "clear heat," and a cloud of dew at harvest would produce mildew and great crop loss. *Judgment is coming!*

The Time of the Judgment

"For afore the harvest, when the bud is perfect and the sour grape is ripening . . ." (v. 5)—at a time when the country under consideration is at the height of its production, when its potential for good is "ripening"—*then* is the time when the judgment of severe pruning is proclaimed against it.

In accordance with this portion of the prophecy, therefore, *the judgment of this nation could come at any moment*, for the prophesied status of "this nation" fits America today.

The Source of the Judgment

Read carefully now, for real discernment will reveal much here. Take a careful review of the nouns and pronouns of the great proclamation of this prophecy.

(1) The proclamation is not against a particular leader nor any particular regime. This is a proclamation of judgment on "the land" which consists of "a nation" made up of its component parts, states, and people. In actuality this judgment is on ". . . a people . . . whose land the rivers have spoiled!" (Isa. 18:2). The ecologists tell us today that the rivers of refuse and poisons have spoiled not only the land of America, but also the surrounding seas far out into the Gulf Stream. Yes, this description fits the United States.

(2) In reference to its identity, the country is referred to, not in the female gender as would be the case with so many of the nations in Bible history and prophecy, but in the masculine gender: ". . . see ye, when he [Uncle Sam, so to speak] lifteth up an ensign . . . and when he bloweth a trumpet, hear ye" (v. 3).

(3) In verse 4, Isaiah recorded: "So the Lord said unto me, I will take my rest, and I will consider. . . ." The reference here is to the Lord, Himself; and, significantly, He is identified by the specific pronoun "I."

(4) In verse 5, as we come to the actual statement of the judgment against this nation, the terminology merits some serious reflection, for the statement is: "For afore the harvest, when the bud is perfect, and the sour grape is ripening in the flower, he shall both cut off the sprigs [some unnecessary or insignificant portions of the vine] with pruning hooks, and take away and cut down the branches." Here is a declaration that someone other than the Lord God is destined to "prune" and "cut" this vine—*this nation.*

The Destiny of This Nation

As to the destiny of this nation, we find a solacing statement in verse 6 which states: "They shall be left together. . . ." Thus

83

the declaration is that America, even though it is to be severely "cut" and "pruned" at the time of its greatest productivity, *shall not be utterly destroyed.*

The last two verses of Isaiah 18 read: "They shall be left together unto the fowls of the mountains, and to the beasts of the earth: and the fowls shall summer upon them, and all the beasts of the earth shall winter upon them. In that time shall the present be brought unto the Lord of hosts of a people outspread and polished, and from a people terrible from their beginning hitherto; a nation meted out and trodden under foot, whose land the rivers have spoiled [traversed], to the place of the name of the LORD of hosts, the mount Zion" (vv. 6,7).

Truly, God has laid out the destiny of the nations, and in accordance with the documentation presented in this chapter, He has portrayed for all to see the ultimate destiny of America.

The people of America will survive the holocaust of being "pruned" and "cut" in that thermonuclear war we term World War III, and they will survive the other judgments to come in the prophesied tribulation period of which that war is a part. They will survive and be delivered.

Full deliverance will come when Christ returns to earth as the Messiah of Israel, and as King of kings and Lord of lords (Zech. 14:4,5,9; Rev. 19:11–20:4). When He establishes His perfect kingdom of peace on earth, the surviving nations will praise and honor Him and ". . . shall even go up from year to year to worship the King, the Lord of hosts, and to keep the feast of tabernacles" (Zech. 14:16).

Sing unto the LORD, O ye saints of his, and give thanks at the remembrance of His holiness. For His anger endureth but a moment; in his favour is life: weeping may endure for a night, but joy cometh in the morning (Ps. 30:4,5).

Section II

FURTHER INFORMATION ON THE DESTINY OF THE UNITED STATES

Declaration

Two secular visions have been selected for comment in this writing due to the evidence of their accuracy and accountability which I attribute to divine revelation. Careful analysis shows that they do not contradict Bible prophecy.

The intent in quoting and commenting on these visions is to show the power and the absolute *foreknowledge* of God.

Bible prophecy has been found to be true based on current scientific facts. Many historical developments already have been given which have verified the authenticity and the accuracy of these Bible prophecies.

No secular vision or revelation would even be considered for comment which would be in any way contrary to those facts which already have been established. Consider the presentation of the correlation of these recorded prophecies, therefore, with assurance and with confidence in their reality.

The evidence in this section of the book is presented so that you may know when these things come to pass that you can fully trust in the directions for survival which are given at the end of this writing.

Capable of both pre-attack and post-attack strategic reconnaissance missions, the SR-71 carries a wide variety of advanced observation equipment. Flying at 2,000 m.p.h., it can survey 60,000 square miles of the earth's surface in one hour from an altitude of 80,000 feet. (U.S. Air Force information sheet)

8

GEORGE WASHINGTON'S
VISION

Great caution must be taken in accepting the authenticity of any visions or dreams of men. The following vision, however, does have some very remarkable factors which seem to be fully true to U.S. history as well as to the potential history of today. The occurrences depicted are also in accord with the prophecies of the Bible.

The story of the occurrence and the content of this vision was first published in the American war veterans' paper *The National Tribune* in December, 1880. That paper is now known as *The Stars and Stripes*. The vision account was reprinted again in *The Stars and Stripes* dated December 21, 1950. The occasion of the vision, as told to publisher Wesley Bradshaw, is as follows:

The last time I ever saw Anthony Sherman was on the fourth of July, 1859, in Independence Square. He was then ninety-nine years old, and becoming very feeble. But though so old, his dimming eyes rekindled as he gazed upon Independence Hall, which he had come to visit once more.

"Let's go into the hall," he said. "I want to tell you of an incident of Washington's life—one which no one alive knows of except myself; and if you live, you will before long see it verified. Mark the prediction, you will see it verified.

"From the opening of the Revolution we experienced all phases of fortune, now good and now ill, one time victorious and another conquered. The darkest period we had, I think, was when Washington after several reverses, retreated to Valley Forge, where he resolved to pass the winter of 1777. Ah! I have often seen the tears coursing down our dear commander's care-worn cheeks, as he would be conversing with a confidential officer about the condition of his poor soldiers. You have doubtless heard the story of Washington's going to the thicket to pray. Well, it was not only true, but he used often to pray in secret for aid and comfort. And God brought us safely through the darkest days of tribulation.

"One day, I remember it well, the chilly winds whistled through the leafless trees, though the sky was cloudless and the sun shone brightly. He remained in his quarters nearly all the afternoon, alone. When he came out I noticed that his face was a shade paler than usual, and there seemed to be something on his mind of more than ordinary importance. Returning just after dusk, he dispatched an orderly to the quarters of an officer, who was presently in attendance. After a preliminary conversation of about half an hour, Washington, gazing upon his companion with that strange look of dignity which he alone could command, said to the latter:

An Uninvited Guest

" 'I do not know whether it is owing to the anxiety of my mind, or what, but this afternoon, as I was sitting at this table engaged in preparing a dispatch, something in the apartment seemed to disturb me. Looking up, I beheld standing opposite me a singularly beautiful being. So astonished was I, for I had given strict orders not to be disturbed, that it was some moments before I found language to inquire the cause of the visit. A second, a third, and even a fourth time did I repeat the question, but received no answer from my mysterious visitor except a slight raising of the eyes.

90

" 'By this time I felt strange sensations spreading over me. I would have risen but the riveted gaze of the being before me rendered volition impossible. I assayed once more to speak, but my tongue had become useless, as if paralyzed. A new influence, mysterious, potent, irresistible, took possession of me. All I could do was to gaze steadily, vacantly at my unknown visitor.

" 'Gradually the surrounding atmosphere seemed to fill with sensations, and grew luminous. Everything about me seemed to rarefy, the mysterious visitor also becoming more airy and yet more distinct to my eyes than before. I began to feel as one dying, or rather to experience the sensations which I have sometimes imagined accompany death. I did not think, I did not reason, I did not move. All were alike impossible. I was only conscious of gazing fixedly, vacantly at my companion.

The Revolutionary War as Seen in the Vision

" 'Presently I heard a voice saying, "Son of the Republic, look and learn," while at the same time my visitor extended an arm eastward. I now beheld a heavy white vapor at some distance rising fold upon fold. This gradually dissipated, and I looked upon a strange scene. Before me lay, spread out in one vast plain, all the countries of the world—Europe, Asia, Africa and America. I saw rolling and tossing between Europe and America the billows of the Atlantic, and between Asia and America lay the Pacific. "Son of the Republic," said the same mysterious voice as before, "look and learn."

" 'At that moment I beheld a dark, shadowy being, like an angel, standing, or rather floating in mid-air, between Europe and America. Dipping water out of the ocean in the hollow of each hand, he sprinkled some upon America with his right hand, while with his left he cast some over Europe. Immediately a cloud arose from these countries, and joined in mid-ocean. For awhile it seemed stationary, and then it moved slowly westward, until it enveloped America in its murky folds. Sharp flashes of lightning gleamed through it at intervals, and I heard the smothered groans and cries of the American people. [This may be interpreted to have been the Revolutionary War then in progress.]

" 'A second time the angel dipped water from the ocean and sprinkled it out as before. The dark cloud was then drawn back to the ocean, in whose heaving billows it sank from view.

Prediction of the Civil War

" 'A third time I heard the mysterious visitor saying, "Son of the Republic, look and learn." I cast my eyes upon America and beheld villages and towns and cities springing up one after another until the whole land from the Atlantic to the Pacific was dotted with them. Again, I heard the mysterious voice say, "Son of the Republic, the end of the century cometh, look and learn."

" 'And this time the dark shadowy angel turned his face southward. From Africa I saw an ill-omened spectre approach our land. It flitted slowly and heavily over every town and city of the latter. The inhabitants presently set themselves in battle array against each other. As I continued looking I saw a bright angel on whose brow rested a crown of light, on which was traced the word "Union." He was bearing the American flag. He placed the flag between the divided nation and said, "Remember, ye are brethren."

The Republic Develops as "A Nation"

" 'Instantly, the inhabitants, casting down their weapons, became friends once more and united around the National Standard.

Frightful – Incredible – World War III

" 'Again I heard the mysterious voice saying, "Son of the Republic, look and learn." At this the dark, shadowy angel placed a trumpet to his mouth, and blew three distinct blasts; and taking water from the ocean, he sprinkled it upon Europe, Asia and Africa.

" 'Then my eyes beheld a fearful scene. From each of these continents arose thick black clouds that were soon joined into one. And through this mass there gleamed a dark red light by which I saw hordes of armed men. These men, moving with the cloud, marched by land and sailed by sea to America, which country was enveloped in the volume of the cloud. And I dimly saw these vast armies devastate the whole country and burn the villages, towns and cities which I had seen springing up.

" 'As my ears listened to the thundering of the cannon, clashing of swords, and the shouts and cries of millions in mortal combat, I again heard the mysterious voice saying, "Son of the Republic, look and learn." When this voice had ceased, the dark shadowy angel placed his trumpet once more to his mouth, and blew a long and fearful blast.

Heaven Helps the U.S.A.

" 'Instantly a light as of a thousand suns shone down from above me, and pierced and broke into fragments the dark cloud which enveloped America. At the same moment the angel upon whose head still shown the word "Union," and who bore our national flag in one hand and a sword in the other, descended from the heavens attended by legions of white spirits. These immediately joined the inhabitants of America, who I perceived were well-nigh overcome, but who immediately taking courage again, closed up their broken ranks and renewed the battle.

" 'Again, amid the fearful noise of the conflict I heard the mysterious voice saying, "Son of the Republic, look and learn." As the voice ceased, the shadowy angel for the last time dipped water from the ocean and sprinkled it upon America. Instantly the dark cloud rolled back, together with the armies it had brought, leaving the inhabitants of the land victorious.

The Destiny of the United States

" 'Then once more, I beheld the villages, towns and cities springing up where I had seen them before, while the bright angel, planting the azure standard he had brought in the midst of them, cried with a loud voice: "While the stars remain, and the heavens send down dew upon the earth, so long shall the Union last." And taking from his brow the crown on which blazened the word "Union," he placed it upon the standard while the people kneeling down said, "Amen."

" 'The scene instantly began to fade and dissolve, and I at last saw nothing but the rising, curling vapor I at first beheld. This also disappeared, and I found myself once more gazing upon the mysterious visitor, who, in the same voice I had heard before, said, "Son of the Republic, what you have seen is thus interpreted. Three great perils will come upon the Republic. The most fearful for her is the third. But the whole world united shall not prevail against her. Let every child of the Republic learn to live for his God, his land and Union." With these words the vision vanished, and I started from my seat and felt that I had seen a vision wherein had been shown me the birth, the progress, and destiny of the United States.'

"Such, my friends," the venerable narrator concluded, "were the words I heard from Washington's own lips, and America will do well to profit by them."

Commentary

The commentary concerning this vision will be given after

the text of the other vision is quoted. Both vision accounts will then be discussed in their relation to history, their potentiality for fulfillment, and their coordination with the recorded specific prophecies of the Bible. The resulting comparison is very striking and amazing.

9

THE AMERICAN EVANGELIST'S VISION

An American evangelist recorded the following supernatural vision in the year 1954. Research reveals that not only are the prophecies of this vision true to the Scriptures quoted therein, but scientific and military leaders today are aware that these things are coming to pass or are very plausible in light of modern technological advances. The evangelist remains anonymous. (It was not this author.)

The Background

"As I stepped inside the elevator at the Empire State Building, I never dreamed of the experience which awaited me just 86 stories up.

"My ears began to close, due to the sudden increase of altitude, as the elevator shot upward to the first observatory 86 floors above the ground. This was the first time I had gone atop the Empire State Building, and it was a trip I had been eager to take, since no visit to New York City can be considered complete without a trip to the observatories up the 1472 foot tall building . . .

"As I stepped off the elevator and went onto the outside terrace, I went expecting to see all of New York City, New Jersey, Manhattan, the Bronx, and on across the Hudson

River to Westchester in a great panoramic view. But little did I realize that God had an even greater view awaiting me there; as, through a supernatural vision, He would let me see that which is soon to take place on the whole North American continent.

The View

"As I stood there . . . , just to the south of me, on Bedloe's Island, I could see the Statue of Liberty illuminating the gateway to the new world. To people everywhere, this 300 foot statue has become the symbol of liberty. It was presented to the people of the United States by the freedom-loving people of France in 1883 . . .

"I looked to the east. There I could see the United Nations Building, which has been called 'The last sacred temple for the rediscovery of human brotherhood.' The great statesmen of the world have declared we must remain at peace with one another or die. . . .

"The Empire State Building, located at the intersection of 34th Street and Fifth Avenue, covers only about two acres of ground, yet it is so high that people in the observatories can see the sun rise a half-hour sooner and set a half-hour later than people on the street . . . From the 86th floor observatory, if you look up, you will see the huge television tower rising 222 feet above the previous height of the building. This tower sends the signals of all of Manhattan's important TV broadcasters, who have their transmitters in the building.

"The 102nd floor observatory, 1,250 feet above the street, is glass enclosed so that one may see in all directions the surrounding areas of the city.

"The 86th floor observatory has both indoor and outdoor terraces. When you step out on the 86th floor terrace, you are standing where famous people from every country of the world have been before you . . . As I stood there, I was aware that I was only one of 10 million people representing every nation on earth who have visited the Empire State Observatories. But I still did not realize that I was to be the only one of that ten million to whom God had chosen to give such a revelation as I was to receive atop that great building.

A Giant Telescope — And The Spirit of the Lord

"There, on the east side of the terrace, I noticed a giant telescope, of the kind into which you can drop a dime and see for approximately fifteen miles. I knew that a dime slipped into that telescope would enable me to see much farther than the natural eye could reach. I got a dime from my pocket and held it in my hand, ready to drop it into the telescope when the man in front of me was through viewing the scene . . . As I stood with my dime between my fingers, waiting my turn, suddenly the Spirit of the Lord came upon me. I noticed the two giant eyes of the telescope as the man who was manipulating it turned it in my direction. I was amazed that the Spirit of the Lord should so move upon me, there, atop the Empire State Building. Why should I feel such a surge of His Spirit and power there?

"Thou Shalt Have Wars"

"Then suddenly I heard the voice of the Lord. It was as clear and as distinct as a voice could be. It seemed to come from the very midst of the giant telescope. But when I looked at the telescope, I knew it hadn't come from there, but directly from heaven. The voice said,

'The eyes of the Lord run to and fro throughout the whole earth, to shew himself strong in the behalf of them whose heart is perfect toward him. Herein thou hast done foolishly: therefore from henceforth thou shalt have wars.' [This was a direct quotation from 2 Chronicles 16:9.]

"Immediately, when I heard the voice of God, I knew this was a quotation of Scripture. But never before had I had a thing come to me so forcefully by the power of the Spirit. The ticking of the telescope stopped. The man before me had used up his dime's worth. As he stepped away I knew that I was next. As I stepped to the telescope and dropped in my dime, immediately the ticking started again. This ticking was an automatic clock which would allow me to use the telescope for a definitely limited time only.

"As I swung the telescope to the north, suddenly the Spirit of God came upon me in a way that I had never thought of before. Seemingly in the Spirit I was entirely caught away. I knew that the telescope itself had nothing to do with the distance which I was suddenly enabled to see, for I seemed to see things far beyond the range of the telescope, even on a bright, clear day. It was simply that God had chosen this time to reveal these things to me, for as I looked through the telescope, it was not Manhattan Island that I saw, but a far greater scene . . .

An Amazing Vision

[*Note: The next portion of this vision-revelation is in the form of an allegory wherein the evangelist sees a struggle and the fall of the Statue of Liberty. His vision of the action of World War III comes at and after the fall of the statue.*]

"That which I was looking upon was not Manhattan Island. It was all of the North American continent spread out before me as a map is spread upon a table. It was not the East River and the Hudson River that I saw on either side, but the Atlantic and the Pacific Oceans. And instead of the Statue of Liberty standing there in the bay on her tiny island, I saw her standing far out in the Gulf of Mexico. She was between me and the United States.

[*Note: As though he was looking at North America from the northern coast of South America.*]

The U.S.A., as Viewed from the South

"There, clear and distinct, lay all the North American continent, with all its great cities. To the north lay the Great Lakes. Far to the northeast was New York City. I could see Seattle and Portland far to the northwest. Down the West Coast, there was San Francisco and Los Angeles. Closer in the foreground, there lay New Orleans, at the center of the Gulf Coast area. I could see the great towering ranges of the Rocky Mountains, and trace with my eye the Continental Divide. All this and more, I could see spread out before me as a great map upon a table.

God's Portrayal of Judgment to Come

"As I looked, suddenly from the sky I saw a giant hand reach down. That gigantic hand was reaching out toward the Statue of Liberty. In a moment her gleaming torch was torn from her hand, and in it instead was placed a cup. And I saw protruding from that cup a giant sword, shining, as if a great light had been turned upon its glistening edge. Never before had I seen such a sharp, glistening, dangerous sword. It seemed to threaten all the world. As the great cup was placed in the hand of the Statue of Liberty, I heard these words:

'Thus saith the Lord of hosts . . . Drink ye and be drunken, spue, and fall, and rise no more, because of the sword which I will send. . . .'

"As I heard these words, I recognized them as a quotation from Jeremiah 25:27.

"I was amazed to hear the Statue of Liberty speak out in reply, 'I will not drink.'

"Then, as the voice of thunder, I heard again the voice of the Lord, saying:

. . . 'Thus saith the LORD of hosts, Ye shall certainly drink' (Jer. 25:28).

"Then suddenly the giant hand forced the cup to the lips of the Statue of Liberty, and she became powerless to defend herself. The mighty hand of God forced her to drink every drop of the cup. As she drank the bitter dregs, these were the words that I heard:

'. . . should ye be utterly unpunished? Ye shall not be unpunished: for I will call for a sword upon all the inhabitants of the earth, saith the LORD of hosts' (Jer. 25:29).

"When the cup was withdrawn from the lips of the Statue of Liberty, I noticed the sword was missing from the cup, which could mean but one thing. The contents of the cup had been completely consumed! I knew that the sword merely typified war, death, and destruction, which is no doubt on the way.

[*Note: A cross-reference to the above statement is found in Ezekiel 21:28: "And thou, son of man, prophesy and say, Thus saith the LORD GOD . . . . The sword, the sword is drawn, for the slaughter it is furbished to consume because of the glittering."*]

"Liberty" Staggers

"Then, as one drunken on too much wine, I saw the Statue of Liberty become unsteady on her feet and begin to stagger and to lose her balance. I saw her splashing in the Gulf, trying to regain her balance. I saw her stagger again and again, and fall to her knees. As I saw her desperate attempts to regain her balance, and rise to her feet again, my heart was filled with compassion for her struggles. But as she struggled there in the Gulf, once again I heard these words:

'Ye shall drink and be drunken, and spue, and fall, and rise no more because of the sword that I shall send among you.'

"As I watched, I wondered if the Statue of Liberty would ever be able to regain her feet—if she would ever stand again. And as I watched, it seemed that with all her power she struggled to rise, and finally staggered to her feet again, and stood there swaying drunkenly. I felt sure that any moment she would fall again—possibly never to rise again. I seemed overwhelmed with a desire to reach out my hand to keep her head above water, for I knew that if she ever fell again she would drown there in the Gulf.

The Skeleton-Shaped Cloud

"Then as I watched, another amazing thing was taking place. Far to the northwest, just over Alaska, a huge, black cloud was arising. As it rose, it was as black as night. It seemed to be in the shape of a man's head. As it continued to rise, I observed two light spots in the black cloud. It rose further, and a gaping hole appeared. I could see that the black cloud was taking the shape of a skull, for now the huge, gaping mouth was plainly visible. Finally the head was complete. Then the shoulders began to appear, and on either side, long, black arms.

"It seemed that what I saw was the entire North American continent, spread out like a map upon a table with this terrible skeleton-formed cloud arising from behind the table. It rose steadily until the form was visible down to the waist. At the waist, the skeleton seemed to bend toward the United States, stretching forth a hand toward the east and one toward the west—one toward New York and one toward Seattle. As the awful form stretched forward, I could see that its entire attention seemed focused upon the United States, overlooking Canada—at least for the time being. As I saw the horrible black cloud in the form of a skeleton bending toward America, bending from the waist over, reaching down toward Chicago and out toward both coasts, I knew its one interest was to destroy the multitudes.

Three Puffs of Searing Vapors

[*Note. This part of the vision refers to a MIRV-type distribution, unknown in 1954*]

"As I watched in horror, the great black cloud stopped just above the Great Lake region, and turned its face toward New York City. Then out of the horrible, great gaping mouth began to appear wisps of white vapor which looked like smoke, as a cigarette smoker would blow puffs of smoke from his mouth. These whitish vapors were being blown toward New York City. The smoke began to spread until it covered all the eastern part of the United States.

"Then the skeleton turned to the west, and out of the horrible mouth and nostrils came another great puff of white smoke. This time it was blown in the direction of the West Coast. In a few minutes, the entire West Coast and Los Angeles area was covered with its vapors.

"Then toward the center came a third great puff. As I watched, St. Louis and Kansas City were enveloped in its white vapors. Then it came toward New Orleans. On they swept until they reached the Statue of Liberty where she stood staggering drunkenly in the blue waters of the Gulf. As the white vapors began to spread around the head of the Statue, she took in but one gasping breath and then began to cough as though to rid her lungs of the horrible vapors she had inhaled. One could tell readily by the painful coughing that those white vapors had seared her lungs.

"What were these white vapors? . . . Could they be the horrible nerve gas recently made known to the American public?

[*Note: Nerve gas works on humans in the same way insecticides work on bugs. The parallel is more than a coincidence. In the middle thirties, Dr. Gerhard Schrader of Germany discovered nerve gas during a search for new insecticides. The Nazis immediately realized the potential of Dr. Schrader's discovery and in 1939 built a plant to produce various nerve gases at Dyhernfurth, near the Polish border. Production got under way in 1942, but the Germans did not use nerve gas during World War II, presumably because the Allies' air superiority gave them the power to retaliate. After the war, the Russians took over the Dyhernfurth factory and its trained personnel. It has been producing nerve gas for the Soviets ever since.*

Possession of the plant gave the Russians a head start over the United States in nerve gas research. After years of research, we're now abreast and may have passed them.

After three years of research and experiments, Army and Civil Defense scientists, chemists, and technicians have produced the type of gas masks that apparently give adequate protection against nerve gas, but more tests are needed before the masks can be turned over to industry for mass production.

Authorities want to be sure that the masks will give protection against not only nerve gas, but all forms of gases, bacteriological warfare agents, and radioactive particles from atomic explosions. "We can't recommend the masks to the American people until they are foolproof," a spokesman said. What is holding up the tests? Lack of funds for research.]

The Vision: God Speaks Again

"As I looked with wonder upon the vision God had given me, I wondered: 'Could it be that it was the horrible nerve gas which was causing the Statue of Liberty to react so violently as it floated about her head, looking like an innocent cloud?'

"Then I heard the voice of God as He spoke again:

'Behold, the LORD maketh the earth empty, and maketh it waste, and turneth it upside down, and scattereth abroad the inhabitants thereof.

'And it shall be, as with the people, so with the priest; as with the servant, so with his master; . . . as with the buyer, so with the seller; as with the lender, so with the borrower; as with the taker of usury, so with the giver of usury to him.

'The land shall be utterly emptied, and utterly spoiled: for the LORD hath spoken this word.

'The earth mourneth and fadeth away, the world languisheth and fadeth away, the haughty people of the earth do languish.

'The earth also is defiled under the inhabitants thereof; because they have transgressed the laws, changed the ordinance, broken the everlasting covenant.

'Therefore hath the curse devoured the earth, and they that dwell therein are desolate; therefore the inhabitants of the earth are burned, and few men left' (Isa. 24:1–6).

The End of "Liberty"

"As I watched, the coughing grew worse. . . . The Statue of Liberty was moaning and groaning. She was in mortal agony. The pain must have been terrific, as again and again she tried to clear her lungs of those horrible vapors. I watched her there in the Gulf as she staggered, clutching her lungs and her breast with her hands. Then she fell to her knees. In a moment she gave one final cough, made a last desperate effort to rise to her knees, and then fell face forward into the waters of the Gulf and lay still—still as death. Only the lapping of the waves, splashing over her body, which was partly under the water and partly out of the water, broke the stillness.

"Run For Your Lives"

"Suddenly the silence was shattered by the screaming of sirens, sirens that seemed to scream, 'Run for your lives!'

Never before had I heard such shrill, screaming sirens. They seemed to be everywhere—to the north, the south, the east and the west. There seemed to be multitudes of sirens. And as I looked, I saw people everywhere running; but it seemed none of them ran more than a few paces, and then they fell. And even as I had seen the Statue of Liberty struggling to regain her poise and balance, and finally falling for the last time, to die on her face, I now saw millions of people falling in the streets, on the sidewalks, struggling. I heard their screams for mercy and help. I heard their horrible coughings, as though their lungs had been seared with fire [*Note: brimstone?*]. I heard the moanings and groanings of the doomed and dying. As I watched, a few finally reached shelters; but only a few ever got to the shelters, and above the groaning and the moaning of the dying multitudes, I heard these words:

'A noise shall come even to the ends of the earth; for the LORD hath a controversy with the nations, he will plead with all flesh; he will give them that are wicked to the sword, saith the LORD. . . . Behold, evil should go forth from nation to nation, and a great whirlwind shall be raised up from the coasts of the earth, and the slain of the LORD shall be at that day from one end of the earth even unto the other end of the earth: they shall not be lamented, neither gathered, nor buried; they shall be dung upon the ground' (Jer. 25:31–33).

Destructive Rockets Rise From the Sea

"Then suddenly I saw from the Atlantic and from the Pacific, and out of the Gulf, rocket-like objects that seemed to come up like fish leaping out of the water. High into the air they leaped, each heading into a different direction, but every one toward the United States. On the ground, the sirens screamed louder. Up from the ground I saw similar rockets beginning to ascend. To me, these appeared to be interceptor rockets although they arose from different points all over the United States. However, none of them seemed to be successful in intercepting the rockets that had risen from the ocean on every side. These rockets finally reached their maximum height, slowly turned over, and fell back to earth in defeat. Then suddenly, the rockets which had leaped out of

the oceans like fish all exploded at once. The explosion was
ear-splitting. The next thing which I saw was a huge ball of
fire. The only thing I have ever seen which resembled that
which I saw in my vision was the picture of the explosion of
the H-bomb somewhere in the Pacific some months ago. In
my vision, it was so real I seemed to feel a searing heat from
it.

Devastation by Terrific Explosions

"As the vision spread before my eyes, and I viewed the
widespread desolation brought about by the terrific explosions, I could not help thinking, 'While the defenders of our
nation have quibbled over what measures of defense to use,
and neglected the only true defense, faith and dependence
upon the true and living God, that which she has greatly
feared has come upon her! How true it has been proven that
"except the Lord keep the city, the watchman waketh but
in vain." '

A Very Significant, Final, Bible Quotation

"Then, as the noise of the battle subsided, to my ears came
this quotation from Joel, the second chapter:

'Blow ye the trumpet in Zion, and sound an alarm in my holy
mountain: let all the inhabitants of the land tremble: for the day of
the LORD cometh, for it is nigh at hand;
'A day of darkness and of gloominess, a day of clouds and of thick
darkness, as the morning spread upon the mountains: a great people
and a strong; there hath not been ever the like, neither shall be any
more after it, even to the years of many generations.
'A fire devoureth before them; and behind them a flame burneth:
the land is as the Garden of Eden before them, and behind them a
desolate wilderness; yea, and nothing shall escape them.
'The appearance of them is as the appearance of horses; and as
horsemen, so shall they run.

'Like the noise of chariots on the tops of the mountains shall they leap, like the noise of a flame of fire that devoureth stubble, as a strong people set in battle array. Before their face the people shall be much pained: all faces shall gather blackness.

'They shall run like mighty men; they shall climb the wall like men of war; and they shall march every one on his ways, and they shall not break their ranks: Neither shall one thrust another; they shall walk every one in his path: and when they fall upon the sword, they shall not be wounded.

[*Note: Observe the change of pace here, for the next verse indicates a very definite change from organized assault to looting, rioting, and acts of anarchy.*]

'They shall run to and fro in the city; they shall run upon the wall, they shall climb upon the houses; they shall enter in at the windows like a thief.

'The earth shall quake before them; the heavens shall tremble: the sun and the moon shall be dark, and the stars shall withdraw their shining' (Joel 2:1–10).

"Then the voice was still. The earth, too, was silent, with the silence of death.

Concluding View: God's Protection

"And then to my ears came another sound—a sound of distant singing. It was the sweetest music I had ever heard. There was joyful shouting, and sounds of happy laughter. Immediately I knew it was the rejoicing of the saints of God. I looked, and there high in the heaven, above the smoke and poisonous gases, above the noise of battle, I saw a huge mountain. It seemed to be of solid rock, and I knew at once that this was the mountain of the Lord. The sounds of music and rejoicing were coming from a cleft, high up in the side of the rock mountain.

"It was the saints of God who were doing the rejoicing. It was God's own people who were singing and dancing and shouting with joy, safe from all the harm which had come upon the earth, for they were hidden away in the cleft of the rock. There in the cleft, they were shut in, protected by a great, giant hand which reached out of the heavens, and which was none other than the hand of God, shutting them in, until the storm was over-passed."

10

U.S. HISTORY, WASHINGTON'S VISION, AND THE BIBLE

The Declaration of Independence was the first real document of "the people" of "the land" of the United States. It was drafted by Thomas Jefferson with the aid of an assigned committee consisting of John Adams, Benjamin Franklin, Robert R. Livingston, and Roger Sherman. It was adopted by the Continental Congress assembled in Philadelphia, Pennsylvania, on July 4, 1776. John Hancock was the president of that congress, and the original document was "signed by Order and in Behalf of the Congress, John Hancock, President. Attest. Charles Thomson, Secretary."

The members of the Continental Congress did not sign it lightly. The *World Almanac* states that eighty-six changes were made and 480 words eliminated, leaving the present 1,337 words. Following its approval, "The unanimous Declaration of the thirteen united States of America" was ordered engrossed on parchment and directed to be signed by all members of Congress. Although adopted by unanimous vote on the evening of July 4, 1776, the last signature was not affixed then (Thomas McKean [Del.] rejoined Washington's Army before signing and said later that he signed it in 1881). The original engrossed Declaration is preserved in the National Archives Building in Washington.

These details have been given to verify the history and authenticity of the document. It was printed by John Dunlap at Philadelphia for the Continental Congress. Note especially the wording of the first paragraph quoted verbatim (the odd capitalization is as it is in the Declaration):

> When in the Course of human Events, it becomes necessary for one People to dissolve the Political Bands which have connected them with another, and to assume among the Powers of the Earth, the separate and equal Station to which the Laws of Nature and of Nature's God entitle them, a decent Respect to the Opinions of Mankind requires that they should declare the causes which impel them to the Separation.

A People Terrible From Their Beginning

In Isaiah 18, that prophet was led to describe "a nation" composed of "a people" who were to be "terrible from their beginning." The history of "the people" of the United States shows that they fit that description. If you have any doubts as to the veracity of that statement, read the long list of grievances quoted in vociferous words throughout the 1,337 words of the Declaration of Independence! Follow also the exploits of the American people from the first battle at Concord on through such episodes as the crossing of the Delaware and the defeat of Cornwallis on October 19, 1781. Recall also Patrick Henry's famous declaration, "Give me liberty, or give me death!" Such has been, and still is, the nature of the true patriots of the "people" of the United States.

Under the heading, "The Revolutionary War as Seen in the Vision" as recorded in Chapter eight of this book, note that the sprinkling of the waters of the Atlantic Ocean over Europe and America was indicative of the battles of the Revolutionary War. In the following paragraph it was portrayed that "the dark cloud was then drawn back to the ocean, in whose heaving billows it sank from view." Not only did the Revolutionary

Army defeat the European tyrants on land, but John Paul Jones won decisive victories over the British Navy at sea. Yes, "a vision fulfilled" and another portion of Bible prophecy verified. It has been proven on the fields of battle and upon the high seas as well that the American people are, indeed, "terrible" (Hebrew—*yare*—"to be feared") even "from their beginning hitherto."

A Nation

The Declaration of Independence was that of "the thirteen united States of America." As of 1776, the thirteen colonies were functioning as "free and independent States." Not until the ratification of the Constitution of the United States did the colonies become, in fact, "a more perfect Union." For clarification of this fact, note the wording of the Preamble to the Constitution of the United States as adopted and declared to be in effect as of March 4, 1789:

> We, the people of the United States, in order to form a more perfect Union, establish justice, insure domestic tranquility, provide for the common defense, promote the general welfare, and secure the blessings of liberty to ourselves and our posterity, do ordain and establish this Constitution for the United States of America.

Seven specific Articles of the Constitution were listed and were then adopted. Thus was officially established "a nation," by "the people."

The Civil War Predicted

In George Washington's vision at Valley Forge in 1777, he was given to foresee "an ill-omened spectre" approach our land from Africa. Obviously indicative of the slavery of negroes brought from Africa, this spectre "flitted slowly and heavily over every town and city," and "The inhabitants presented themselves in battle array against each other."

It is notable that the actual time of such an occurrence, which General George Washington could not possibly have known, was predicted unto him by the words: "Son of the Republic, the end of the century cometh, look and learn." A Civil War was set to take place before the first century of United States' history was over.

Even dating the United States from 1776, the Civil War did occur just before the close of that first century. Several of the southern states had officially seceded from the Union, and they adopted a provisional constitution on February 8, 1861. On the next day they elected Jefferson Davis as President. He was inaugurated at Montgomery, Alabama, on February 18, 1861. General Robert E. Lee surrendered to General Ulysses Grant at Appomattox Court House in Virginia, April 9, 1865.

It happened just as predicted. The "ill-omened spectre" of slavery was abolished by the adoption of the thirteenth amendment to the Constitution, effective December 18, 1865—just eleven years short of "the end of the century." By this official act, a marvellous non-Bible but angelic prophecy was thus fulfilled.

Also, "The inhabitants, casting down their weapons, became friends once more and united around the national standard." As the Civil War came to its close, this specific portion of George Washington's vision likewise saw its fulfillment. It could be said that the union was sealed by the first official national Memorial Day on May 30, 1868, still nine years before the close of the first century of the history of the United States.

"A Nation Meted Out . . ."

The description of the measurements of America by way of its county areas, its roadways, its railway and river transportation systems has already been documented in Chapter six of this book.

The population has grown, likewise, from the 1790 census total of 3,929,214. The 1979 figure is estimated to be in excess of 219 million.

Around the world, the United States is still recognized as the mightiest nation on earth. Its Gross National Product is the highest in the world ($1,379,000,000,000 as of August, 1978).

The Truth of the Bible

All ye inhabitants of the world, and dwellers on the earth, see ye, when he lifteth up an ensign on the mountains; and when he [Uncle Sam, so to speak] bloweth a trumpet, hear ye (Isa. 18:3).

Thus reads the declaration written by the prophet Isaiah when he wrote concerning this nation in the eighth century before the birth of Christ.

11

CORRELATION OF PROPHECIES AND VISIONS AS THEY RELATE TO AMERICA'S "DEVASTATION"

"Correlation" is, by definition, "to connect by disclosure of a mutual relation."

We have before us, at this point, three distinctly different sources of information. Each was recorded—written down as a permanent testimony—apparently by divine inspiration or revelation. Since only by way of foreknowledge of the course of all human events could they possibly have any accuracy of relationship to each other, we now face the true test of establishing the absolute fact of that divine inspiration. Or, we face the fact of the possibility of fallacy.

There is one true test of their credibility. Do they correlate? Is there the evidence of divine inspiration present which can be proven?

Can the Prophecies Stand the Test?

Permanently recorded prophecies from three sources are now before us:

1. The various recorded prophecies written in the Bible.

2. The written testimony of George Washington's vision at Valley Forge.

3. The written declaration of the vision of the American evangelist.

Since they all pertain to the destiny of America, only if they coincide do they have validity.

If it is found that they do correlate to the extent that a proper correlation of the texts of these written documents gives evidence that an amalgamation of the facts presented in them blends into a mutually presented oneness of declaration, then it can be stated: These prophecies must have, and could only have, originated by way of actual revelations of advance knowledge to the men who wrote them; and such extensive foreknowledge could only have come from the only One who could possibly know it—the eternal and living God.

The Impossibility of Collusion

The evangelist's vision-revelation was made known to him and recorded in 1954. George Washington's vision-revelation was made known to him in 1777. The Bible prophecies were recorded by various prophets, teachers, and apostles of both Old and New Testament times ranging from at least the eighth century B.C. until about the close of the first century after the advent of Christ.

None could have known the other person or persons by individual contact because of the timespan of over 2,700 years. Neither could one have copied from the other due to the fact that the evangelist's vision centered around the apparent destruction of liberty as we know it today, as typified by the fall of the Statue of Liberty prior to the great "explosions." Washington's vision had to do with the total history of the United States. Bible prophecies cover international events concerning many countries of the world, including the United States. The messages differ completely in the nature of their contents, yet they coincide as to the proclamations and declarations of "woe," or of the "burning" of the many cities of this highly developed country.

Chronological Order to Arrive at Logical Conclusions

You will note that I first quoted both of the secular visions in their entirety so as not to lose one whit from their chronological order. This is also true of the Isaiah 18 prophecy. I believe by preponderance of facts that this Scripture passage pertains to the United States. Additional prophecies were quoted from the Bible to show the international aspects and to clarify that one third of the earth will be greatly devastated in World War III.

There has been a specific purpose for such a special presentation. First, it is to warn every reader of the impending great holocaust. Second, it is also to prove the verity of the prophecies. Finally, and of even greater importance, it is to reassure all who read this book that the Bible is absolutely true—regardless of what they may have been told to the contrary by those who seek to undermine their faith and trust in the living God. What better way can there be than to back up truth with truth so that the deceived ones—and even the deceivers—can have no other alternative but to acknowledge and believe documented truth?

Before giving the amazing documentation of specific prophecies regarding the order of events to occur in the actual attacks on the United States, let us note the correlation of past history with the visions of George Washington and the evangelist.

1. Correlated Historical Chronology

George Washington's vision starts our chronology with the founding of this nation, and the historical reliability of this vision was illustrated in Chapter ten. The record was documented from the signing of the Declaration of Independence step by step through the vision account. It portrayed the Civil War both as to its occurrence and also as to the time—proclaiming even in 1777 that it would occur before "the end of the century cometh." All of the first part was fulfilled. It also portrayed the great growth of this nation, for Washington stated that he "beheld villages and towns and cities springing up one after the other until the whole land from the Atlantic to the Pacific was dotted with them."

The evangelist expressed virtually the same fulfillment of growth when he stated:

> There, clear and distinct, lay all the North American continent, with all its great cities. To the north lay the Great Lakes. Far to the northeast was New York City. I could see Seattle and Portland far to the northwest. Down the West Coast, there was San Francisco and Los Angeles. . . .

Isaiah pictured it in the words of his day (740-680 B.C.). Since America was not yet established, let alone named, he described it in Isaiah 18 as follows:

> . . . a nation scattered and peeled, to a people terrible from their beginning hitherto; a nation meted out and trodden down, whose land the rivers have spoiled (v. 2)!
>
> . . . the land . . . beyond the rivers of Ethiopia: That sendeth ambassadors by the sea . . . (vv. 1,2).
>
> All ye inhabitants of the world, and dwellers on the earth, see ye, when he lifteth up an ensign on the mountains; and when he bloweth a trumpet, hear ye (v. 3).

His message was sent to a nation which was to be highly developed and to be a leading nation recognized throughout the whole earth. And such is "America" today.

2. Correlated Declarations of Judgment Upon America

Washington's vision:

> Then my eyes beheld a fearful scene. From each of these continents [Europe, Asia, and Africa] arose thick black clouds that were soon joined into one. And throughout this mass there gleamed a dark red light by which I saw hordes of armed men. These men, moving with the cloud, marched by land and sailed by sea [The means of transportation in Washington's day and time] to America.

And I saw these vast armies devastate the whole country and burn the villages, towns and cities which I had seen springing up.

Evangelist's vision:

Then, as the voice of thunder, I heard again the voice of the Lord, saying, "Thus saith the Lord of Hosts; Ye shall certainly drink" [Jer. 25:28]. Then suddenly the giant hand forced the cup to the lips of the Statue of Liberty, and she became powerless to defend herself. The mighty hand of God forced her to drink every drop from the cup. As she drank the bitter dregs, these were the words that I heard, ". . . should ye be utterly unpunished? Ye shall not be unpunished: for I will call for a sword upon all the inhabitants of the earth, saith the LORD of hosts" [Jer. 25:29].

When the cup was withdrawn from the lips of the Statue of Liberty, I noticed the sword was missing from the cup, which could mean but one thing. The contents of the cup had been completely consumed! I knew that the sword typified war, death, and destruction, which is no doubt on the way. . . .

Then suddenly I saw from the Atlantic and from the Pacific, and out of the Gulf, rocket-like objects that seemed to come up like fish leaping out of the water [Note: Submarine launching of missiles was as yet unheard of at the time of this recorded vision in 1954]. High into the air they leaped, each heading into a different direction, but every one of them toward the United States. . . . Then suddenly, the rockets which had leaped out of the oceans like fish all exploded at once. The explosion was earsplitting. The next thing which I saw was a huge ball of fire . . . and I viewed the widespread desolation brought about by the terrific explosions. . . . [Note: The following is a portion of the final Bible quotation recorded in the Evangelist's account of his vision.] "A day of darkness . . . a day of clouds and thick darkness . . . a great people and a strong. . . . A fire devoureth before them; and behind them a flame burneth: the land is as the Garden of Eden before them, and behind them a desolate wilderness" [Joel 2:2,3].

As documented in Chapter five of this book, America will be a part of the one third of the earth terribly devastated by fire . . . and so will the U.S.S.R.—according to the Bible prophecies recorded in Revelation 8.

Isaiah 18:

> For the LORD said unto me . . . I will consider . . . like a clear heat upon herbs, and like a cloud of dew in the heat of harvest. For afore the harvest, when the bud is perfect, . . . he shall both cut off the sprigs with pruning hooks, and take away and cut down the branches (vv. 4,5).

The devastating effects portrayed here are better understood when compared with the preceding prophecy recorded in Isaiah 13:4–19:

> . . . a tumultuous noise of the kingdoms of nations gathered together: the LORD of hosts mustereth the host of the battle. They come from a far country, . . . the weapons of his indignation, to destroy the whole land, . . . as a destruction from the Almighty (Isa. 13:4–6).
>
> They shall be amazed one at another; their faces shall be as flames (v. 8).
>
> . . . I will cause the arrogancy of the proud to cease, and will lay low the haughtiness of the terrible. I will make a man more precious [Hebrew: *yaqar*, rare] than fine gold. . . . in the wrath of the LORD of hosts, and in the day of his fierce anger (Isa. 13:11–13).

Clarification of "The Weapons of His Indignation"

Isaiah 13:5 quoted above, states:

> They come from a far country, from the end of heaven, even the LORD, and the weapons of his indignation, to destroy the whole land.

Please note what a close examination of this statement reveals, when compared with other biblical statements.

A prime example of another Bible use of this term ("his indignation") is found in Jeremiah 50:25 which reads: "The LORD hath opened his armory, and hath brought forth the weapons of his indignation: for this is the work of the Lord GOD of hosts in the land of the Chaldeans [Babylonia]." Jeremiah 51:6 reads: "Flee out of the midst of Babylon . . . for this is the time of the LORD's vengeance; he will render unto her a recompense." Verse 11 reads: ". . . the LORD hath raised up the spirit of the kings of the Medes: for his device is against Babylon, to destroy it; because it is the vengeance of the LORD, the vengeance of his temple."

The terminology "the vengeance of his temple" is explained by Daniel 5:22-31, which reads, in summary:

> And thou . . . O Belshazzar, hast not humbled thine heart, though thou knewest all this; But hast lifted up thyself against the Lord of heaven; and they have brought the vessels of his house [taken from Solomon's Temple] before thee, and thou and thy lords, thy wives, and thy concubines, have drunk wine in them; and thou hast praised the gods of silver, and gold, of brass, iron, wood, and stone, which see not, nor hear, nor know: and the God in whose hand thy breath is, and whose are all thy ways, hast thou not glorified. . . .
>
> In that night was Belshazzar the king of the Chaldeans slain. And Darius, the Median, took the kingdom. . . .

The Medes were thus used of the Lord in this instance as "the weapons of his indignation" against the wicked king of Babylon, just as he had specified through Jeremiah.

One of the things which Belshazzar "knew" was that God had declared unto his grandfather Nebuchadnezzar, the first king of the first great Gentile empire, "Thou, O king, art a king of kings: for the God of heaven hath given thee a kingdom, power, and strength, and glory" (Dan. 2:37).

In relation to the expansion of Nebuchadnezzar's kingdom, Ezekiel, a contemporary of Jeremiah and of Daniel, had recorded in Ezekiel 30:25,26:

> . . . I will strengthen the arms of the king of Babylon and the arms of Pharaoh shall fall down; and they shall know that I am the LORD,

when I shall put my sword into the hand of the king of Babylon, and
he shall stretch it out upon the land of Egypt . . . and they shall
know that I am the LORD.

In fulfillment of the above, Nebuchadnezzar defeated
Pharaoh-Neco of Egypt at Carchemish in 605 B.C., taking all of
Egypt's conquered land. After Babylon was overrun by the
Medes, Egypt was again conquered by the king of the East, in
538 B.C.

There are other similar references throughout the Scriptures, but the two given above show specifically that the Lord
does open His armory and bring forth out of it other nations to
serve as the "weapons of his indignation."

"From the End of Heaven"

A very interesting observation can also be made in relation to
that key verse of Isaiah 13:5. Recall that the statement reads:
"They come from a far country, from the end of heaven. . . ." A
brief reflection on the countries to be involved in World War
III, plus the declared statement that only the U.S.S.R. and the
United States have the super-bombs and the capability to
deliver them in tremendous quantities upon each other (or
anywhere else in the world), reveals two specific armed camps
at enmity with each other. According to the Bible prophecies,
the U.S.S.R. is to be devastated when God shall "send a fire on
Magog [which is the area of southern, industrial, Russia]"
(Ezek. 39:6). That same verse also specifies that devastation by
fire shall come upon those who "dwell carelessly in the
isles. . ." which would include countries such as America.
This takes on added ominous meaning in the light of the next
information.

In the original Hebrew text of the Isaiah 13:5 prophecy, the
prophet chose to use the Hebrew word *qatseh* which is translated into the English word *end*. Over thirty different Hebrew
and Greek words are variously translated "end" in the Bible.

U.S. Bases Abroad

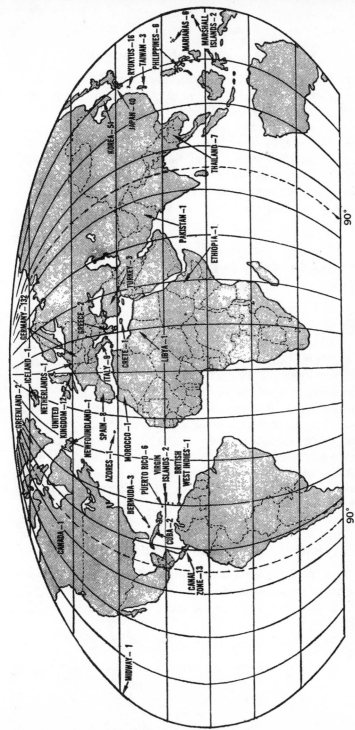

Figures indicate the number of major U.S. bases in each country shown. (Copyright 1969, *Los Angeles Times*. Reprinted by permission.)

The significance is in the fact that this particular Hebrew word, *qatseh*, means "extremity" in the sense of being "from the opposite end." If you will check any atlas you will find that the center of the United States is almost exactly ninety longitudinal degrees west of Greenwich, England, from which all meridian lines are figured. The center of the U.S.S.R. (Russia and Siberia) is almost precisely 90 longitudinal degrees east, making these two "super-powers" exactly "from the (opposite) end of heaven" one from the other. God's prophecies are tremendous!

The U.S. and U.S.S.R. as "The Weapons of His Indignation"

In all the world, the only entity that would dare to attack the United States today would be the U.S.S.R. It now has the power to do so, and it has the oft-expressed determination and desire to do such an act. It would thus be in a sense "the weapon of God's indignation" against this now very sinful land. In similar manner, since the United States is fully committed to the protection of Israel against any aggression, it would thus become "the weapon of God's indignation" against atheistic Russia and her satellite partners. In the process, we would also have the cooperation of the NATO countries in the event of a thrust against Israel; and, according to Bible prophecy, that is precisely what will happen—and the time thereof seems, by way of news documentations, very near at hand.

Documented Progression Toward World War III

In layman's terms, here is a summary of what the Bible says will be the order of events which will bring about World War III (a few news items, showing the trend in that direction are included):

1. "The king of the south" will make the first move (Dan. 11:40).

CORRELATION OF PROPHECIES AND VISIONS

(August 31, 1970, *Daily Breeze* Wire Service, Torrance, Calif.): Cairo—Egypt's war minister announced today the formation of a supreme command of *all* Arab fronts under his headquarters in Cairo [italics mine].

(October 7, 1977, *Los Angeles Times*) The Egyptian armed forces are estimated by most observers to number 345,000, but by some close to 1 million including police and paramilitary groups. . . .

Western military observers say there are numerous signs that the Egyptian military machine may be even stronger today than it was when Sadat launched the 1973 war. Logistical capabilities reportedly have been substantially improved with the addition of a large number of Mercedes transport trucks.

Armored equipment remains in good enough shape for the military to run full-scale desert maneuvers every two months or so. "That tells you something," a military source said. "An army that can maneuver as often as this one isn't hurting for spare parts or equipment on the ground."

He added that the maneuvers have been extremely well planned and executed.

(November 23, 1977, *Jerusalem Post*) What could have prompted Chief of Staff Mordechai Gur into making his public statement that Egypt was preparing for war . . . ? In his interview, he himself cited the fact that the Egyptian army was conducting military offensive maneuvers on an unprecedented level. . . .

But what Gur did not mention was a report in the American "Armed Forces Journal" that a two-year $6 billion arms modernization plan has just been launched by the Egyptians. The "Journal" quotes one Western observer as claiming that the plan will make Egypt "a military powerhouse."

Points covered by the plan include:

* Purchase of 200 Alpha Jets from Britain, 185 of which will be built at a new Egyptian plant to be constructed on a turn-key basis.
* Transfer of 36 Mirage 111E and 40 Mirage F-1 fighters to Egypt from Saudi Arabia.
* Overhaul of all of Egypt's 200 Mig-21 fighters. . . .
* Purchase of 400 British-made Lynx helicopters.
* Modernization of 12 Hawker-Siddeley 748 short-field transports.

* Purchase of 21,000 Swingfire anti-tank missiles mounted on new Landrovers.

* Overhaul of Egypt's missile-boat fleet, providing them with new fire-control systems.

* Refurbishing all Egypt's Soviet T-55 tanks. . . .

* New fuses for all 122mm and 130mm artillery shells, greatly improving overall artillery capability and efficiency.

* Purchase of another 14 Lockheed C-130 transports from the U.S.

Israeli Phantom jets flying in formation

This kind of preparation certainly gives "the king of the south" the capability to "strike."

2. "The king of the north" will enter the conflict "like a whirlwind," according to the same verse, Daniel 11:40.

(August 18, 1970, *Los Angeles Times*) Cairo—The Soviet Union in recent days and weeks has been moving into Egypt a wide variety of military hardware—including the largest artillery cannon in

Moscow's arsenal—and it is being deployed in the field. Authoritative sources describe the big weapon as a 203-mm gun with a range of at least 20 miles, packing an extremely powerful conventional shell. . . .

Another new weapon added to the growing list of sophisticated Russian military hardware in Egypt is the ZSU-2 anti-aircraft battery which has been seen outside of the Soviet Union only in Poland. This four-barreled, radar-controlled, armor-mounted weapon can fire at the extraordinary rate of 4,000 rounds per minute at maximum. It is still *manned only by Russian gunners . . .*" [italics mine].

(November 20, 1973, *Jerusalem Post*) Washington (Reuter)—The Soviet Union has provided Egypt and Syria with double the tonnage of war supplies that the U.S. has sent to Israel since the Middle East war erupted, according to figures released last Monday by the Pentagon. . . . The Pentagon pointed out that the Russians had delivered more than 100,000 tons of arms and ammunition to the Arabs since the war began.

(April 1, 1977, *Christian Anti-Communism Crusade*) During the years prior to the Second World War, Winston Churchill warned England and the U.S.A. about the increasing dangers of war due to the doctrines and armament practices of Nazi Germany. . . .

His mantle has now fallen upon his nephew Winston Spencer Churchill, who is warning England and the U.S.A. about the dangers faced because of communist doctrines and increasing Soviet might. The following is from a speech Winston Churchill made to a meeting of the National Association of Freedom:

"Thirty years ago, when the last survivors of the Nazi concentration camps were liberated, we thought we had world freedom. . . . Alas, it was not to be. . . . The Soviet Red Army came not as liberators but as enslavers. . . . and they are there not as a defensive force but as an Army of Occupation. . . .

"Although the Soviet Union has already achieved strategic and tactical nuclear parity with the United States and has established a preponderance in conventional forces in Europe of approximately 3:1 in tanks, aircraft and manpower over NATO, Soviet factories are at this minute churning out modern aircraft at the rate of 150 per month and tanks at 300 per month. . . . *The Soviet buildup is far beyond any requirements of self-defense—indeed the Soviets are building the greatest war-machine the world has ever seen.* This is more than a challenge to the West—*it is the most deadly threat to freedom and to peace any generation has ever known"* [italics mine].

(October 16, 1977, *Los Angeles Times*) United Nations (UPI)— Strategic nuclear warheads in the United States and Soviet Union ready to be unleashed at the push of a button and destroy mankind now total 12,000 and "their combined explosive power is believed to be equivalent to 1.3 million Hiroshima-size bombs," a recent U.N. report on the arms race estimated.

In addition, there are about four times as many smaller tactical nuclear weapons in the arsenals of the two superpowers amounting to 50,000 more Hiroshima atom bombs. . . .

The arms race costs about $350 billion annually at present prices. . . . Since World War II, the report said, direct costs of the arms race have exceeded $6 trillion.

3. "And I will send a fire on Magog [Russia] and among them that dwell carelessly in the isles [coastlands of Western Europe and America] . . . Behold, it is come, and it is done, saith the Lord GOD; this is the day where of I have spoken" (Ezek. 39:6,8; note also Joel 1:15–2:6; Isa. 13:6–16; Rev. 8:7–12).

3. Correlated: Manner of the Attack Against the United States

Washington's vision: "Three great perils will come upon the Republic. The most fearful for her is the third." This is an awesome prediction of judgment to come. In consideration of the tremendously destructive potential of the weapons of today, there is no question as to the accuracy of that prophecy. Hear his words again:

Then my eyes beheld a fearful scene. From each of these continents [previously described as Europe, Asia and Africa] arose thick black clouds that were soon joined into one. And through this mass there gleamed a dark red light by which I saw hordes of armed men. . . . And I dimly saw these vast armies devastate the whole country and burn the villages, towns and cities which I had seen springing up.

The prediction is that the attack will originate from "red" Russia (and from its satellite countries of Eastern Europe), from Siberia, the "red" dominated Arab countries of Asia (not including China whose tremendous armies shall come forth later as the armies of "the kings of the east" . . . to the battle of Armageddon), and from the "red" dominated Arab countries of North Africa.

Reports abound as to the vast amount of armaments which Russia has poured into Syria, Iran, and Iraq of Asia as well as into Algeria, Libya, Egypt, and Sudan of North Africa. Arab Mediterranean seaports have been made wide open for the fast-growing "Russian Sixth Fleet," and Russia's floating supply bases and ships abound in the Mediterranean and the Atlantic Ocean, even reaching now into the Caribbean Sea around the perimeter of Cuba. They are in the Pacific Ocean also.

Millions of People in the Conflict

A notable prediction is also evident in the portion of Washington's vision where he related, "My ears listened to the thundering of the armaments and the shouts and cries of millions in mortal combat."

The 1790 census report of the United States showed only 4,000,000 inhabitants. The 1978 census, however, totals in excess of 219,000,000 inhabitants (218,575,000 as of July 1, 1978). It is no wonder that George Washington proclaimed as "a fearful scene" the view of "millions in mortal combat."

The Evangelist's vision:

It seemed that what I saw was the entire North American continent, spread out like a map upon a table, with this terrible skeleton-shaped cloud arising from behind the table. It rose steadily until the form was visible down to the waist. At the waist, the skeleton seemed to bend toward the United States, stretching

129

forth a hand toward the east and one toward the west—one toward New York City and one toward Seattle. As the awful form stretched forward, I could see that its entire attention seemed to be focused upon the United States, overlooking Canada, at least for the time being. As I saw the horrible black cloud in the form of a skeleton bending toward America, I knew its one interest was to destroy the multitudes.

As I watched in horror, the great black cloud stopped just above the Great Lake region, and turned its face toward New York City. . . . Then the skeleton turned to the west, and out of the horrible mouth and nostrils came another great puff of white smoke. This time it was blown in the direction of the West Coast. In a few minutes time, the entire West Coast and Los Angeles area was covered with its vapors.

Then toward the center came a third great puff. As I watched, St. Louis and Kansas City were enveloped in its white vapors. Then it came toward New Orleans . . . reached the Statue of Liberty where she [as previously explained] stood staggering in the blue waters. . . . As the white vapors began to spread around the head of the Statue, she took in but one gasping breath, and then began to cough as though to rid her lungs of the horrible vapors she had inhaled. One could see readily by the painful coughing that those white vapors had seared her lungs. . . . What were these white vapors?

Two Extra Factors: MIRV Warheads — Chemical Warfare

Many years before the first MIRV (Multiple Independently-targeted Reentry Vehicle) rockets were known of or tested, this evangelist declared that he saw such an element come from the north, stop over the Great Lakes region, and then send its deadly cargo in three different directions. (How interesting that it should be specifically three, which was the original payload on an ICBM rocket! Also, that its "cargo" was quite evidently the dreaded nerve gas which has now been used in combat tests.)

The first MIRV announcement I have on file refers to the missile as a new "space bus." This news item appeared in

1967—thirteen years after the vision of the evangelist was first published!

Nerve gas was discovered in 1939, put into production by the Germans in 1942, and first used in combat action in Yemen in 1967. (See scientific report in Chapter three of this book.)

Pentagon Says Chemical Warfare Deterrent Vital

(September, 1969, *Los Angeles Times*) Washington—World War III is over. The Soviet Union won. The Soviets won, according to military experts who analyzed the results of numerous war games fought by computer at the Pentagon, because they used deadly chemical weapons while North American Treaty Organization (NATO) forces shunned them.

That is the argument cited by the Defense Department for continued research and development of lethal chemical and biological weapons (CBW). . . .

The Pentagon argument is based to a large degree on World War III scenarios played through computers by the Joint Chiefs of Staff war gaming group. Such "wars" have been fought repeatedly on miles and miles of tape. . . .

NATO Preparing for Chemical Attack

(September 23, 1978, *Los Angeles Times*) Neumuenster, West Germany (AP)—North Atlantic Treaty Organization military units are pushing their preparations to survive chemical warfare but officers say they are deeply troubled over Western shortcomings in the field.

NATO's supreme European commander, U.S. Gen. Alexander M. Haig Jr., said Friday the military alliance's protection from chemical attack is "still highly unsatisfactory. . . ."

Protection against chemical warfare has been a major part of the current NATO exercise involving 200,000 troops, including 11,400 marines.

Haig and many other Western specialists have accused the Soviet Union of stepping up its ability to wage chemical war. They say the Soviet-led Warsaw Pact forces can deliver heavy amounts of gas and sprays from planes, rockets and artillery shells that could immobilize or kill troops. . . .

U.S. Nerve Gas

American chemical research has existed for many years. It entered the modern age when Dugway Proving Ground was established in Utah in 1942 as a center for chemical weapons' research.

Considered too potent for safe keeping in the United States, our stockpile of nerve gas was transported to Johnston Island in the Pacific Ocean where it is held on stand-by alert. The quantity kept there is classified information. But it is held as a deterrent to discourage the U.S.S.R. which was reported to have fifty thousand tons of nerve gas stockpiled by the late 1950s.

When Israel captured over $1 billion worth of Russian-supplied armament from the Arabs in 1967, they discovered huge quantities of nerve gas in the Sinai arsenal. In 1973, even more potent nerve gas was captured, along with a new discovery: The Russians now are prepared for its use!

(June 5, 1974, *Daily Breeze*, Torrance, Calif.) Washington (UPI)—Rep. Samuel S. Stratton, D-NY, said today Soviet equipment captured by Israeli forces showed that Russian units were prepared to resort to chemical warfare "if the appropriate opportunity" arose. . . .

Stratton said he viewed last November a vast display of latest Russian battle equipment captured by Israel in the Mideast. "One of the most startling revelations of that display . . . was the fact that every Soviet equipped unit goes into battle with a full set of defenses against chemical, biological and radiological attack," Stratton said.

The United States has developed a "safe" type of potent nerve gas called binary gas. It can be stored most anywhere and reportedly is ready for production to compensate for the vast Soviet supply.

CORRELATION OF PROPHECIES AND VISIONS

(October 20, 1978, *The Register*, Orange Co., Calif.) Washington (AP)—The military budget that will go to Congress next January reportedly will contain a request for funds to develop a new nerve gas system.

Pentagon sources said Thursday that Deputy Defense Secretary Charles Duncan has sent the Army a secret memo telling them to include money for the nerve gas in its budget request for the fiscal year beginning Oct. 1, 1979. Duncan's memo reportedly asks for production of a "binary" nerve gas weapon which would be produced at the Pine Bluff Arsenal in Arkansas.

(September 1979, *Reader's Digest*) . . . Today we have perhaps 3,500 officers and enlisted men involved with chemical-warfare tasks, and nothing remotely resembling an adequate retaliatory capability.

By contrast, the Red army includes a chemical-warfare contingent fully ten percent as large as the entire U.S. Army—80,000 to 100,000 officers and enlisted men. At some 40 sites in Eastern Europe, these forces train intensively for chemical warfare—day and night, in all kinds of weather, on all kinds of terrain. Every Soviet tank and personnel carrier is equipped with chemical detection and alarm systems that automatically close all apertures, and with efficient air-filtration systems. Every Soviet foot soldier is issued a gas mask made of lightweight, rubberized material resistant to all known chemical and biological agents. He also carries gloves, leggings, boots and a thin cape quickly convertible into an overall suit, all of the same protective material.

Approximately every third Soviet missile and rocket warhead, and up to ten percent of artillery projectiles, mortar shells, land mines and aerial bombs, are loaded with a chemical agent. These weapons—between 300,000 and 700,000 tons of them—have a higher kill ratio (per shell or missile fired) than any military device short of nuclear bombs.

Would the Soviets really use their chemical weapons? To my mind, it is naïve in the extreme to think that they would go to the immense trouble and expense of constructing history's most impressive offensive chemical-warfare capability, and then not use it.*

*(CREDIT: Richard H. Ichord, "The Deadly Threat of Soviet Chemical Warfare," *Reader's Digest* (September 1979.).

4. Further Correlation: Direction of Attack vs. the United States

George Washington related that in his vision he saw an attack from Europe, Asia, and Africa. Such an attack, being made by missiles today, would come the shortest distance which would be over the polar region and Canada, because of launching from Russia or Siberia. As to Africa, Russian Poseidon-type nuclear submarines roam at will across the Atlantic from known sub bases in North Africa.

In the vision of the evangelist we have the factor of a MIRV-type poison gas attack over the polar region just previous to the thermonuclear attack. We do, therefore, have a very definite *co-relationship* between these two visions in this regard.

Millions of Americans Scream and Die

Washington's vision: "My ears listened to the . . . cries of millions . . ."

The evangelist's vision:

Suddenly the silence was shattered by the screaming of sirens, sirens that seemed to scream, "run for your lives!"

Never before had I heard such shrill, screaming sirens. . . . There seemed to be multitudes of sirens. And as I looked, I saw people everywhere running; but it seemed none of them ran more than a few paces, and then they fell. [Even as he had seen the Statue of Liberty's struggle to survive, "liberty," such as America has known it over the years, shall very evidently be likewise engulfed in just such a struggle. Its efforts shall be tremendous, but America's "woe" shall have come upon it, and it shall be "pruned" and shall see its productive branches "cut down."]

I now saw millions of people falling in the streets, on the sidewalks, struggling. I heard their screams for mercy and help. I heard their horrible coughings, as though their lungs had been seared with fire [nerve gas or "brimstone"?]. I heard the moanings and groanings of the doomed and dying. As I watched, a few finally reached shelters; but only a few ever got to the shelters. And above the groaning and the moaning of the dying multitudes, I heard these words:

A noise shall come even to the ends [both ends] of the earth; for the LORD hath a controversy with the nations. He will plead with all flesh; He will give them that are wicked to the sword, saith the LORD . . . Behold, evil shall go forth from nation to nation, and a great whirlwind [thermonuclear] shall be raised up from the coasts of the earth (Jer. 25:31,32). . . .

Then suddenly I saw from the Atlantic and from the Pacific, and out of the Gulf, rocket-like objects that seemed to come up like fish leaping out of the water. [Recall that this vision was recorded in 1954, previous to the time of the development of submarine-launched missiles. Thus they "seemed" like fish leaping out of the water.] High into the air they leaped, each heading in a different direction, but every one toward the United States. . . .

Then suddenly, the rockets which had leaped out of the oceans like fish all exploded at once. . . . The explosion was earsplitting. The next thing which I saw was a huge ball of fire. . . .

As the vision spread before my eyes, and I viewed the widespread desolation brought about by the terrific explosions, I could not help thinking, "While the defenders of our nation have quibbled over what measures of defense to use, and neglected the only true defense, faith and dependence upon the true and living God, that which she has greatly feared has come upon her! How true it has been proven that 'except the LORD keep the city, the watchman waketh but in vain' " [Ps. 127:1].

Conclusion of "Phase I" of the Devastation of America

The vision of the evangelist drew near its close, and he stated:

As the vision spread before my eyes, and I viewed the widespread desolation brought about by the terrific explosions. . . .

After the immense shock of the "earsplitting" explosion of the first super-bomb attack, it is indicated that other explosions followed in rapid succession. Note the subsequent statement: "The widespread desolation brought about by the terrific explosions." When the "first strike" actually takes place, the all-out nuclear exchange will follow in just a matter of minutes. Since it will be "kill, or be killed," every missile and bomb on land or in the air or in the sea will "go."

Section III

KNOWN FACTS MUST PRECLUDE PREDICTION

Note

Apart from verified divine inspiration, no prediction of any event on this earth could be valid other than from positively known facts or a vast preponderance of equivalent evidence. It is, however, within the scope of reason to analyze known facts and such prophecies as are verified by the divinely inspired Scriptures, and—by carefully comparing these with each other—to set them into chronological order as a total scenario of events.

Correlations Involved

Seven topics concerning known factors have been presented for correlation.

1. Past, and thus established, history.
2. Documented statistics of world geography.
3. Established facts of science.
4. Written, unchangeable, recorded Bible prophecies.
5. The written, and thus unchangeable, recorded testimony of the vision-revelation as seen and heard by General George Washington at Valley Forge, Pennsylvania, in 1777.
6. The written, unchangeable, report of the vision-revelation of an American evangelist in 1954.
7. Documented, and thus verifiable, news events of the past.

New Evidence to be Presented

In order to establish the proper base for a scenario of past, present, and future events, even more related evidence must be presented. This has been retained to this point only so I could first establish the fact of World War III. The alignments of the nations to be involved and the written prophecies on the nature of the attack have been correlated with Bible prophecies and with scientific, topographic, and historic facts. Now let us look into the future.

12

THE PARTICIPANTS OF WORLD WAR III

"At the time of the end," there are to be two men who shall lead two great alignments of nations. They are to come from two separate places, have two separate purposes, and do two separate things.

The individual identity of each can easily be clarified by the context of Scripture references.

The Isaiah 18:5 "He" Who Shall "Cut" America. In the context of this passage it is obvious that God is proclaiming through Isaiah that some person, referred to simply as "he," will cause great harm to "this nation," America. This person will be "brought forth" as a "weapon" of God's indignation against this country, and it will be at a time when this country is at the very peak of its productive capacity and potential power.

Note the context of Isaiah 18:4,5:

> . . . I will consider in my dwelling place . . . (v. 4).
> . . . he shall both cut off the sprigs with pruning hooks, and take away and cut down the branches (v. 5).

The devastation is to be done by another. Note that this is a parallel to the illustration given in Jeremiah 50:25:

> The LORD hath opened his armory, and hath *brought forth the weapons of his indignation,* for this is the work of the Lord GOD of hosts . . . (italics mine).

The clarification of this statement is found in Jeremiah 51:11:

> . . . the LORD hath raised up the spirit of the kings of the Medes: for his devise is against Babylon, to destroy it; because it is the vengeance of the LORD. . . .

The fulfillment came one hundred years later when the Medes conquered Babylon in 539 B.C., serving, in this instance, as "the weapons" of God's indignation against sinful Babylon. In like manner, God is proclaiming that a military leader ("he") is going to "cut" this nation.

From Which Nation?

As to the United States, what person from which nation would like the most to see America "cut"? Also, which nation of all the nations on the earth today would be in a position of power sufficient to endeavor to "prune with pruning hooks" this country that notably has been "terrible (tenacious) from its beginning hitherto"?

Only the mighty military and strategic warfare combine of the U.S.S.R. would even dare to consider such an action.

This is amazingly important, for there are only two personages of power within the end-time period whom God is against. One is the Antichrist "beast" referred to in Revelation 13, 17, and 19 and also referred to as "the prince that shall come" in Daniel 9:26 and as "the king" of Daniel 11:36. The other person is the one who shall be the military leader of the land of Russia "in the latter years" in accordance with the prophecy recorded in Ezekiel 38:2–9.

From Russia

Note the proclamation against the leader of the Soviet Union starting with Ezekiel 38:2.

Son of man, set thy face against Gog, [of] the land of Magog [Russia], the chief prince of Meshech and Tubal [Moscow and Tobolsk], and prophesy against him, And say, *Thus saith the Lord GOD; Behold, I am against thee, O Gog, the chief prince of Meshech and Tubal* [God knew they would combine to form the U.S.S.R. in 1923]: And I will turn thee back, and put hooks in thy jaws, and I will bring thee forth, and all thine army, horses and horsemen, all of them clothed with all sorts of armor, even a great company . . . Persia, Ethiopia and Libya with them; all of them with shield and helmet: Gomer and all his bands; the house of Togarmah of the north quarters, and all his bands: and many people with thee.

Be thou prepared, and prepare for thyself, thou, and all thy company that are assembled unto thee, and be thou a guard unto them [Gog will lead them all].

After many days thou shalt be visited: in the latter years thou shalt come into the land that is brought back from the sword, and is gathered out of many people, against the mountains of Israel, which have been always waste: but it is brought forth out of the nations, and they shall dwell safely all of them [ultimately].

Thou shalt ascend and come like a storm, thou shalt be like a cloud to cover the land [Ezekiel apparently saw air power, but he could not grasp the significance of it in the chariot-racing days in which he lived], thou, and all thy bands [armies], and many people with thee (Ezek. 38:2–9; italics mine).

In plain and simple language, and as a mighty testimony to the divine inspiration of the biblical text, Ezekiel, writing in the sixth century before Christ, recorded for all time that "in the latter years" of international history the head of the Russian military colossus, referred to as "the chief prince of Meshech and Tubal," would be in alignment with and "a guard unto" the Arab nations—the exact nations arrayed against the people of Israel, who have been "gathered out of many people," today.

Our primary concern here, however, is to point out specifically that God will be "against" this "chief prince of Meshech [Moscow]."

There is another reason for God to be against the leader from Moscow—besides the fact that the "chief prince" is set in great battle array against the Promised Land of Israel. Russian policy and doctrine propagate atheism and are thus diametrically opposed to God and Christianity. This is probably best documented by the classic declaration of Commissar Lunarcharsky, the Soviet Commissar of Public Instruction, recorded as follows:

> And you must always remember this, that we hate Christianity and the Christians. Even the best of them must be regarded as our worst enemies. They preach love to one's neighbor and pity (mercy) which is contrary to our principles. Christian love is a hindrance to the development of the revolution. Down with love of one's neighbor!
>
> What we need is hatred. We must know how to hate, for only at this price can we conquer the universe.*

This Marxist-Leninist doctrine was echoed in our country by Jerry Rubin of the Students for Democratic Society (SDS) at Kent State University on July 20, 1970, according to a *TARS* newsletter which quoted his statement as follows:

> The first part of the Yippie program is to kill your parents. And I mean that quite literally, because until you're prepared to kill your parents, you're not ready to change the country. Our parents are our first oppressors.

Top U.S. Communist, Gus Hall, once said: ". . . Slit the throats of Christian children and drag them over the mourner's bench and the pulpit and allow them to drown in their own blood." (This is a direct quote from Gus Hall, which he made at the 1961 funeral of Eugene Dennis, National Chairman of the Communist Party. More of his statements are unprintable due to their vileness.)

Is it any wonder that the Lord God directed His prophet to write: "I am against thee, O Gog, the chief prince of Meshech (Moscow)"?

NAE Action (May, 1962).

The Identity of "Gog"

The military leader of Russia, whomever he is "at the time of the end"—at the time of the beginning of World War III—will be the "he" referred to in Isaiah 18:5 who shall order the land of the United States to be "burned," "cut," and devastated.

Many have been the threats and proclamations of Russian officials against the United States. Those quoted most often are the tirades of former Premier Nikita Khrushchev and the classic formula of Dimitry Z. Manuilski.

At various times Khrushchev boasted: "Whether you like it or not, history is on our side. We will bury you."

Dimitry Manuilski, professor at the Lenin School of Political Warfare in Moscow, made his most famous declaration in 1930:

> War to the hilt between communism and capitalism is inevitable. Today, of course, we are not strong enough to attack. *Our time will come in thirty or forty years.* To win, we shall need the element of surprise. The Western world will have to be put to sleep. So we shall begin by launching the most spectacular peace movement on record. There shall be electrifying overtures and unheard of concessions. The capitalist countries, stupid and decadent, will rejoice to cooperate to their own destruction. They will leap at another chance to be friends. *As soon as their guard is down, we shall smash them with our clenched fist* [italics mine].

"Stupid and Decadent" America Cooperates

The concessions made by the various administrations of the U.S. government could fill a book. It is unnecessary to repeat or review them to any thinking American. It has been an American disgrace approaching the very height of stupidity. We have given or sold to Russia everything from truck factories to sophisticated calculators. One example:

> (July 1978, *The Truth Crusader*, Harrisonburg, Va.) It is an established historic fact that much of the material used by our enemies to destroy us came from the United States.

For instance, we gave the Soviets a 40 ton magnet—which happens to be the largest in the world. It generates a magnetic field 250,000 times greater than that of the earth. (*New York Times*, June 21, 1977). This magnet will undoubtedly be used in making the exclusively Soviet-controlled famous Nekola Tesle Particle Beam Death Ray. . . .

Soviet Military Power

(June 12, 1978, *Newsweek*) The Russians are now able to challenge the West in a way they were unable to do for lack of global reach during the Cuban missile crisis in 1962.

The Kremlin's muscle-building has been a long, steady process. By the CIA's reckoning, the Soviets have devoted 12 to 13 per cent of their gross national product to military spending for years now. . . .

The Pentagon says the U.S. is now outnumbered 5-to-1 in tanks, 4-to-1 in artillery pieces and 3-to-1 in submarines. . . .

U.S. and British estimates declare that the Soviets have 4.4 million men under arms, 8,653 combat aircraft, 1,500 transport planes and 1,300 aeroflot planes. They list 1,700 ships in their merchant marine plus 230 major surface-combat ships, 234 attack submarines and cruise missile ships. They list 19,000 artillery pieces, 43,000 tanks and 1,477 ICBM's. Russia's total military budget for 1978 is estimated to be $150 billion. . . .

Soviet military doctrine on how to use this power makes frightening reading for Westerners. The "bible" of Soviet doctrine, a 1962 book called "Military Strategy," asserts: "A third world war will be a missile and nuclear war. . . . Entire states will be wiped off the face of the earth." But the Soviets insist that they can survive and win a nuclear conflict. . . .

Considering the awesome size of the Soviet military machine, some responsible Western analysts conclude that, despite their frequent disclaimers, the Russians mean to attack first. . . .

(February 21, 1978, *Los Angeles Times*) The British government said the Soviet military buildup is outstripping that of the North Atlantic Treaty Organization in the air, on land and at sea. In its annual expense report, the government said the Soviets are spending between 11% and 13% of their resources on the buildup. "Soviet forces have in many areas been strengthened in size and quality on a scale which goes beyond the need of any purely defensive posture," it said. Moscow's military capability goes well beyond Europe. . . .

Soviet "Killer" Satellites and Missiles

(October 27, 1977, *The Register*, Orange Co., Calif.) Washington (AP)—The Soviet Union has staged its second apparently successful test of a new system that could threaten destruction of U.S. reconnaissance and other military satellites, the Pentagon disclosed today.

"We have preliminary indications that the Soviets launched an antisatellite interceptor on Wednesday against a target satellite," a Pentagon statement said. "Presumably, a successful intercept occurred."

The new intercept apparently was made in a relatively low orbit, which suggests that the Soviet weapon could be used against U.S. satellites carrying cameras and infrared and other sensors. . . .

The Soviets conducted antisatellite experiments in the 1960s. They resumed the tests early last year. Since then, there have been seven tests monitored by U.S. radar, three of them rated successful.

(June 20, 1978, *Los Angeles Times*) Washington—The White House has ordered that all future U.S. satellites with national security importance be protected against anti-satellite weapons such as those demonstrated by the Soviet Union, it was disclosed Monday.

(June 1, 1978, *The Register*, Orange Co., Calif.) Washington (AP)—A new long-range missile now deployed by the Soviet Union is more accurate than any previous nuclear weapon aimed from Russian submarines against the United States, according to U.S. intelligence officials. . . .

The new missile has been test-fired with multiple warheads over a 4,700-mile range and has traveled up to 5,750 miles with a single warhead. This means SS-N-18s could strike targets in the United States from Delta submarines stationed relatively close to Soviet home ports. . . .

The SS-N-18 is the third major new Soviet missile to become combat-ready in the last six months.

(July 30, 1978, *Los Angeles Times*) The first Soviet sea-based missile with multiple warheads is in operation, tripling the number of targets the newest type of Soviet submarines could attack with nuclear weapons, U.S. intelligence sources said. Latest evidence indicates the SS-N-18 missile, with a range of more than 4,900 miles, is being deployed on Delta 3 submarines as the vessels enter the Soviet fleet. . . .

(January 26, 1979, *Los Angeles Times*) Washington—Defense Secretary Harold Brown said Thursday that the Soviet Union is building its nuclear missile force at a faster pace than was anticipated a year ago, increasing the danger that the 1980s may become an era of Soviet strategic superiority.

"He" Is Almost Ready!

Great numbers of news items could be quoted. The ones just listed show that on land, in the air, from satellites or from submarines, Russia is equipping itself for global war. "Gog" is on the move. No other nation on earth has this extensive capacity to attack America.

The "chief prince of Meshech [Moscow]" is almost ready, and time is running out. World War III is "just around the corner."

The Way It Will Happen

Bible prophecy indicates that Russia *will* strike at the United States, but it will be in conjunction with another military goal. Russia wants control of the Middle East. To get that control, it must help the Arabs in their showdown fight with Israel. And Russia knows that any time it strikes at Israel, it is going to have to deal with the United States and with the Western European nations—all have proclaimed their support of Israel. Always pro-Israel to a certain extent, the Western European nations made it official policy following the Arab attack against Israel on Yom Kippur, 1973.

(November 20, 1973, *Jerusalem Post*) Paris—Supporters of Israel from 11 Western European parliaments decided here on Friday to act together in order to back Israel against political pressure from the Arab and Soviet countries. . . .

(October 29, 1977, *The Register*, Orange Co., Calif.) United Nations, N.Y. (AP)—The General Assembly censured Israel on Friday for establishing Jewish settlements in occupied Arab territories. . . .

The nine European Common Market countries and other traditional supporters of Israel . . . announced support for the resolution.

A Common Market spokesman, Belgian Ambassador Andre Arnemann, said Thursday the Israeli settlements "aggravate tensions in the area and prejudge future over-all negotiations. *We remain fully committed to the security of Israel*, but every unilateral move could eventually harm Israel's security," he said [italics mine].

The Common Market countries remain fully committed to the security of Israel, but until the advent of a strong military leader in Europe, the backing is strictly for show. That, however, is going to change in the very near future, for the Bible predicts that "at the time of the end" there will be a mighty military king over ten nations of the western region of the old Roman empire (the eastern region of it to be conquered as a result of World War III).

America's Role in World War III

America's role in World War III, as far as Israel is concerned, will be to send a rain of fire and brimstone on the land of Magog, industrial Russia, effectively cancelling it out from a production standpoint.

Unfortunately, in the vast thermonuclear exchange that will

take place, the United States also will be greatly "cut" and devastated. It will survive, but it will be severely damaged.

Bible prophecy proclaims that the bulk of the Soviet military forces will be sent to, and fall on, "the mountains of Israel," but the nuclear destruction will be primarily in the Soviet Union and in the United States.

One of the key verifications of this is found in Ezekiel 39:6,8.

> And I will send a fire on Magog, and among them that dwell carelessly in the isles [Heb. *ee*, a habitable, desirable coast]: and they shall know that I am the LORD. . . . Behold, it is come, and it is done, saith the Lord GOD, this is the day whereof I have spoken.

The nature of the fire and the extent of the damage will be explained later. Ezekiel 39:8 stipulates that the nuclear exchange will take place in one horrendous day.

After that massive attack, although America will endure and continue as a nation, it will no longer be a super-power. World leadership will transfer to the new military king of Western Europe, the Antichrist.

The Daniel 11:40 "He" Who Shall Fight Against "Gog" in World War III

There are many Bible descriptions of the end-time despotic king, "the beast," the one commonly called "the Antichrist."

He is introduced in Daniel 11:36 as "the king" who "shall do according to his will, and he shall exalt himself. . . ." In verse 38 it is said of him, ". . . in his estate shall he honor the God of forces: and a god whom his fathers knew not shall he honor with gold, and silver, and with precious stones, and pleasant things." This man will possess a very costly but highly effective weapon (god of force), and with it he will project himself into a place of great prominence. He will gain the confidence of the leaders of the ten-nation European (Common Market) community and become their leader ("king").

The apostle John referred to this when he wrote in Revelation 17:12,13:

> And the ten horns which thou sawest are ten kings, which have received no kingdom as yet; but receive power as kings one hour with the beast.
> These have one mind, and shall give their power and strength unto the beast.

That this man is to become the head of an empire is self evident. Further proof of this is given, however, in the manner of his introduction in Revelation, chapters 13 and 17.

The beast of Revelation 13 and the scarlet-colored beast of Revelation 17 portray the same picture: Both are seen to have seven heads and ten horns. The meaning of the picture is that the beast of the end time is the seventh (and final) Gentile empire and that it will be a coalition of ten nations.

Historically, six Gentile empires have had dominion over Jerusalem and the land of Israel. They are as follows:

Babylon:	586–539 B.C.
Media	539–530 B.C.
Persia	530–334 B.C.
Greece	334–323 B.C.
Egypt	323–30 B.C.
Rome	30 B.C.—A.D. 70

The Jews were greatly persecuted by Titus the Roman who burned and destroyed the Hebrew temple and the city of Jerusalem in A.D. 70. They had no further territorial rights in Palestine until the revival of the nation of Israel in 1948.

The seventh Gentile empire to have dominion over Jerusalem and Israel will be the end time revived Roman Empire ruling as the beast with ten horns. It will be dominated and led by the Antichrist king of the Tribulation period.

In Daniel 7, this end time revived Roman Empire is again portrayed as a "dreadful and terrible" beast having ten horns, and then a little horn is seen to come up into prominence. Daniel 7:8 reads:

> I considered the horns, and, behold, there came up another little horn, before whom there were three of the first horns plucked up by the roots: and, behold, in this horn there were eyes like the eyes of a man, and a mouth speaking great things.

When Daniel asked the Lord for a clarification of the meaning, it was defined as follows:

> And the ten horns out of this kingdom are ten kings that shall arise: and *another* shall arise *after them;* and he shall be diverse from the first, and he shall subdue three kings (Dan. 7:24; italics mine).

The three kings that are to be "plucked up by the roots" will be replaced by three others of the choice of the Antichrist king. Daniel 11:39 reads, ". . . and he shall cause them to rule over many, and shall divide the land for gain."

That there still are to be ten kings is proven by two texts. Revelation 17:16 declares that the ten kings will "hate the whore, and shall make her desolate . . . and burn her with fire." This refers to the destruction of the wicked one-world false church system that will have its headquarters in rebuilt Babylon during the *first half* of the Tribulation period. At the middle of the Tribulation (after three and one half years), the ten kings will not only give their power and strength unto the beast, but when he becomes indwelt by Lucifer (Satan) and demands worship as God, they will destroy the apostate church headquarters (evidently by an atomic explosion, for it is to be "in one hour" that Babylon the great is to be burned with fire—Revelation 18), and they will actually worship the beast-king of the end time. Also, Revelation 17:14 specifies that at the end of the seven-year reign of the Antichrist, "These [ten kings] shall make war with the Lamb [the Lamb of God, the Lord Jesus Christ], and the Lamb shall overcome them; for he is Lord of lords and King of kings . . ." Their dominion will end at the battle of Armageddon.

"At The Time of the End"

It has been declared that the Antichrist king will be the leader of a coalition of ten Western European nations. We can see the foundation of that end-time empire today.

The ten-nation coalition began with the signing of the Benelux Agreement in 1948 (the same year Israel was revived as a nation). Luxembourg, Belgium, and The Netherlands signed the agreement that united their countries' economic and domestic policies.

With the signing of the Treaty of Rome, March 25, 1957, the Benelux three expanded to the Common Market six, bringing in Italy, France, and West Germany. Great Britain, Denmark, and Ireland joined the European Economic Community (EEC), the Common Market, on January 1, 1973.

Greece Makes Number Ten

(February 10, 1976, *Los Angeles Times*) The nine governments of the European Common Market unanimously endorsed Greece's membership application.

(May 29, 1979, *Los Angeles Herald Examiner*) Athens, Greece—Greece became the 10th member of the European Common Market yesterday, culminating 22 years of efforts by Premier Constantine Caramanlis to join his country economically with Europe. . . .

Greece's active membership is scheduled to start Jan. 1, 1981, after the 10 member parliaments ratify the agreement.

European Parliament Election

Anticipating Greece's entry, but not waiting for it, the Common Market countries took the next big step toward consolidation. They called for a special universal election to select representatives for a European Parliament.

(April 8, 1978, *Los Angeles Times*) Copenhagen, Denmark— Heads of government of the European Common Market countries agreed here Friday to schedule the long-planned direct elections for the nine-nation European Parliament for June 7, 8 and 9, 1979. . . .

The parliament which Europeans will elect by popular vote will be important symbolically even though it will have few real powers. But the simple fact that its members will be elected from all over Europe instead of appointed by governments as at present is bound to enhance its importance and its impact on the conduct of Common Market business.

It will be a body of 410 members—81 seats each for Britain, France, West Germany and Italy, 25 for The Netherlands, 24 for Belgium, 16 for Denmark, 15 for Ireland and 6 for Luxembourg—to meet monthly 10 months of the year, alternating between assembly halls in Luxembourg and Strasbourg.

(June 12, 1979, *Los Angeles Times*) Final returns in Europe's first multinational election gave a coalition of Liberals, Christian Democrats and British Conservatives a working majority in the European Parliament of the Common Market. The center-right bloc won 207 seats in the 410-member Parliament. Socialists won 111 seats, and Communists 42—24 from Italy and 18 from France. The remaining seats will be held by Progressive Democrats and other small and diverse factions from across Europe.

(June 18, 1979, *Los Angeles Times*) Strasbourg, France (AP)—The European Parliament, history's first directly elected multinational assembly, opened its inaugural session Tuesday and elected as its first president Simone Veil, a Jewish Frenchwoman who survived the Auschwitz death camp. . . . It is a measure of how far Europe has evolved democratically from the Hitler years.

Ready For "The Prince"

I had anticipated the election of a pro-Israel president for the new European Parliament, but the selection of a Jewess who bears a Nazi number (78651) tattooed on her arm and who survived the dreadful Auschwitz death camp was even beyond expectation. Who could possibly be more willing to make a *covenant for the protection of Israel?*

We now are at the threshold of "the time of the end." The prophesied ten-nation empire is practically complete and the Western European military king is about to come on the international scene. When he does, he will become the one who will oppose the mighty war machine of "Gog, of the land of Magog." This king will be destined to fight for the protection of the land of Israel.

"The Prince Who Shall Come"

> . . . and *the people* of the prince that shall come shall destroy the city and the sanctuary . . . And *he* shall confirm the covenant with many [Israelis] for one week: and in the midst of the week [of years] *he* shall cause the sacrifice and the oblation to cease . . . (Dan. 9:26,27; italics mine).

"The people of the prince" were the Romans who destroyed the city of Jerusalem and its Hebrew temple in A.D. 70.

"He" is to be the head of a revived Roman Empire in the last days, beginning with the aforementioned ten-nation entity as defined by other prophecies.

One of his first acts is to be the establishment of a seven-year covenant with the Jewish nation wherein he will guarantee Israel's security and also assure the Jews the right to perform animal "sacrifice and oblation."

It will be as a result of this covenant of guarantee that the Antichrist king will fight on behalf of Israel when that nation is attacked by the combined forces of the Arabs and the Soviets. We can pick up the chronology of these end-time events by referring to Daniel 11:40–43.

> And at the time of the end shall the king of the south [Arabs] push *at him:* and the king of the north [Soviets] shall come *against him* like a whirlwind, with chariots, and with horsemen, and with many ships; and *he* shall enter into the countries, and shall overflow and pass over.

He shall enter also into the glorious land [Israel, ostensibly to protect it], and many countries shall be overthrown . . . and the land of Egypt shall not escape.

But *he* shall have power over the treasures of gold and silver, and over all the precious things of Egypt: and the Libyans and the Ethiopians shall be at his steps [italics mine].

The Arab nations are to be defeated and the Soviet armies destroyed. The one who will claim credit for the victory will be the one who guaranteed Israel's security—the Antichrist king of Western Europe.

America? It will be reeling from the devastating effect of hundreds if not thousands of nuclear bombs rained upon it by the Soviet Union.

But there is another great reason that America will no longer be a prominent nation, at least not until after the beginning of the one thousand-year reign of Christ on earth as King of kings. Millions of Bible believing, born-again Christians from the United States will have been "caught up" to the glories of heaven in the event called the Rapture of the church. The ones who remain, therefore, will not be the true and the strong. They will be the unbelievers who are apt to be weaker in character. We can only trust that their patriotism will be strengthened by their adversity, and that in the course of events they will turn to the Lord for their salvation.

13

A NATION MARKED FOR JUDGMENT

The prophecy-related history of the United States has been given from its official beginning to the present. As "a nation" it stands in a position of power and strength. It could well be said of America now the same words declared by the prophet Isaiah over 2,700 years ago:

> All ye inhabitants of the world, and dwellers on the earth, see ye, and when he lifteth up an ensign on the mountains; and when he bloweth a trumpet, hear ye (Isa. 18:3).

From the conception of this nation at the signing of the Declaration of Independence in Philadelphia on July 4, 1776, and its birth through the pangs of the Revolutionary War, this nation has indeed been as prophesied, "a nation, terrible from its beginning hitherto," as stated in Isaiah 18:2.

"Woe" Proclaimed—When America Is Affluent

According to Isaiah "this nation" is to be severely "cut" and pruned "with pruning hooks" and to see its very productive branches "cut down" and "taken away" when the nation is approaching the peak of its productivity: "For afore the harvest, when the bud is perfect, and the sour grape is ripening in the flower . . ." (v. 5). Today with its gross national production measuring close to two trillion dollars; with its boats and yachts numbering in the millions; with Los Angeles County having an average of over 2.5 cars per family; with campers on every highway and the average income nearly eight thousand dollars per year per person across this nation, it certainly can be said that we are a "wide, highly developed, outspread and polished" nation—an affluent society.

Yet, in the face of all this, we are a nation that has become "careless." Anyway you look at it, Americans are "living carelessly in the borders and coastlands."

O that the people of our land would heed the examples of the Scriptures and would cry a prayer of contrition as did Daniel. Note his prayer:

> . . . O Lord, the great and dreadful [Hebrew *yare*: "reverenced"] God, keeping the covenant and mercy to them that love him, and to them that keep his commandments; we have sinned, and have committed iniquity, and have done wickedly, and have rebelled, even by departing from thy precepts and from thy judgments: neither have we hearkened unto thy servants the prophets, which spake in thy name to . . . our fathers, and to all the people of the land.
>
> O Lord, righteousness belongeth unto thee, but unto us confusion of faces, as at this day . . . O Lord, to us belongeth confusion of face, to our kings, to our princes, and to our fathers, because we have sinned against thee.
>
> To the Lord our God belong mercies and forgivenesses, though we have rebelled against him; Neither have we obeyed the voice of the LORD our God, to walk in his laws, which he set before us by his servants the prophets.
>
> Yea, all Israel have transgressed thy law, even by departing, that they might not obey thy voice; therefore the curse is poured upon us . . .
>
> As it is written in the law of Moses, all this evil is come upon us; yet made we not our prayer before the LORD our God, that we might turn from our iniquities, and understand the truth.
>
> Therefore hath the LORD watched upon the evil, and brought it

upon us: for the LORD our God is righteous in all his works which he doeth: for we obeyed not his voice . . . (Dan. 9:4–14).

It's so evident: The people of America have sinned grievously. Lawlessness and iniquity abound; drunkenness and prostitution are on every hand; drug addiction, pot, perversion, and lewdness are flaunted. The "new morality" is nothing more than an excuse for slipping back into the cesspools of the iniquities of ancient Babylon. Witchcraft and Babylonian astrology are the order of the day, deluding hearts and minds and tending more and more to Satanism. America stands indicted and is guilty as charged; and who can deny it?

It is not without cause, therefore, that God declared in Isaiah 18:4, ". . . I will consider . . . like a clear heat upon herbs, and like a cloud of dew in the heat of harvest."

This nation is marked for judgment, even as are many other nations of the world; and the time for that judgment is almost at hand.

Bible prophecy does declare that America will be delivered, but first it shall go through the crucible of a "hell on earth." World War III is prophesied and shall come to pass. There is also much evidence that our beloved country will suffer not only from nuclear attack, but will endure the pangs of treason, anarchy, and internal revolution as the reactionary groups, trained by professional insurgents, try to take control of the shattered remains. Everyone would do well to heed the oft-repeated warning, "Prepare to meet thy God," or, in the words that were said so often to George Washington, "Look, and learn." God *is* warning the people of this nation.

14

WORLD WAR III
AND
THE BATTLE OF ARMAGEDDON

World War III will precede the battle of Armageddon by nearly seven years. The Bible record shows this to be a fact. There are hundreds of prophecies that pertain to world-shaking events that are to happen in this generation. Many of these prophecies concern these two great wars.

The first of these conflicts, World War III, is often referred to as "the battle of fire" due to many references concerning fire, flame, blackness, etc. The closing war of this portion of the history of mankind is the one commonly called the battle of Armageddon. It is not to bring about the end of the world, but it is to be the last battle fought before the true Prince of Peace, the Messiah, establishes His reign of absolute peace on earth. Jesus, appearing in power and great glory, will be revealed as the true Lord of hosts, the "KING OF KINGS, AND LORD OF LORDS" (Rev. 19:16; see Rev. 19:11–20:6).

CONTRASTS BETWEEN WORLD WAR III AND THE BATTLE OF ARMAGEDDON

A. REALMS IN THE BATTLES

World War III

1. "Alignments" of nations involved.

A complete and specific list of the nations to be involved in World War III is given in Ezekiel 38:1–6.

Description of the Bible terms is as follows:

"Gog" is the "chief prince" ruler of Magog (Russia) of the land controlled by Meshech and Tubal (Moscow and Tobolsk: the U.S.S.R.).

"Persia" is the ancient Persian Empire area from West Pakistan to Turkey to Egypt, except Saudi Arabia which was never conquered.

"Ethiopia" is Ethiopia, Somalia, and Sudan of today.

"Libya" is the North African Arab nations of today.

"Gomer and his bands" is the Warsaw Pact area of Eastern Europe.

"Togarmah of the north quarters" is the Baltic States area of Russia which was Estonia, Lithuania, and Latvia.

Togarmah was a son of Gomer who was a grandson of Noah. Part of his family settled in Turkey, and part went

Armageddon

1. All nations of the world involved.

"For they are the spirits of devils, working miracles, that go forth unto the kings of the earth and of the whole world, to gather them to the battle of that great day of God Almighty . . . And he gathered them together into a place called in the Hebrew tongue Armageddon" (Rev. 16:14–16).

"For I will gather all nations against Jerusalem to battle . . . Then shall the Lord go forth, and fight against those nations, as when he fought in the day of battle" (Zech. 14:2,3).

"And I saw heaven opened, and behold a white horse; and he that sat upon him was called Faithful and True, and in righteousness he doth judge and make war . . . And He was clothed with a vesture dipped in blood; and his name is called The Word of God. And the armies which were in heaven followed him. . . . And he hath on his vesture and on his thigh a name written, KING OF KINGS, AND LORD OF north to the Baltic region, thus referred to as being "of the north quarters."

Daniel 2:42–45 and 7:7, and Revelation 17:12 all refer to ten "kings" of the ten nations of the Old Roman Empire area of Western Europe who shall "give their power and strength" unto the beast-despot who shall be the end-time dictator called the Antichrist.

The U.S., bound by the NATO alliance, will be involved and be "cut," etc. in fulfillment of Isaiah 18.

LORDS. . . . And I saw the beast, and the kings of the earth, and their armies, gathered together to make war against him that sat on the horse, and against his army" (Rev. 19:11–19).

B. REGIONS IN THE BATTLES

World War III

Ezekiel 38:8 reads: ". . . in the latter years thou shalt come into the land that is brought back from the sword, and is gathered out of many people, against the mountains of Israel. . . ."

Ezekiel 39:4: "Thou shalt fall upon the mountains of Israel, thou, and all thy bands, and the people that is with thee."

Armageddon

Revelation 16:16 reads: "And he gathered them together into a place called in the Hebrew tongue Armageddon."

The Valley of Megiddo (2 Chron. 35:22). Stalls for hundreds of Solomon's chariots and horses have been found by archaeologists at the fortress of Megiddo on the edge of that valley in north-central Palestine. Multiplied thousands of troops could assemble and encamp in this three hundred-square-mile valley.

C. REASONS FOR THE BATTLES

World War III

Ezekiel 38:12: "To take a spoil, and to take a prey; to turn thine hand upon the desolate places that are now inhabited, and upon the people that are gathered out of the nations. . . ."

Armegeddon

Revelation 16:14, ". . . go forth unto the kings of the earth and of the whole world, to gather them to the battle of that great day of God Almighty."

D. RESULTS OF THE BATTLES

World War III

1. Ezekiel 39:4: "Thou shalt fall upon the mountains of Israel. . . ."

2. Ezekiel 39:6,7: "And I will send a fire on Magog [the land of Russia and its hordes], and among them that dwell carelessly in the isles [coastlands of the Mediterranean and Atlantic seacoasts; Arabian North African coasts; revived portion of Old Roman Empire area of Western Europe including England, and, a "young lion thereof," the United States of America. The "coastlands" would also include the Red Sea coast and the Persian Gulf coast, taking in the "Persia and Ethiopia" areas listed in Ezekiel 38:5]. . . ."

Armageddon

1. Revelation 19:19–21. "And I saw the beast, and the kings of the earth, and their armies, gathered together to make war against him that sat upon the horse, and against his army.

"And the beast was taken, and with him the false prophet that wrought miracles before him, with which he deceived them that had received the mark of the beast, and them that worshipped his image. These were both cast alive into a lake of fire burning with brimstone.

"And the remnant were slain with the sword of him that sat upon the horse, which sword proceeded out of his mouth [Clarification: Hebrews 4:12 reads, "The word of God is quick, and powerful, and sharper than any two-edged sword."]; and all the fowls were filled with their flesh."

3. ". . . and they shall know that I am the LORD. So will I make my holy name known in the midst of my people, Israel, and I will not let them pollute my name any more; and the uttermost parts of the north [Russia and her invading hordes] shall know that I am the LORD, the Holy One in Israel."

The true Jewish people will, indeed, worship the Lord; and they shall never again falter from His way.

4. Ezekiel 39:14,16, "And they shall sever out men of continual employment passing through the land to bury . . . those who remain upon the face of the earth, to cleanse it; after the end of seven months shall they search . . . Thus shall they cleanse the land."

This cleansing of the land is a vital factor, for immediately after the end of World War III the orthodox Jews will build a temple for "oblation and sacrifice," and before the priests can perform their duties the dead must be buried to comply with the Law of Moses recorded in Leviticus 21:1, "And the LORD said unto Moses, Speak unto the priests . . . There shall none be defied for the dead. . . ."

2. Zechariah 14:12, "And this shall be the plague wherewith the LORD will smite all the people that have fought against Jerusalem: Their flesh shall consume away while they stand upon their feet, and their eyes shall consume away in their holes, and their tongue shall consume away in their mouth. And it shall come to pass in that day, that a great tumult from the LORD shall be among them. . . ."

3. True is the written prophecy of the Lord which is recorded in Hebrews 10:31, "It is a fearful thing to fall into the hands of the living God."

4. Revelation 19:21 concludes: ". . . and all the fowls were filled with their flesh."

This occurrence is at the immediate end of the battle of Armageddon.

The "consuming away" of "the peoples who have fought against Jerusalem," prophesied by Zechariah, takes place at the next instance—the judgment of the nations in fulfillment of Matthew 25:31–46. The description of the judgment is verified by Malachi 4:1, which states:

"For behold, the day cometh that shall burn like an oven, and all the proud, yea, and all that do wickedly, shall be stubble: and the day that cometh shall burn them up, saith the LORD of hosts. . . ."

E. REGAL RESULTS OF THE BATTLES

World War III	Armageddon

World War III

1. "And then shall that Wicked be revealed, whom the Lord shall [ultimately] consume with the spirit of his mouth and shall destroy with the brightness of his coming:

"Even him, whose coming is after the working of Satan with all power and signs and lying wonders, And with all deceivableness of unrighteousness in them that perish; because they received not the love of the truth, that they might be saved.

"And for this cause God shall send them strong delusion, that they should believe the lie: That they all might be damned [judged] who believed not the truth, but had pleasure in unrighteousness" (2 Thess. 2:8–12).

2. "And the king [despot-king of the tribulation "time of Jacob's trouble"] shall do according to his will; and he shall exalt himself, and magnify himself above every god, and shall speak marvellous things against the God of gods, and shall prosper till the indignation be accomplished: for that that is determined shall be done" (Dan. 11:36).

3. "He shall enter also into the glorious land [Israel—ostensibly to protect it from the Arab-Russian onslaught] . . . but

Armageddon

1. "In that day shall the LORD defend the inhabitants of Jerusalem; . . . [like] the angel of the LORD before them . . . to destroy all the nations that come against Jerusalem" (Zech. 12:8,9).

2. "And the beast was taken, and with him the false prophet that wrought miracles before him. . . . These both were cast alive into a lake·of fire burning with brimstone" (Rev. 19:20).

3. "And I will pour upon the house of David, and upon the inhabitants of Jerusalem, the spirit of grace and of supplications: and

165

these shall escape out of his hand, even Edom and Moab, and the chief of the children of Ammon" (Dan. 11:41).

The ancient areas of Edom, Moab, and Ammon constitute almost precisely the area of Jordan of today. For these to escape "his" hand indicates a fulfillment of the prophecy of Ezekiel 25 wherein God declares that He will lay His vengeance upon them "by the hand of my people, Israel: and they shall do in Edom according to mine anger and according to my fury . . ." (Ezek. 25:14). Thus, Israel is destined to conquer Jordan!

Verification is found in Zephaniah 2:9, 10:

"Therefore, as I live, saith the LORD of hosts, the God of Israel, Surely Moab shall be as Sodom, and the children of Ammon like Gomorrah . . . a perpetual desolation: the residue of my people shall spoil them, and the remnant of my people shall possess them. This shall they have for their pride, because they have reproached and magnified themselves against the people of the LORD of hosts."

4. "The king" shall be the military leader of the ten-nation revived Roman Empire area of Western Europe. He shall assuredly enter "into the glorious

they shall look upon me whom they have pierced, and they shall mourn for him, as one mourneth for his only son, and shall be in bitterness for him, as one that is in bitterness for his firstborn [Christ, when He arose, became "the firstborn from the dead"].

"In that day shall there be a great mourning in Jerusalem, as the mourning of Hadadrimmon, in the Valley of Megiddon [Josiah, the great reformer King of Judah, died as a result of a battle wound he had received at Hadadrimmon in the Valley of Megiddo, and all of Jerusalem had mourned their beloved king].

"And the land shall mourn [when Israel finally realizes that their forefathers slew the Lord, who died for their sin, but who arose as their redeemer and as the eternal King of kings and Lord of lords], every family apart; and the family of the house of David apart . . ." (Zech. 12:10–13).

4. "And it shall come to pass that in all the land, saith the LORD, two parts therein shall be cut off and die [evidently those who have followed after the

land," as prophesied, and will thus be on hand and in a position of authority, having made the infamous "covenant with many for one week" (—seven years) as recorded in the prophecy of Daniel 9:27.

Having gained his position of power and authority "after the working of Satan with all power and signs and lying wonders, And with all deceivableness of unrighteousness . . . ," as stated in 2 Thessalonians 2:9,10, he shall indeed deceive and delude many. He shall also claim full credit for the victory over the mighty Russian alignment, and in so doing will "guarantee" Israel's safety and allow them to build a Hebrew Temple in Jerusalem. He shall, also, "in the midst of the week" (after three and a half years), set his own image in their temple and shall sit "in the temple of God, showing himself that he is God," in direct fulfillment of 2 Thessalonians 2:4.

Satan Restrained After the Seven Years of Tribulation

5. "And I saw an angel come down from heaven, having the key of the bottomless pit and a great chain in his hand.

"And he laid hold on the dragon, that old serpent, which is the Devil and Satan, and bound him a thousand years, And cast

"beast," the Antichrist]; but the third shall be left therein.

"And I will bring the third part through the fire, and will refine them as silver is refined, and will try them as gold is tried: they shall call on my name, and I will hear them: I will say, It is my people: and they shall say, The LORD is my God" (Zech. 13:8,9).

5. "And I saw thrones, and they sat upon them, and judgment was given unto them: and I saw the souls of them that were beheaded for the witness of Jesus, and for the word of God, and which had not worshipped the beast, neither his image, neither had received his mark upon their foreheads, or in their hands; and they lived and reigned with Christ a thousand years" (Rev. 20:4).

By identity, these can only be the ones who were slain during the last half of the seven-year Tribulation period, for not until then is the image set up and the death penalty established for any who will not worship the beast nor his image. These saints, slain too late to appear at the judgment seat of Christ for their rewards, now receive their commendations, and ". . . they shall be him into the bottomless pit, and shut him up, and set a seal upon him, that he should deceive the nations no more, till the thousand years should be fulfilled . . ." (Rev. 20:1–3).

priests of God and of Christ, and shall reign with him a thousand years" (Rev. 20:6).

God's prophecies are specific and they shall surely come to pass.

Summary of Revealed Differences of the Battles

Based on these contrasts, any honest and thinking person can see that it is impossible for the two great wars depicted to be considered as one and the same battle. In summary:

A. World War III involves but one third of the world. The battle of Armageddon sees the whole world involved.

B. World War III will have its climaxing battle on "the mountains of Israel" (to include the Lebanese and the Syrian area anti-Lebanese Mountains.)

The battle of Armageddon will have its climaxing battle in the valley of Megiddo, called Armageddon, and at Jerusalem (see Rev. 16:16; Zech. 14:2–5).

C. In World War III the full-scale battle takes place when the U.S.S.R., as "the king of the north," comes "against him" (Israel's pseudo-protector, the selected king or leader of the Western European revived Roman Empire area and probable commander of the Western European Union and/or NATO forces which would, by treaty, involve and include the United States) "like a whirlwind," as portrayed in the prophecy recorded in Daniel 11:40.

In the battle of Armageddon the real battle takes place when "the kings of the earth" are gathered at a place called Armageddon, near Jerusalem, "to make war against him that sat on the horse [Christ], and against his army" (Rev. 19:19).

D. The results of the battles conflict completely. In World War III "the king" becomes identified with "the beast" referred to in Revelation 13 and with "the scarlet-colored beast" described in Revelation 17 when he usurps his power for his own glory, claiming full credit for the victory wherein "many countries shall be overthrown." The land of Egypt shall not escape, but he shall have power over the treasures of gold and of silver, and over all the precious things of Egypt, and the Libyans and Ethiopians (the other Arab League nations) shall be at his steps (see Dan. 11:41–43).

The end result of the battle of Armageddon is the destruction of this "beast" when Christ and His army of saints come forth from heaven. Christ, as "KING OF KINGS AND LORD OF LORDS" (Rev. 19:16), defeats the armies of the whole world gathered together, and casts the "beast" and his false prophet into the lake of fire and brimstone (Rev. 19:11–21).

E. World War III establishes the end-time king-despot in his place of power. The battle of Armageddon brings about his defeat and establishes the real rule of peace on earth by the real King of kings and Lord of lords, the resurrected and glorified Lord Jesus Christ.

The Conclusion of the Matter

Satan's counterfeit king, the Antichrist, has no power against "the Way, the Truth and the Life," the Lord Jesus Christ, when He will come at His appointed time to establish true peace on the earth. Satan and his cohorts may be able to conquer the world and to call all of the armies of the world together to fight against God and His Christ, but in "the great day of God Almighty" (Rev. 16:14), his efforts will be shown for what they really are: utter fallacy.

Satan is to be chained up by one of God's angels (Rev. 20:1,2). He shall be loosed again after the thousand-year peaceful reign of Christ upon the earth (Rev. 20:7–10); but after that "little season" in which Satan shall again try to raise up an army to fight against God, he shall be permanently defeated and disposed of by being "cast into the lake of fire and brimstone, where the beast and the false prophet are, and shall be tormented day and night for ever and ever" (Rev. 20:10).

The end of the matter is that Satan and all of his followers shall be judged and punished eternally for all of the evil which has been perpetrated against God and mankind.

Choose Your Own Leader and Destiny

Joshua, the man chosen of God to lead the children of Israel into the Promised Land, gave a great message to the people when they had, with the mighty help and deliverance of God, conquered the various tribes and peoples who had dwelt in the land of Canaan. He said to them:

> Now, therefore, fear the LORD, and serve him in sincerity and in truth: and put away the gods which your fathers served on the other side of the flood, and in Egypt; and serve ye the LORD. And if it seem evil unto you to serve the LORD, choose you this day whom ye will serve . . . but as for me and my house, we will serve the LORD (Josh. 24:14,15).

Joshua's Prophetic Warning

Having led the people, preached to the people, challenged and given to them a clear-cut choice as to the course of their destiny, and declared unto them his own choice to "serve the Lord," Joshua added this sage admonition:

> . . . Ye cannot [lightly] serve the LORD; for he is an holy God, he is a jealous God, he will not forgive your transgressions nor your sins [of falsehood and idolatry and following after sorcerers, astrologers, and "familiar" spirits].
>
> "If ye forsake the LORD, and serve strange gods, then he will turn and do you hurt, and consume you, after he hath done you good . . . Now, therefore, put away . . . the strange gods which are among you, and incline your heart unto the LORD God . . ." (Josh. 24:19,20,23).

An Admonition

This book has been written not only to be a book of verified history, science, geography, and a coordination of all of these with the prophecies of the Bible; but it has been written also as a firm testimony unto the truth.

If you choose to serve God by trusting in His Son as your Savior and by believing the words written concerning Him; and if you choose to oppose Satan and his antiChrist imposter who is soon to be revealed and foisted upon the unsuspecting people of this world, take a firm stand for God; for it is written in God's Word:

> . . . without faith it is impossible to please him: for he that cometh to God must believe that he is, and that he is a rewarder of them that diligently seek him (Heb. 11:6).

The time will come when the Satan-empowered antiChrist leader will gain more and more power and authority upon this earth. Furthermore, it is prophesied that he will receive a head wound that will kill him (Gen. 3:15; and Rev. 13:3–5); but he shall be revived therefrom, and as a result of this, he shall be greatly admired and be worshipped. Worship him not!

If you ever submit to the worship of that Satan-in-dwelt counterfeit "deliverer" or receive the "mark of the beast" which he will require all to receive if they are to be able to buy or sell anything in his world domain, it will signify your rejection of the true and the living God and it will seal your destiny forever as a worshipper of Satan, which will not be forgiven (Rev. 14:9–11).

Now—or Later—or Never

If you believe in God and in His true Deliverer, the Messiah and Savior, Jesus Christ, your destiny will be sealed with God, and you will have eternal rejoicing and peace together with God and with His angels and saints forever. If you should delay too long, you will be forced by the Antichrist of the end time to "worship him, or die." Should you ever be faced with that decision, choose death, for in so doing, you will save your soul for all eternity.

If you submit, and worship the man or his image or receive

his "mark," your own destiny will subsequently be sealed with his, and your ultimate destruction will be assured when he is defeated at the battle of Armageddon at the close of the Tribulation period—that terrifying time which is biblically referred to as "the time of Jacob's trouble." Even as he will be judged, so will all of his followers be judged, and the ultimate end is eternal separation from God and everlasting punishment in the lake of fire and brimstone.

Thus it is that, faced with specific factors, each person is confronted with a specific decision, each person is given a free choice. The admonition of this author is that you follow the great example of Joshua, and say: "As for me and my house, we will serve the Lord."

The only time that you are sure of is *now*. You might have an opportunity *later*, if you survive through World War III and all of its tremendous devastations. You may *never* have time to even finish the reading of this book, for your life and soul are just one push-button away from eternity.

God provided salvation by dying in your place. "To wit, that God was in Christ, reconciling the world unto himself, not imputing their trespasses unto them, and hath committed unto us the word of reconciliation . . . as though God did beseech you by us: we pray you in Christ's stead, be ye reconciled to God" (2 Cor. 5:19,20).

It is written, "If thou shalt confess with thy mouth the Lord Jesus, and shalt believe in thine heart that God hath raised him from the dead, thou shalt be saved" (Rom. 10:9). Also, "Whosoever shall call upon the name of the Lord shall be saved" (Rom. 10:13).

My admonition is, "Do it now." Let your signature be your confession of faith in Jesus as *your* Savior:

Section IV

A DESCRIPTIVE SCENARIO OF EVENTS PRECEDING WORLD WAR III

Submarine tender refitting U.S. Polaris submarine in Holy Loch, Scotland.
(U.S. Navy photo)

15

CURRENT PREPARATIONS FOR WORLD WAR III

The two great superpowers and their vast alignments of nations (identified in Chapter five) shall most certainly engage in a fast and furious world-encircling all-out war. Both the war and its results are graphically outlined in the Bible.

Nearly six hundred years before Jesus walked on earth, Ezekiel recorded the God-given prophecy that God in judgment would "send a fire on Magog" (the land of Russia). He recorded that five sixths of the vast Russian military forces would "fall on the mountains of Israel." This shall surely come to pass.

It is prophesied just as graphically that the nations which God shall use to fight against the Russian alliance shall be greatly devastated in that war, especially the nation that has been "terrible from its beginning," the United States.

How soon shall these prophecies be fulfilled? Great preparations are underway today for exactly that kind of war.

Russia's Preparations

Navy

(August 29, 1970, *Los Angeles Times*) London (AP)—The U.S. Navy will end this fiscal year next June 30 with 175 fewer active ships and 732 fewer aircraft than it had at the end of fiscal 1968, Jane's Fighting Ships reports in its 1970-71 edition.

By contrast, it says, the Soviet Navy is undergoing "spectacular growth."

Editor Raymond Blackman wrote in his forward to the authoritative annual review that while the U.S. and British fleets were spread thin and growing obsolete, the Soviet fleet was growing so rapidly that "there is no hiding place from the hammer and sickle."

He said the Soviet merchant fleet rose from 1,000 ships in 1955 to 7,000 in 1970 and that the increase in the Russian's fighting fleet "has been no less spectacular, particularly in the late 1960s."

"The U.S.S.R. is no longer copying and emulating," Blackman wrote. "She is initiating and inventing. Regularly there appears a new class of warship peculiar to Soviet requirements. Each year for the past few years a new type of rocket cruiser or missile destroyer has appeared."

He said a new class of Soviet submarine has been observed each year and that "for years improvements have progressively been made in a series of deadly little missile boats running into hundreds of units" . . . .

(July 29, 1977, *Los Angeles Times*) Brussels, Belgium—Nearly 100 Soviet submarines went into the Atlantic Ocean recently in a massive show of naval strength that stretched western surveillance

Soviet nuclear submarine

forces to their limits, Atlantic Alliance Intelligence sources revealed Thursday.

"More Soviet submarines were deployed between North America and Europe than ever before," according to a senior intelligence officer in the North Atlantic Treaty Organization.

American and British submarines which usually trail Soviet submarines were unable to cope with the rush and the alliance had to resort to other, less effective, means to keep track of many of the Soviet vessels. . . .

In April, 89 Soviet submarines . . . swept into the Norwegian Sea and the Atlantic. . . . The submarines were accompanied by a large force of surface warships, including the aircraft carrier, Kiev, which bears vertical takeoff and landing jet fighters.

Long range warplanes, including some of the 400 supersonic Backfire bombers that the Russians now operate, flew over the maneuvering fleet from their bases in the Murmansk area, the sources said.

The NATO submarines concentrated on keeping track of the Russian ballistic submarines, the sources said.

(January 12, 1978, *Los Angeles Times*) The Soviet Union is expanding its naval forces in the Far East at an unexpectedly rapid pace, sources close to the Japanese Defense Agency said. They said two of the most modern Soviet missile-carrying warships were spotted by Japanese patrol planes in the East China Sea. . . .

As of last July, the Soviets had 755 warships in their Far East fleet, including 10 cruisers, 80 destroyers and 125 submarines.

(July 30, 1978, *Los Angeles Times*) The first sea-based missile with multiple warheads is in operation, tripling the number of targets the newest type of Soviet submarines could attack with nuclear weapons, U.S. intelligence sources said.

Latest evidence indicates the SS-N-18 missile, with a range of more than 4,900 miles, is being deployed on Delta-3 submarines as the vessels enter the Soviet fleet. Five Delta-3 submarines have been counted in the Soviet fleet, but more are being built.

Army

(July 6, 1978, *Los Angeles Times*) The biggest Soviet military maneuvers in Central Europe since the 1975 Helsinki Security

177

Conference start today in East Germany, with the West barred from sending observers. About 30,000 Soviet troops will take part in war games for five days across a 125-mile swath of East Germany.

(February 24, 1978, *The International August Review*) Scottsdale, Ariz.—The prestigious Foreign Affairs Institute (London) recently released a seven page report entitled Chemical and Bacteriological Warfare: The Threat Facing NATO. Within that report is the following:

"Recent disclosures by Western intelligence, based on satellite reconnaissance, confirm that the Soviet Union is currently engaged in an extensive research and development programme in the field of bacteriological warfare. . . .

"There is no doubt of their ability to wage chemical warfare at any time. Every Soviet division has one chemical warfare battalion as part of its organic structure and elaborate exercises in chemical warfare are conducted at regular intervals.

"All Soviet troops are issued with protective clothing and masks and carry pocket-sized detection meters in addition to small dosimeters for detecting nuclear radiation. They are equipped with first-aid kits specially designed to counter the effects of CW weapons.

"The latest addition to their stockpile of chemical weapons is B gas, which affects human beings in much the same manner as DDT affects insects: it demolishes their nervous system."

Stragetic Buildup Summary

The immensity of the Soviet strategic buildup is causing alarm in many Western capitals. Britain's Winston Spencer Churchill stated in an address to a meeting of the National Association for Freedom: "The Soviet buildup is far beyond any requirements of self defense—indeed the Soviets are building the greatest war-machine the world has ever seen.This is more than a challenge to the West—it is the most deadly threat to freedom and to peace any generation has ever known."

Statistics are mountainous pertaining to the Soviet buildup of its overall strategic attack capability. By way of a brief summary, consider the following information, gleaned from many sources.

The Soviet army boasts 4.4 million men. Pentagon reports indicate that the U.S. is outnumbered 2-to-1 in armed forces, 4-to-1 in artillery pieces and 5-to-1 in tanks.

In missiles, Russia reportedly has 1,400 ICBMs plus 1,015 sub-launched missiles with over 4,500 nuclear warheads. In March, 1977, the Soviets test-fired two major submarine-launched missiles from a Russian submarine in the Barents Sea. They travelled 5,700 miles over Russia and Siberia, landing in a target area in the Pacific Ocean. This gives full evidence that Russia has the capability to blast any U.S. city from Soviet submarines deployed close to Soviet shores.

A third major Soviet aircraft carrier has been launched, bringing their surface combat fleet to 243 ships compared to 172 in the U.S. fleet. In submarines, the U.S.S.R. has the U.S. outnumbered 3-to-1.

While in Australia to attend a seminar conducted by the Australian Naval Institute in February 1979, Admiral Elmo R. Zumwalt, former Navy chief of operations, stated:

> It is the professional judgment of senior officials in the U.S. that our Navy has only a 35 percent probability of winning a conventional naval war against the Soviet Union. Our military knows this, and so does theirs. About the only people who do not seem to know it are the general public in the United States and Australia.
>
> Nor do they know that a nuclear exchange in 1981 on present trends would result in about 160 million dead in the United States. . . .
>
> Unless we begin immediately to redress the imbalance, by 1981–85 Moscow will have what it has long wanted, a strategic war-winning capability in which it might never even have to fire a shot.*

(January 26, 1979, *Los Angeles Times*) Washington—Defense Secretary Harold Brown said Thursday that the Soviet Union is

Spotlight, February 26, 1979.

179

building its nuclear missile force at a faster pace than was antici-pated a year ago, increasing the danger that the 1980s may become an era of Soviet strategic superiority. . . .

He cited the growth in the Russian military as "potentially very dangerous to us." As a result, he said, by 1982 a Soviet first strike could destroy 80% of this country's Minuteman intercontinental ballistic missiles in their silos. . . .

"After 1982," he said, "if the United States pursues a vigorous program of developing the Trident submarine and missile, the MX missile and cruise missiles, it could 'reverse' the Soviet lead by the end of the decade."

(February 1, 1979, *Los Angeles Times*) The Soviet Union deto-nated a record 27 nuclear underground blasts in 1978, more than all other nuclear powers combined, according to a Swedish defense agency.

Commentary

Bible prophecy shows that we are at the point of climax and at the very threshold of "the time of the end." Prophecy reveals that the Soviet colossus will strike—and that it will be horribly defeated.

Consider now a few of the material reasons as to *why* the Kremlin's forces will fall.

America's Preparations

The United States is prepared for war: It has been and it will be. Here are some evidences of that preparation.

Armaments

(September 6, 1967, *Los Angeles Times*) (AP Science Editor) Washington—The United States has a powerful and versatile stockpile of tens of thousands of individual nuclear weapons.

The stockpile includes such novel things as nuclear antisubmarine rockets, torpedoes and depth charges—weapons that have had little mention in the past.

. . . In questions submitted by the Associated Press . . . answers to the queries—in which the Defense Department collaborated with the Atomic Energy Commission—brought out that:

Our weapons stockpile consists of tens of thousands of nuclear weapons. . . .

Yields range from subkilotons to megatons. (A kiloton is the explosive equivalent of 1,000 tons of TNT. A megaton is equal to 1 million tons.) . . .

The United States has artillery-fired atomic projectiles, atomic demolition munitions, antisubmarine rockets, torpedoes, depth charges, strategic and tactical missiles, and bombs.

Soviet Superiority?

"Superiority" is a relative term meaning "having an advantage." For an aggressive nation to have an advantage is dangerous in that it invites exploitation and adventurism. The Soviets are known for both.

When the Soviets do strike (Bible prophecies declare that they will), it will be with great fury, causing extreme damage to America, Western Europe, and Israel. In the course of the brief but devastating war, Russia and its satellite nations will also suffer greatly, being rained upon by atomic fire.

Although dropping to second place numerically, the U.S. is still the leader in delivery systems and in the accuracy thereof. The Soviets would do well to notice the prophecy of Ezekiel 39:6, "I will send a fire on Magog [Russia]. . . ."

U.S. government reports indicate that in 1978 we had 1,054 ICBMs, 656 sub-launched missiles, 432 strategic bombers, 4,500 tactical aircraft, 172 surface combat ships, 41 Polaris-Poseidon nuclear powered, nuclear-missile-firing submarines, plus a large number of attack and cruise-missile-firing submarines. Yes, we are capable of launching an all-out barrage of *thousands* of nuclear warheads against any proverbial enemy.

We have enough nuclear firepower to make a cinder of Russia.

I'll take you now "behind the scenes" to describe some of the manners in which our strategic strength is deployed.

Aerial Command Post

(January 18, 1970, Exclusive to *The Times* from Reuters)
Omaha—A lone Boeing 707 circles Omaha every hour, every day of
the year, carrying a general whose job means life or death for
millions. The plane is an aerial command post for the Strategic Air
Command, a flying trigger that could send nuclear missiles into
action if a sneak attack wiped out SAC's subterranean control
centers.

This reporter (Howard Sibler) was the first newsman to fly
aboard an aerial command post. It was a routine mission, routine
day—guarding against the chance that the routine one day might be
for real.

At 7:15 a.m. Maj. Gen. Sherman F. Martin left the warmth of an
automobile and stepped into the sub-zero cold and 30 m.p.h. wind
that swept across Offutt Air Force Base, SAC headquarters. A knot
of heavily clothed men, several of them armed, parted to make way
for him and he hurried up the steps to the door of the 707.

Close Security

Waiting aboard was Lt. Col. Robert L. Standerwick of Mankato,
Kan., armed with a holstered .38-caliber revolver. Standerwick
followed the general into a large compartment, made certain they
were alone and closed the door behind them. The room was lined
with electronic communications consoles, each with a telephone
instrument. Mounted at table height at the right side of the cabin
was a steel box painted red, secured by two heavy padlocks.

Chain on Neck

Without a word each officer produced a key from a chain around
his neck and opened a lock. As the box lid was lifted a raucous
clacking filled the airplane. The alarm was shut off quickly.

For 20 minutes Martin examined documents from the box. The
information they contained represented most of the strategic deterrent strength of the Western world—the means of implementing the
Strategic Air Command war plan. He checked the availability of
1,054 Minuteman and Titan II intercontinental ballistic missiles,
nearly 450 B-52 bombers and numerous tanker aircraft used to
refuel bombers in flight.

Then he made a careful appraisal of one of the most secret

documents of all. This had the SAC "go-codes"—words that could unleash thermonuclear weapons . . .

The plane was the SAC airborne command post (code name— Looking Glass).

Martin replaced the papers in the box. The lid closed, the locks snapped shut. If it were reopened during the ensuing 8 hours and 20 minutes the act would signal either an emergency exercise or the serious threat of a nuclear war. The compartment door was opened and more men entered. With Standerwick they would serve as the battle staff during the flight, now minutes away.

General Handles Controls

A few minutes later Martin slid into the pilot's seat of the four-engined plane. Every SAC general who is a pilot takes his turn aboard the airborne command post. Most handle the controls for the takeoff and landing. . . .

Looking Glass has top priority. The command post planes take off precisely at 8 a.m., 4 p.m. and midnight. Martin eased the four turbofan engines toward full power. At exactly 8 a.m. the plane shot forward. It carried 20 men, a heavy load of communications and data-processing equipment and enough fuel to remain aloft for at least 12 hours without refueling in flight.

The plane leveled off at 24,000 feet. It would remain at this altitude for eight hours unless a war threat crisis developed. In that event it would go higher.

Martin returned to his desk. The battle staff was busy. Communications tests were being made. War plans documents were being examined. This was not a training exercise. The battle staff and the support personnel on the plane had to be ready for any eventuality. Martin said they were.

Since 1961

Looking Glass has been on an airborne alert since Feb. 3, 1961. With what SAC describes as "very few and brief exceptions" a command post plane has been in the air at all times, always with a general aboard.

The command post orbits Omaha usually at a distance of about 100 miles. If the SAC underground command post were destroyed or lost its ability to communicate with SAC forces, Looking Glass would go into action. First, said Martin, the staff would determine the status of secondary command posts in California and Louisiana.

If these were out of action the airborne command post would take control of surviving elements of the SAC force.

"But even while we are inquiring about the other command posts we could alert the force," the general said, "and give the orders for SAC bombers to take to the sky."

Bombers, Missiles

At the direction of the President or his successor, Looking Glass could send the bombers on retaliatory attacks and order the launching of missiles. And, since 1967, SAC has been capable of triggering a growing number of Minuteman ICBMs from Looking Glass and certain other aircraft.

Martin said that before the end of this year it would be possible to launch all 1,000 Minutemen from aloft—but only if it is no longer possible to control the missiles from the ground. Looking Glass is the nucleus of SAC's post-attack command and control system.

Other Planes

Crisis conditions would send three auxiliary command post aircraft, each with a general aboard, and six relay planes into the air. All are cousins of the Boeing 707. The auxiliary command posts would circle over the South, New England and the Southwest. They are based in Louisiana, Massachusetts and California. The radio relay planes would be deployed from South Dakota and Indiana. Looking Glass and its nine companions would fly random courses at high altitudes. The chances of an enemy destroying any, even with a nuclear burst, are almost nonexistent.

The entire fleet takes to the air for regular exercises. But Looking Glass is the only one that is always aloft. . . .

Two battle staff members paid considerable attention to the world situation . . . intelligence officers had brought with them sheaves of news dispatches. They maintain an information file for Martin. Under post-attack conditions they would identify targets to be hit in retaliation.

The operations plans officers would advise the general on the best means to strike those targets and, where bombers were to be used, the route for them to take. Two logistics officers would maintain a file on the availability of various weapons systems. "It is a small, compact battle staff but it can do the job," Martin said.

Routine Course

For eight hours Looking Glass flew a routine course. . . . This was one of the possible courses . . . Shortly before 4 p.m. Martin put away a sheaf of papers labeled "top secret" and went forward to the pilot's seat.

A few minutes later a radio message brought word that the relief airborne command post had taken off. At 4:08 p.m., assured that the partner was climbing to its planned altitude and was establishing its communications, Martin began to take his plane home. Soon Looking Glass was on the ground—and Looking Glass was in the sky. This is the way it has been for nearly nine years. . . ."

The Boeing 747 U.S. flying command post. (The arrow indicates the bulge where the super high frequency communications system is housed.)

New Flying Command Post

(June 15, 1978, *Seattle Post-Intelligencer*) An "improved version" of an airborne command post 747, designed for use by the president and other top officials in national emergencies, has begun an 11-week flight test program at Boeing Field.

The main apparent difference in the "B" version is a bulge atop the forward fuselage. The bulge contains a "super high frequency" communications system designed to receive and transmit satellite signals.

The big plane also has a "very low frequency system that requires a trailing antenna cable up to five miles long which winds up inside the plane," said the spokesman Jim Grafton.

"This new plane . . . also features nuclear thermal shielding and the largest power-generator system ever flown," officials said.

This blue and white 747, with *United States of America* emblazoned on its fuselage, is one of six command post planes stuffed with elaborate electronics and communications gear that can be utilized to conduct an entire nuclear war. One of the six is in the air over the U.S.A. every hour of every day.

(December 1978, *The Washington Monthly*) . . . That's the Plane.

At Andrews Air Force base, just outside Washington, it sits apart from the other presidential planes. The main field is littered with assorted Special Mission Air Force jets that could carry Chip Carter to Peking or a congressional group to Taipei. To the left, over by the VIP area, are the planes that shuttled Henry Kissinger around the world—those oft-televised beauties, Air Force One and Air Force Two. But there, over on the right, far away from the other planes sits the big one. A 747 bigger than Air Force One, with a proud UNITED STATES OF AMERICA emblazoned in four-and-a-half-foot high letters where an ordinary plane's windows would be.

It costs $250 million. One quarter of a billion dollars. It's the most expensive aircraft ever. The Joint Chiefs already own four of them, and there are many who think that we need twice that number to insure the nation's survival.

The plane goes by the title of E-4 Advanced Airborne Emergency Command Post (AAENCP). But if you've heard of it at all, you most likely know it as the Doomsday Plane, the name reporters gave it last February when Carter took them along on the Plane's first presidential dry-run—a trip back home to Georgia. After going along for the ride, the press painted the Plane as a sort of electrified Fairy Godmother that can swoop down and bear our Leader away from the nuclear unpleasantness. Good copy, but not quite true.

Even when swept clean of classified equipment (so the press could take a peek), the Plane is as impressive inside as out . . . Computers, transmitters, conference rooms, map rooms, and a situation room with electronic screens ready to flash pictures of battle theaters in any part of the world. All this and more.

There's a relatively spacious cabin with an imperial gold color scheme. In the rear, bunks of a more Spartan quality accommodate the 15-man battle staff that operates the radar and computers and

27-man crew that actually flies the Plane and feeds its precious cargo.

The Plane is not supposed to accommodate only the President. It can also take along 94 passengers. The guest list is a print-out of those who are essential to the President, the ultimate Who's Who. It is classified. . . .

U.S. Secrets: The Big Three

(June 8, 1970, *Newsweek*) The three topmost U.S. military secrets are the Single Integrated Operations Plan (SIOP), which outlines how a nuclear war would be conducted; the National Strategic Target List (NSTL), which lists the targets in such a nuclear war; and the National Military Command Authorities (NMCA), from the President on down to the chairman of the Joint Chiefs of Staff, who would hold the cryptographic key to the nuclear trigger—the nuclear line of succession, so to speak. Their identities have never been disclosed."*

Secret Mount Weather

(March 1, 1977, *Chicago Tribune*) Washington—One of the capital's best known top secrets concerns a hidden city, about 40 miles west of the White House, built under the Appalachian foothill called Mount Weather.

The underground city—complete with three-story buildings, streets and a lake for drinking water—would shelter thousands of selected government managers if the Soviet missiles ever rain down on Washington. When the topic is Mount Weather, questions at the Pentagon, CIA, even at the Social Security Administration draw a terse "no comment." Mount Weather is something like the U.S. government's safe deposit box. Its buildings contain computers which duplicate the data stored elsewhere in the country— information crucial *for rebuilding*. Current records, census data, Social Security files, military intelligence, even income-tax data are stored in the system.

Similar but much smaller hardened nuclear shelters at Ft. Ritchie, Md., Colorado Springs, Omaha, and probably a few truly

*Copyright, Newsweek, Inc., 1970.

secret locations, make up the United States' efforts to build special wartime shelters. These are designated for military and government leaders. If the unthinkable comes, civilians will be directed to 235,000 buildings with fallout shelter signs throughout the country.

If there is time, Pentagon civil defense officials say, the government will attempt a massive evacuation of most cities with the terrified residents relocating to host communities in the rural countryside. . . .

(November 16, 1978, *The Register*, Orange Co., Calif.) New York (AP)—Where do you put eight million New Yorkers in the face of a nuclear attack—shuffle them off to Buffalo?

The federal government has spent $500,000 and state and federal officials have taken three years trying to come up with a disaster evacuation plan. The plan . . . calls for evacuating residents to "host areas" in upstate New York.

Caspar Kasparian of the federal Defense Civil Preparedness Agency, a division of the Defense Department, said the plan assumes there will be up to a two-week warning. When asked if the plan could work, Kasparian said: "We're not talking about anything practical. Practical is not the name of the game. The name of the game is survival."

Crisis Relocation

The Pentagon is currently developing plans to use abandoned mines as nuclear fallout shelters and to move millions of Americans into them during times of crisis.

"Our estimates now," says a researcher for the Defense Department's Civil Defense Preparedness Agency (DCPA), "are that under Crisis Relocation Planning criteria, there is a potential for sheltering 50 million people in dry, level and readily accessible mines."

The DCPA says it has already found space for "6 million in some 2,000 mines" around the country . . . A study in Pennsylvania, which is considered a prime location because of its coal mines, "demonstrated that the entire population of Pittsburgh could be sheltered in mines within 70 miles of the city."

Retaliation Emphasized

Although Washington D.C. has its Mount Weather and the rest of the U.S. has its caves and mines, the primary Pentagon emphasis is on retaliation rather than protection. The costs of truly adequate civilian protection from sustained nuclear attack are generally considered unacceptable to the American taxpayer. "Grin and bear it" seems to be a philosophy more palatable. Americans evidently take heart in hope and in the thought of "revenge." We don't want to talk or even think about the possibility of immense nuclear damage or danger. Military planners, instead, talk of retaliation.

(July 2, 1978, *Los Angeles Times*) Washington (UPI)—A retaliatory strike by the United States could devastate the Soviet Union even after a massive, surprise Russian attack aimed at destroying U.S. nuclear forces, congressional studies released Saturday said. . . .

The report said at least 120 bombers, 17 Poseidon submarines and 700 land-based ICBMs would survive, or about 5,000 nuclear weapons. Even holding 1,000 in reserve, the second-strike would destroy 80% of the Soviet industrial target base and 90% of the military facilities other than missile silos.

"This retaliation could kill between 20 million and 95 million people in the Soviet Union, depending on the effectiveness of Soviet civil defense efforts," the study said.

Polaris—Poseidon Power

America's "triad of power" consists of its bombers, its ICBMs, and its submarine-launched missiles. To give you a view of the potency of such power, let me show you just one portion of it, our submarine-launched nuclear warhead capacity.

The U.S. has 41 nuclear ballistic missile submarines. Thirty-one of these are Poseidon submarines containing ten warheads per missile. This gives the U.S. the following strike capacity: 10×16 (Polaris) $+ 31 \times 16 \times 10$ (Poseidon) $= 5,120$ nuclear warheads. They can incinerate 5,120 targets; and these

The USS James Madison, a Poseidon Nuclear submarine. It can launch 16 Poseidon missiles in 8 minutes that can obliterate 160 targets—many hundreds of miles apart—over 3,000 miles from its launch location.

(U.S. Navy photo)

are backed up by almost exactly 6,000 more nuclear warheads carried by our bombers, on our ICBMs, or in tactical field use.

To help you grasp the awesomeness of this power, I am including two graphic descriptions by American reporters who witnessed first-hand the U.S. nuclear strike capability.

1. The Nuclear Sub Tender "Simon Lake"

(April 3, 1970, *Life Magazine*) Half-hidden in the frigid waters of the Scottish cove, the nuclear submarines cluster around the mother ship. This is Holy Loch, home of 10 of America's Polaris missile subs, a place rarely seen by outsiders but one of enormous interest and importance today. . . .

Holy Loch is not the usual sort of naval base—it has almost no onshore facilities—but for practical purposes the sub tender "Simon Lake" is a base in herself. A floating shipyard and storehouse, she can haul anchor and head for the open sea if attack should threaten. Her subs cruise for two months at a time beneath the Atlantic and the Mediterranean, then return to Holy Loch to be repaired, resupplied and—as exclusive photographs by Life's Bill Ray show—rearmed by the mother ship.

A Gathering of Nuclear Firepower

. . . The wind is so fierce sailors call it The Hawk. It can blow a man overboard as though he were a leaf. One stormy night in 1968 the wind gusted at 140 mph. . . .

The only thing at Holy Loch more awesome than the elements is the nuclear firepower gathered there. It was raining—horizontally, as usual—as Photographer Bill Ray and I braced ourselves on the flying bridge of the "Simon Lake" and surveyed the deadly array. To port were four Polaris subs, a total of 64 missiles. Amidships on the tender, additional missiles were stored in a maximum security magazine. To starboard was a Navy transport just in from the U.S. with food, machinery and still more missiles. We were standing among enough nuclear warheads to account—give or take a few megatons—for 5,000 Hiroshimas. The missiles are safe, of course. While in the loch, special devices make it impossible to fire them—either deliberately or by mistake.

For a week we watched the skilled crew of the "Simon Lake" work night and day to maintain the exacting month-long "refit" schedule on the four subs. While the machine shop turned out and installed parts that normally would have kept a sub immobilized in a shipyard for three months, the optics shop replaced the crosshairs of a navigational periscope and medical took out a sailor's appendix. Altogether the "Simon Lake" carries 105,000 items a sub might need, from toilet paper to a spare engine screw. Its staff even includes a peridontist. A Navy-trained safecracker is on hand to maintain the scores of safes containing classified material. If one malfunctions, this fellow can polish his fingertips and crack it. . . .

Uncompromising Security

Shipboard security is uncompromising. Armed deck guards have orders to shout "Halt!" once and then fire at any intruder. We were topside on the sub "Thomas Jefferson" one afternoon when the "Simon Lake's" public address system erupted with a shrill whistle and the terse announcement, "Security violation! Security violation!" Suddenly guards materialized at every gangway and we were ordered to "freeze." As it turned out, some sailor had inadvertently opened a forbidden hatch.

The Russians have shown an understandable interest in Holy Loch. Their electronic intelligence trawlers have poked nosily around in the nearby Atlantic and in 1967 an East German agent was arrested in nearby Dunoon. . . . To make it harder for foreign agents to compile arrival and departure schedules, the subs carry no hull numbers or other distinguishing marks. There are other precautions too. Every few hours wetsuited skin divers go into the frigid waters of the loch (six degrees above freezing when we were there) to inspect the bottoms of the subs, especially those about to go on patrol. A secretly planted homing device could make a sub susceptible to tracking by a Soviet attack sub or destroyer. . . .

Early one morning we noticed sparks flying from the deck of the "Abraham Lincoln." Her superstructure hatches were being welded shut to prevent any possible noise while operating at great depths and flank speed. It meant the refit was over. She had taken on 17 tons of supplies. The "Simon Lake" repair department had put in 6,000 manhours on her, replacing, aligning, fixing, overhauling. Her 16 missiles had received another 2,000 hours of checking out. Now she was ready to rejoin the 20 to 25 other Polaris subs normally on patrol throughout the world at any given time.

Two tugs nudged her away from the tender and she got up speed. Once under way, her skipper would tear open the red Top Secret envelope containing "transit orders" for the two-month, 2,000-mile journey. No one on the "Simon Lake" paused even to wave. The "Lincoln" had been the 256th refit at Holy Loch. Now the important thing was the 257th.*

2. The Polaris Submarine USS Henry Clay

(July 12, 1970, *Daily Breeze*, Torrance, Calif.). . . Exactly where she said she would surface and only one minute away from her estimated time of arrival, the Polaris submarine USS Henry Clay arrived off Long Beach Harbor Saturday. . . . She traveled submerged from the Panama Canal, and Saturday's 1 p.m. arrival marked the beginning of a four-day port call. . . .

(July 19, 1970, *Daily Breeze*, Torrance, Calif.) Polaris—According to Webster it means a star of the second magnitude. To the Navy it is a weapon of the first magnitude.

A ghostly shadow knifes through the cold, northern ocean hundreds of feet below the surface. Like a circling shark, the Polaris submarine banks into a smooth turn.

It has no specific destination; it is just on the move as it has been for weeks. Hidden . . . silent . . . waiting.

In the navigation center, the first officer scans readout tapes from the Navigation Data Assimilation Computer. One deck below a technician stares at the blinking lights of a Digital Automatic Tape Intelligence (DATICO) and tries to decide if it's worth the effort to go up to the enlisted mess for a cup of coffee.

Aft in the missile compartment a fire control technician is beating the chief of the boat at pinochle.

Suddenly the rasping scream of the warning alarm shatters the tranquility.

Now hear this! Now hear this! All hands man their battle stations. Proceed to status 2SQ.

*Abridged from "Inside Holy Loch," by Richard B. Stolley, *Life* Magazine, April 3, 1970, © 1970 Time, Inc.

Instant Reflex Action

Instant reflex action gained from thousands of drills galvanizes the boats' crew into action and they race to their stations. Missile technicians in blue jump suits scramble to the Missile Compartment and Missile Control Center, and put on headsets. The jump suits are made of dacron so they won't build up static electricity if they brush against the bulkheads covered with electrical gear.

A seaman readies himself at the ballast control panel, with checkout list already in hand, waiting for orders that will bring the atomic-powered submarine up to optimum missile firing depth.

The attainment of 2SQ alert is the first step in launching the 16 Polaris missiles that can lay waste to a continent. It takes four minutes for the crew to reach its station and begin actuating and checking out the infinite electronic and mechanical systems.

The missiles are spun up—their internal guidance system gyros humming, linking their computerized brains into SINS, the ships inertial navigation system. The computers know exactly where the submarine is, after weeks of traveling under the surface, and the missiles are already preset for secret targets. The ballistic plotting between the two points is performed almost instantly.

An ominous silence and intense sense of emergency descends upon the men of Polaris. Silence broken only by the sound of men reporting station status to the Attack Center.

The voice of the ballast control panel operator crackles over the communications system: "Sea valve off, level select switch in upper position." Throughout the sub the countdown in progress continues. Electronically crammed black boxes hum. Lights flash and relays click in and out.

Officers spin combinations on tiny safes and remove the master fire control switch and other hidden top secret items that form final links in the chain of events that releases the missiles. It takes at least five officers and men to set the final sequences; only the captain can turn the key that will arm the nuclear warheads on the giant missiles.

The men have run through this routine many times. But they never know how far it will proceed. The ship's intercom crackles once again with the skipper's voice. "Set condition 1SQ for submerged launch." Men leaning over glowing display boards lick dry lips—a drill seldom goes this far. Condition 1SQ is the next-to-last step in the countdown. The next order in sequence is Missiles Away.

Launch Control Activation

In the missile compartment the launch control panel operator monitors the progress of the launch control sub-system.

"Pressurization switch—to nitrogen."

"Outer tube doors—unlocked!"

The skipper remains close to the Attack Center indicator panel which tells him how the countdown is going. The 1SQ light on its panel flashes on red.

At the launch control console a second 1SQ light turns green. The operator presses the 1SQ button. Both port and starboard banks of missiles are ready for automatic firing in a predetermined sequence.

Devastation Capacities

If aimed and fired at America's West Coast, they would destroy Vancouver, Seattle, Portland, San Francisco, Sacramento, Los Angeles and San Diego. There would be missiles left over for Denver and Salt Lake City. There would be missiles left over for Edwards Air Force Base, March Field, Colorado Springs and Los Alamos.

They can be fired every thirty seconds.

But they are not pointed at the West Coast—they are programmed to fly down range 2,500 miles over frozen tundra. Or over the Himalayas.

Fifteen minutes have passed since the first call to battle stations.

The "permission to fire" indicator flashes green as skipper inserts the key and turns the firing switch to the "fire" position.

The launch control panel operator continues preparing the launch sub-system for firing. In a most serious voice he reports:

"Launch tube No. 1—pressurized!"; "Shocks, launch indicator—green!"; "Prepare to fire indicator—blue!"

On the deck of the submarine, a large muzzle hatch like a giant clam shell springs open, clearing the way for an A-3 Polaris missile to hurtle through the sea.

So far, in the history of the world, the Polaris launch sequence has never been taken beyond this point.

If it is, the Polaris system—America's most effective deterrent program, will have failed. If it is, it means the third World War already has been launched.

In all likelihood the rubble of American cities would already be shining incandescently in the midst of massive firestorms.

If the Polaris crews ever complete the countdown for which they have trained so long—if the miracle of electronics that make up the subsystems of the underwater missile bases are ever completely used—the Polaris crews will have no port to sail home to . . . (Jonathan Beaty).

The Polaris Patrol

(May 15, 1978, *Newsweek*) The Navy's nuclear-powered, nuclear-armed submarines have proved extraordinarily elusive: the Soviets have yet to detect any of the 41 Polaris subs that have carried out 1,500, 60-day patrols in strategic waters since 1960. So says Adm. Hyman G. Rickover, who at 78 is still running the Navy's nuclear-propulsion program. He recently told a Congressional committee: "These missile-carrying submarines are probably the greatest means the U.S. has for averting war. When they are at sea they cannot be detected." The Navy claims that it can keep track of a corresponding Russian fleet, thanks to superior U.S. electronic surveillance and noisier Soviet subs.

(January 10, 1979, *The Register*, Orange Co., Calif.) Washington (AP)—U.S. anti-submarine warfare is becoming so sophisticated that the Soviet Union is responding by protectively convoying its missile-firing submarines and keeping newer, long-range models close to home, it was reported today.

The Washington Post said a study by the Congressional Research Service of the Library of Congress shows U.S. technology developing the capability to possibly destroy Russia's entire underwater missile fleet.

Commentary and Summary

Quotations in the above articles speak for themselves.

As stated by newsman Jonathan Beaty of the Copley publications *South Bay Daily Breeze*, ". . . if the miracle of electronics that make up the subsystems of the underwater missile bases are ever completely used—the Polaris crews will have no port to sail home to."

I have been told by a qualified and unimpeachable source (who must remain anonymous) that our SAC bomber pilots have likewise been told that if or whenever they deliver their nuclear bomb loads over enemy territory, they should fly to some neutral country, for there would by that time be no home fields left to receive them.

Such is the terror of thermonuclear warfare.

This is the war concerning which it is written in Bible prophecy:

> I will send a fire on Magog [Russia], and among them that dwell carelessly [without a care] in the isles [coastlands—U.S.A. et al]: and they shall know that I am the LORD . . . This is the day whereof I have spoken (Ezek. 39:6,8).

The devastation wrought by the use of nuclear armaments will be horrible. It will be a fulfillment of many prophecies such as:

> A day of darkness and of gloominess, a day of clouds and of thick darkness [by atomic clouds!]. . . . : a great people and a strong; there hath not been ever the like, neither shall be any more after it, even to the years of many generations.
>
> A fire devoureth before them; and behind them a flame burneth: the land is as the garden of Eden before them, and behind them a desolate wilderness; . . . Like the noise of chariots on the tops of mountains shall they leap [rockets], like the noise of a flame of fire that devoureth the stubble, as a strong people set in battle array. Before their face the people shall be much pained [burns and radioactivity]: all faces shall gather blackness (Joel 2:2–6).
>
> . . . therefore, the inhabitants of the earth are burned, and few men left" (Isa. 24:6).

Israel To Be Non-nuclear

It is worthy of note that the Bible indicates conventional war in the Holy Land rather than nuclear fire. Consider the following:

> Behold, it is come, and it is done, saith the Lord GOD; this is the day whereof I have spoken. And they that dwell in the cities of Israel shall go forth, and shall set on fire and burn the weapons, . . . and they shall burn them with fire seven years: So that they shall take no wood out of the field, neither cut down any out of the forests; for they shall burn the weapons with fire: and they shall spoil those that spoiled them, . . . saith the Lord GOD" (Ezek. 39:8–10).

If atomic weapons were to be used in Israel, there would be no weapons left for them to burn, and certainly not for seven years, for the flame of the atomic explosions would have consumed them. What is the answer?

Lignostone

It is known that Russia has been making much of its war equipment with a special product developed not long ago in Holland. It is called lignostone.

The origin of this versatile product was not for war use but as a fuel substitute. With no oil or natural gas in Holland, there was a great need for a proper fuel that could be used to produce heat and to burn in their power plants to produce manufactured gas. An inventor in Ter Apel found that by compressing this material (much like the process used in making plywood) it would burn even better than coal, for it is a wood product.

It was found, however, that it had other uses. In its compressed state it was still pliable but was stronger than steel. It had many qualities that made it desirable for use in weaponry. Not being metal, it did not show on radar. Now Russia makes many items out of it, and apparently will make more.

Regardless of the exact material, the weapons will be used by the Israelis for fuel for seven years. ". . . they shall burn the

198

weapons with fire: and they shall spoil those that spoiled them, and rob those that robbed them, saith the Lord God" (Ezek. 39:10).

We have in this statement a double portion. Israel will burn their weapons and the Israelis will get them by robbing "those that robbed them." And they shall do so for seven years.

In order for this prophecy to have its fulfillment, the nuclear war between the Soviets and the Western powers, and the mighty military thrust against the land of Israel, must be at the beginning of the seven-year era called the Tribulation period. Otherwise robbery would be carried over into the millennial reign of Christ, which is contrary to His declaration that ". . . I hate robbery for burnt offering; and I will direct their work in truth, and I will make an everlasting covenant with them" (Isa. 61:8).

With such tremendous preparation for war and with the materials available that will make it all possible, from ligno-stone to satellite warfare, it is very evident that time is running out. The coming of the Lord is near at hand and World War III cannot be far away.

All people, however, will not have to endure the holocaust of the war, nor will they see the terrors that will follow for nearly seven years thereafter, for God in His mercy has provided a means of salvation from it all. To show you that precious provision is one of the purposes of this book.

Section V

EVENTS TO COME

16

THOSE WHO WILL ESCAPE
THE HOLOCAUST

There are millions of people in the world today who shall not be on the earth at the time of the beginning of World War III.

Those who shall escape the horrors of that great war will be the Bible-believing people who have put their faith and trust in the sure promises of God and have given evidence of so doing by acknowledging Jesus Christ as their own Redeemer and Savior.

They are not of any one ancestry nor of any one nation. They are not of any one church denomination or creed. (In fact, beware of any who say that theirs is the only church, for God is no respecter of persons). It will be those who have had strength of character and honesty enough to admit their shortcomings, being willing to confess that they are not righteous in themselves—that they have not "measured up." It will be those who have acknowledged the truth of the Scriptures, that ". . . all have sinned, and come short of the glory of God" and that ". . . there is none righteous, no, not one" (Rom. 3:23,10). They will have found the truth, that ". . . the wages of sin is death; but the gift of God is eternal life through Jesus Christ our Lord" (Rom. 6:23). They will have believed the following Scripture:

> He was in the world, . . . and the world knew him not. He came unto his own, and his own received him not. But as many as received him, to them gave he power to become the sons of God, even to them

that believe on his name: which were born, not of blood, . . . nor of the will of man, but of God (John 1:10–12).

Those who escape will be those who have believed the statement of Jesus:

> That which is born of the flesh is flesh; and that which is born of the Spirit is spirit. Marvel not that I said unto thee, Ye must be born again. The wind bloweth where it listeth and thou hearest the sound thereof, but canst not tell whence it cometh, and whither it goeth: so is every one that is born of the Spirit. . . . And as Moses lifted up the serpent in the wilderness, even so must the Son of man be lifted up [on Calvary's cross]: That whosoever believeth in him should not perish, but have eternal life. For God so loved the world, that he gave his only begotten Son, that whosoever believeth in him should not perish, but have everlasting life. For God sent not his Son into the world to condemn the world; but that the world through him might be saved. He that believeth on him is not condemned; but he that believeth not is condemned already, because he hath not believed in the name of the only begotten Son of God (John 3:6–8; 14–18).

The ones who escape "the day" of the beginning of God's wrath which is to be poured out upon this earth are the ones who have believed the declaration of God through the apostle John:

> He that believeth on the Son [of God, the Lord Jesus Christ] hath everlasting life: and he that believeth not the Son shall not see life; but the wrath of God abideth on him (John 3:36).

The ones who shall be taken up to heaven before "the day of the Lord" and before his "indignation" against the ungodly is poured forth shall be those who have heard and responded to the tender admonition apostle Paul wrote:

> That if thou shalt confess with thy mouth the Lord Jesus, and shalt believe in thine heart that God hath raised him from the dead,

thou shalt be saved. For with the heart man believeth unto righteousness; and with the mouth confession is made unto salvation. . . . For whosoever shall call upon the name of the Lord shall be saved (Rom. 10:9,10,13).

Millions Shall Be Spared

In spite of the apostasy, wickedness, vileness, and blasphemy of multitudes of people of this world, millions of people on earth today do believe in and do earnestly look forward to the coming again of Christ, exactly as He promised:

> Let not your heart be troubled: ye believe in God, believe also in me. In my Father's house are many mansions: if it were not so, I would have told you [for Jesus came from heaven to be righteously born into the human family: Mary having been the virgin whom God chose to honor with "the hope of women" that it might be so. As the Son of God, therefore, and by virtue of his supernatural birth into the human family—being at the same time the Son of man—Jesus could, and did meet and overcome all temptations "yet without sin" as recorded in Hebrews 4:15. In perfect love, then, he gave his perfect life-blood as a supreme sacrifice for the atonement of all who would but put their faith and trust in him, granting to them his merited eternal life and at the same time accepting the added burden of the punishment for their sins in his own bruised and broken body upon the cruel Roman cross. He became the sacrificial Lamb for you and for me. He was, indeed, the perfect One who was to come to suffer and to die, and to rise again from the dead, for death and hell could not hold such a perfect One as He: so that "whosoever" would but believe and trust in Him might have eternal life—might be "saved" from the wages of sin, which is death. He died for you!].
>
> I go to prepare a place for you [He continued] and if I go and prepare a place for you, I will come again, and receive you unto myself; that where I am, there ye may be also (John 14:1–3).

The millions of true believers also trust the words of those who walked and talked with Jesus for forty days after his resurrection, and who on the day of his ascension beheld, as it is recorded:

> . . . he was taken up; and a cloud received him out of their sight. And while they looked steadfastly toward heaven as he went up, behold, two men stood by them in white apparel; Which also said, Ye men of Galilee, why stand ye gazing up into heaven? This same Jesus, which is taken up from you into heaven, shall so come in like manner as ye have seen him go into heaven (Acts 1:9–11).

Millions of Bible-believing Christians anticipate the imminent fulfillment of the recorded prophecies concerning the return of Christ for "the church" which is his body, knowing that:

> And he is the head of the body, the church: who is the beginning, the firstborn from the dead; that in all things he might have the pre–eminence (Col. 1:18).

Their faith, and mine, is based on the above quotations, and upon the even more specific Bible quotations which follow:

> Behold, I show you a mystery; We [Christians] shall not all sleep [die], but we shall all be changed, In a moment, in the twinkling of an eye, at the last trump: for the trumpet shall sound, [1] and the dead shall be raised incorruptible, and [at the second and last sounding of the trumpet] [2] we shall be changed. For this corruptible must put on incorruption, and this mortal must put on immortality . . . then . . . Death is swallowed up in victory.
> But thanks be to God, which giveth us the victory through our Lord Jesus Christ (1 Cor. 15:51–54,57).

God Shall Spare Christians From Wrath

One of the most outstanding passages of Scripture pertaining to the "translation of the church" before the beginning of the very first judgments of God is clearly given in the last chapter of 1 Thessalonians.

Note the contrast in the use of the pronouns, and the people to whom they apply, as quoted from the first eleven verses of 1 Thessalonians 5:

> But of the times and the seasons, brethren, ye have no need that I write unto you. For yourselves know perfectly that the day of the Lord so cometh as a thief in the night. For when *they* shall say, Peace and safety; then sudden destruction cometh upon *them*, as travail upon a woman with child; and *they* shall not escape. But *ye*, brethren, are not in darkness, that that day should overtake *you* as a thief. *Ye* are all the children of light, and the children of the day: *we* are not of the night, nor of darkness. Therefore, let *us* not sleep, as do others; but let *us* watch and be sober. For they that sleep sleep in the night; and they that be drunken are drunken in the night. But let us, who are of the day, be sober, putting on the breastplate of faith and love; and for a helmet, the hope of salvation. For God hath not appointed *us* to wrath, but to obtain salvation by our Lord Jesus Christ, who died for us, that, whether we wake or sleep, we should live together with him. Wherefore comfort yourselves together, and edify one another . . . (italics mine).

Great Reasons for the "Comfort" of Christians

"The translation of the church" is often referred to as "The Rapture of the church" because of the fact of the great rapture and ecstasy of the believers in Christ when they shall at last hear that for which they have longed.

> . . . the Lord himself shall descend from heaven with a shout, with the voice of the archangel, and with the trump of God: and the dead in Christ shall rise first: Then we which are alive . . . [at that precious moment] shall be caught up together with them in the clouds, to meet the Lord in the air . . . (1 Thess. 4:16,17).

"Rapture" also is a transliteration of the Latin word *rapere*, meaning "caught up" or "to snatch away." We shall be "caught up" to meet our Lord.

What a day of rejoicing that will be! It is well expressed in Titus 2:13: "Looking for that blessed hope, and the glorious appearing of the great God and our Savior, Jesus Christ."

Paul wrote of it when he admonished: ". . . sorrow not, even as others which have no hope" (1 Thess. 4:13).

Having described the great event to come, he added in 1 Thessalonians 4:18: "Wherefore, comfort one another with these words."

Paul went on to explain that "the day of the Lord" (which is the day of the beginning of the time of tribulation to come) would, indeed, come "as a thief in the night" to those who looked for all of their happiness in this world and who falsely prophesied and said, "Peace and safety"; for surely "sudden destruction cometh upon them," and "they shall not escape" (1 Thess. 5:3).

But he was quick to remind the "brethren" who believed on the Lord Jesus Christ that "that day" would not overtake them as a thief in the night, for they had the message of the prophets and teachers of the Scriptures and were "children of the day; not of the night, nor of darkness." Therefore they were to "watch" for their Lord, "For God hath not appointed us to wrath, but to obtain salvation [from wrath] by our Lord Jesus Christ" (1 Thess. 5:9).

Because of this great truth, he could exclaim in joy:

"Wherefore comfort one another with these words" and "Wherefore comfort yourselves together, and edify one another, even as also ye do" (1 Thess. 4:18; 5:11).

Of course they could comfort one another and encourage one another, for even though great warfare and times of trouble were prophesied for "the time of the end," the truly born-again children of God would not have to go through or endure those things. Had not Jesus said, "Fear ye not therefore, ye are of more value than many sparrows" (Matt. 10:31)? Furthermore, after he had told them of many things to come, he reassured them with these words: "Heaven and earth shall pass away: but my words shall not pass away" (Mark 13:31).

Summary

With this "blessed assurance" that ". . . all things work together for good to them that love God, to them who are the called according to his purpose," and the statement, "If God be for us, who can be against us?" (Rom. 8:28,31), let us now put all of our information together and observe carefully and assuredly the vast panorama of those things which are about to come to pass upon this earth as we consider from every vantagepoint the step-by-step "scenario" of "World War III and the Destiny of America."

17

THE ORDER OF EVENTS TO COME

The fact of the critical Middle East crisis of "today" is known by all: It was prophesied precisely as it now stands.

The fact that it will lead to an all-out thermonuclear confrontation between the super-powers, and the allies of each, is increasingly evident with every passing news announcement. Daily we all watch—and wonder! The preparations by way of continual arms buildups is astounding.

Many Bible prophecies have already been quoted and explained. The potential for the fulfillments have been given in preceding chapters. Consider now the events to come.

America's Devastation to Come

This country will not be totally destroyed, but the thermonuclear power of the U.S.S.R. and its associates will very evidently be thrust in all of its strength against America to prevent it from coming to the aid of tiny Israel.

If the vision of the American evangelist holds true, America can also expect a first-strike MIRV-warhead-type of widespread nerve gas attack as the first blow.

Russia's Destruction to Come

The leadership of Russia's colossal military power is atheistic. Accordingly, the power of God is not taken into consideration in Russia's plans.

In America and in Western Europe the gospel of salvation has gone forth in great measure in these last days, winning multitudes of souls to Christ. Consequently, when the translation of the church takes place (referred to by many as "the rapture"), the greater confusion caused by the disappearance of millions of people in the Western world will seem like a great opportunity for Russia to order the offensive.

Russia will be held back momentarily, however, due to the fact that, in spite of oppression by the Kremlin authorities, many people there have also received the gospel by radio and literature and by personal testimony and several million people behind the "Iron Curtain" will be "caught up" from Russian territory, too. It will probably mystify Moscow, but as soon as it can "adjust" itself to the situation, according to sure Bible prophecy, it will order the combined Arab and Russian assault against Israel, America, and the allied countries.

In the all-out thermonuclear exchange that will take place, one third of the earth will be affected and greatly devastated. Industrial Russia (the biblical "land of Magog") will be destroyed by "fire" and five sixths of the Russian military will be destroyed in fulfillment of the recorded prophecy of Ezekiel 39:1–12.

This Generation

In Daniel 12:4 it is recorded: ". . . many shall run to and fro, and knowledge shall be increased." How very literally that prophecy has been fulfilled in this generation! Never has there been such a time as this; and it is partially for the sake of this highly technical and very fact-conscious age that God caused men of old to record such amazingly accurate proclamations and prophecies. The Bible is not a myth. It is a book which is packed with scientifically verifiable knowledge and with astounding "history written in advance." It is for this generation.

Unfortunately, great multitudes of Americans stand uninformed. Moreover they have been grossly misinformed by infiltrated subversive elements. They have heeded far too many of the noisy minority who have brought out their slogans and their vile language to attract the restless youth to their rebellious causes. Parental delinquency abounds. It is no wonder that the youth of today, raised by Dr. Spock's program of permissiveness, seek a way out. Their parents have given them no answers, and most have set very poor examples.

For those who want facts; for those who want documentary proof for a foundation that will stand every test; and for those who seek to know the real truth of what is going on in this climactic generation, this book has been written. It is the result of over fifty years of Christian training and of nearly forty years of the observance and study of Bible–prophecy–related news. The wonderfully amazing factor is that it all fits together into a mosaic of eternal truth which can be verified.

I have been only the means by which these facts and documentations have been brought together.

This generation has been termed "a generation of destiny." It is now—in this generation of time—that the climax of history is coming to its apex. Ecology speaks of it. Population explosion speaks of it. The earth speaks of it, even as it is written:

> For nation shall rise against nation, and kingdom against kingdom; and there shall be famines, and pestilences, and earthquakes, in divers places. All these are the beginning of sorrows (Matt. 24:7,8).

Truly, "the coming of the Lord draweth nigh."

The Coming of the Lord

Christ will come, first of all, for his own. They will be the ones who have believed His Word and have trusted in His saving grace and power. They will be "caught up" out of this sin-cursed world. It is at that moment that the deceased Christians who have been "with the Lord" in spiritual bodies will receive their eternal resurrection bodies, and ". . . Then shall be brought to pass the saying that is written, Death is swallowed up in victory" (1 Cor. 15:54).

The physical bodies of the redeemed, buried, or otherwise retained upon this earth until that moment shall be changed, "for . . . this mortal shall put on immortality" (1 Cor. 15:53). It is at that same moment—"in the twinkling of an eye"—that we, who are believers in Christ and who are alive and remain so until then, shall also be changed into resurrection bodies and ". . . shall be caught up together with them . . . to meet the Lord in the air: and so shall we ever be with the Lord" (1 Thess. 4:17).

The Bible promises deliverance and eternal joy to those who believe in God and who have put their trust in Jesus Christ as their Redeemer. The Bible also depicts that there shall come, immediately following the disappearance of the true believers in Christ from this earth, a time of ". . . great tribulation, such as was not since the beginning of the world to this time, no, nor ever shall be" (Matt. 24:21).

Section VI

A CHRONOLOGY: FROM THE RAPTURE TO WORLD WAR III

Note

Historical information concerning the nations is very interesting and vital, and it shall be given; but the readers of this book should be aware that of even greater importance is the eternal destiny of each soul of mankind.

When the Rapture, or, to be more biblically correct, "the translation of the church" takes place, every infant and every person who has trusted in Jesus Christ for the forgiveness of, and atonement for, his or her sins, being born–again by the Spirit of God into the family of God, shall be caught up to be with their Lord and their God in the heavenlies.

God is going to deal with the nations and especially with Israel. The short span of seven years which follows is often referred to as the Tribulation period, and is referred to in the Bible as "the time of Jacob's trouble." One of the first events to happen will be the one-day holocaust of the all-out thermonuclear exchange termed World War III.

Certain adjustments, however, will have to be made before that occurs. It is these adjustments that will be defined in this section.

One hundred policemen slain this year.
—News Item

Paul Conrad's cartoon courtesy of The Register and Tribune Syndicate.

18

CHAOS

Millions of people will suddenly disappear from the face of the earth, including infant children. From all walks of life, there shall be people missing.

The freeways, subways, airports, and streets will be a shambles as many engineers, pilots, busdrivers, and a multitude of private car owners shall suddenly be caught up out of this world. It will be many days before they can unscramble the mangled cars, trains, and fallen aircraft.

Remaining millions of people will be wailing, dazed, and shaken by the event. They shall be frantically striving to locate loved ones in all of the rubble of broken cars, crumbled storefronts, and smashed residences.

Communications will be greatly disrupted. Many key persons shall disappear and lines of communication which are still above ground will be broken by crashes of cars and aircraft. Distraught and searching multitudes will jam and overload the communication lines and systems that do remain.

Dazed and confused pleas from bewildered men over the "alert" systems will try to bring about some semblance of order. Policemen, firemen, and rescue crews will work around the clock. Hospitals will overflow. Emergency shelters and first aid stations will be inadequate. The Red Cross and all other emergency units, plus the army facilities, will still not be enough.

Opportunists will add to the confusion and the misery by looting and killing. They shall feel that under such a total emergency they can get away with anything. Chaos will be on every hand.

Distress Will Be Worldwide

Inasmuch as the "translation of the church" will be worldwide—for there are true believers in Jesus Christ in every country on earth, and they all shall be taken—every country will find itself in turmoil. Each government will have to act as quickly as possible to prevent a wild tide of anarchy and terrorism. Strong measures will be put into effect, and the manner will vary with the nature of the men in power and also in accordance with the fears that they may experience.

Emergency Regulations in the United States

At the time that the Russians were first suspected of putting aggressive missiles in Cuba in 1961, a series of emergency measures were formulated in the event of a full confrontation and possible strategic war. Nikita Khrushchev backed down and withdrew the missiles in 1962, but the emergency measures which were signed into law by the late President John F. Kennedy still stand. They became a part of the vast executive orders when they were signed on February 16 and 27, 1962. Those emergency documents provide that the President, and any succeeding President, shall have complete and final dictatorial control.

The complex society in which we now live necessitates established provision for immediate and decisive action. No time is left for quibbling. A sneak nuclear attack could devastate this land in a matter of minutes. The executive orders are to be carried out through the Office of Emergency Planning, and they may be put into effect in any "time of increased international tension or economic or financial crisis." So all-inclusive are these orders that a listing of them is provided for your information:

220

Executive Order: 10995—Take over all communications media.

Executive Order: 10997—Take over all electric power, petroleum, and gas fuels and minerals.

Executive Order: 10998—Take over all food resources and farms (including farming machinery).

Executive Order: 10999—Take over all methods of transportation, highways, seaports, etc.

Executive Order: 11000—Mobilization of civilians into work forces under governmental supervision.

Executive Order: 11001—Take over all health, welfare and educational functions.

Executive Order: 11002—Postmaster General (member of President's cabinet) will operate nationwide registration of all persons.

Executive Order: 11003—Take over all airports and aircraft.

Executive Order: 11004—Take over housing and finance authorities to relocate communities—to build new housing with public funds—designate areas to be abandoned as unsafe—establish new locations for populations.

Executive Order: 11005—Take over all railroads, inland waterways and public storage facilities.

Executive Order: 11051—Designate responsibilities of Office of Emergency Planning, give authorization to put all other executive orders into effect in times of increased international tension or economic or financial crisis.*

These executive orders grant the President of the United States the absolute power to place every person in this country under absolute dictatorship.

These potential powers are greatly feared by some people, for they see the obvious opportunity for misuse and despotism. Although this danger does exist, it will be these very executive orders which shall prove to be the physical salvation for this country—when the need for them arises. They will greatly expedite stability.

*Copies of these orders are available from the Government Printing Office, c/o Superintendent of Documents, No. Capitol and H Streets N.W., Washington D.C. 20401.

Different Adjustments in the U.S.S.R.

The leadership in Russia is atheistic. Very few, if any, of its top leaders are apt to be even secret believers in Christ. They have no need, furthermore, to pass executive orders for they already have absolute dictatorial power. Therefore, political adjustments will be but minimal.

In the past few years, however, vast numbers of means have been utilized to spread the gospel throughout the iron curtain countries. The result is that millions of people there have been truly converted and will be "taken up" with us to meet the Lord in the air. Their disappearance will cause considerable consternation and chaos in the areas from which they leave, and the bewilderment will be the greater because those remaining will have had very little if any Bible teaching. More prominently there will be the fulfillment of the prophecy, ". . . and none of the wicked shall understand . . ." (Dan. 12:10).

Chaotic conditions in the Communist countries will be less severe simply due to the fact that fewer people in proportion to the populations will be "caught up." The leadership, however, will be caught off guard, and they will not be in position to take full advantage of the vast confusion in the Western world. Russia is, indeed, destined to "think an evil thought" in fulfillment of the prophecy of Ezekiel 38:10, but not until it can adjust itself to the new situation and order the mighty move against the land of Israel. All of this will require a period of time, according to a coordination of Bible references, of about two weeks. This fact will be verified.

Adjustments in the Arab World

Although most of the Arabs are Moslem in religion, many are Socialist-atheists and some are of other religions; but there are also millions of Christians across the wide expanse of the Arab regions. As elsewhere, the Christians will "disappear." The bewilderment among the Arabs will be considerable, but adjustments will probably be minor.

19

"THE KING" GAINS POWER IN WESTERN EUROPE

Multitudes of people will be "caught up to be with the Lord" from Western Europe, for vast Christian campaigns have led to the salvation of many there. The great majority, however, remain non–Christian.

To avoid complete turmoil, and also to brace itself against the potential attack from atheistic Russia and its satellite nations, the leaders of the Common Market area will form a more solid union than the present European Economic Community.

A Ten-nation Empire

Specific Bible prophecies in both Daniel and Revelation predict a ten–nation entity, and each portrays it as the last of the Gentile empires to bear rule over the Promised Land of Canaan (Palestine).

God's prophecy through Daniel is recorded in Daniel 2:27–45. In summary, the Gentile empires were seen in a dream of Nebuchadnezzar, the absolute monarch of the first empire to conquer the land of Israel. He captured Jerusalem and took its last king as a prisoner of war to Babylon in 587 B.C. In his dream-vision, of which the interpretation of the meaning God gave to the prophet Daniel, he had seen the Gentile powers of all time in the form of a multimetallic image of a man with a head of gold, breast and arms of silver, belly and thighs of brass, legs of iron, and the feet and toes a mixture of iron and miry clay. The dream was interpreted and explained by Daniel. The fulfillment is as follows:

1. The Assyrians had taken the northern ten tribes of Israel captive earlier, but the first full conquest of all of Israel was in 597 B.C. when Nebuchadnezzar of Babylon conquered Jerusalem. He carried its last king captive in 587 B.C..

   a) Daniel declared to him, "Thou art this head of gold."

2. The Medes conquered Babylon in 539 B.C., and the combined Medo-Persian Empire controlled Jerusalem until defeated by Alexander the Great of Greece.

   a) The Medes and Persians were represented by "the breast and arms of silver."

3. The Greeks, under Alexander the Great, conquered the Medo-Persian Empire in 334 B.C., putting Jerusalem and all of Israel under the Greek Empire. At the death of Alexander the Great in 323 B.C., the Greek Empire was divided four ways and Jerusalem came under the authority of the Ptolemy dynasties of Egypt. This continued until 198 B.C. when the Seleucid (Syrian area Greek) authority took control, culminating in the desecration of the rebuilt Hebrew temple by Antiochus Epiphanes, and the Maccabean revolt.

   a) "The belly and thighs of brass" of the Gentile empire image was thus fulfilled, with the total Greek rule under Alexander the Great identified as being "the belly of brass" and the Egyptian and Seleucid divisions which both ruled Jerusalem being identified similarly as the "thighs" of brass.

4. The Roman Empire began expanding in 264 B.C., defeated the Greeks in 146 B.C., and it became a "world empire" with the conquest of Egypt in 30 B.C. The Roman Empire lasted until its defeat by the Visigoths in A.D. 410 and the overthrow of its last "emperor" in A.D. 476.

   a) Rome, whose dominion lasted for seven centuries, constituted the longest and the strongest portion of the empire image, "the legs of iron."

5. The "revived Roman empire" is to be a combination of centralized power and of a secondary coalition of ten nations. The last portion of the empire image was described by the prophet Daniel in these words:

"And whereas thou sawest the feet and toes, part of potters' clay, and part of iron, the kingdom shall be divided; but there shall be in it of the strength of the iron, foreasmuch as thou sawest the iron mixed with miry clay.

"And as the [ten] toes of the feet were part of iron, and part of clay, so the kingdom shall be partly strong, and partly broken. And whereas thou sawest iron mixed with miry clay, they shall mingle themselves with the seed of men: but they shall not cleave one to another, even as iron is not mixed with clay" (Dan. 2:41–43).

A Strange Partnership of Powers

A strange partnership shall come forth out of the turmoil which shall be caused by the greatest "air-lift" of all time. All of the Christians of today shall simply disappear. The conservative restraining force of these people shall no longer be felt. Many conservatives and patriots are not born-again Christians, however, and they shall still be here upon the earth—still striving to make a "heaven" out of corruptible man–kind–inhabited earth. They will be anxiously looking for a leader who can be a modern Sir Galahad; and even Jesus spoke of just such a one when He said,

I am come in my Father's name, and ye receive me not: if another shall come in his own name, him ye will receive (John 5:43).

The King to Appear After the Rapture

The king who shall exalt himself shall appear to be a great leader; and he shall have the assistance of God as well as of Satan to cause men to follow after him and to bestow much power and authority upon him. Note how it is written:

. . . because they received not the love of the truth, that they might be saved . . . for this cause God shall send them strong delusion, that they should believe a lie: That they all might be damned who believed not the truth [of salvation by grace through faith in Jesus Christ that they might be "caught up to meet the Lord in the air"], but had pleasure in unrighteousness (2 Thess. 2:10–12).

That same chapter reveals that this king (referred to as "that wicked one") shall be revealed immediately after the removal of the believing Christians from this world. Scripture states in reference to the believing Christians:

> Know ye not that ye are the temple of God, and that the Spirit of God dwelleth in you? (1 Cor. 3:16).

> Hereby know we that we dwell in him, and he in us, because he hath given us of his Spirit . . . the Father sent the Son to be the Savior of the world. Whosoever shall confess that Jesus is the Son of God, God dwelleth in him, and he in God (1 John 4:13–15).

By the Holy Spirit we ". . . are sealed unto the day of redemption [of our bodies]" (Eph. 4:30).

Other similar references could be given, but this is a full witness of the fact.

The restraining power of the Holy Spirit within the body of Christ (the church) *and* Jesus Christ, who is the Head of the body, stand as a bulwark against the forces of evil. Jesus said, ". . . I will build my church; and the gates of hell shall not prevail against it" (Matt. 16:18). In the final analysis, it is Jesus, Himself, the Head of the body of believers, the church (Col. 1:18), who stands in opposition to Satan's Antichrist and hinders (KJV—"letteth"—2 Thess. 2:7) until *he* be taken out of the way. Did not Jesus say, "I am the way" (John 14:6)? When He (Jesus) catches up His body unto Himself in the glories of heaven (John 14:3), then—and only then—can the wicked one, the Antichrist, go forth to fulfill his seven-year destiny of dominion on earth.

The Holy Spirit, being omnipotent and omnipresent, is able to be everywhere, and will not be taken out of the world but remain in His divine capacity throughout the period of the end-time; for men shall be and can be saved during the Tribulation period, Jesus testified concerning the Holy Spirit, and it is worded as follows:

> . . . if I depart [by ascending into heaven], I will send him unto you. And when he is come, he will reprove the world of sin, and of righteousness, and of judgment: Of sin, because they believed not on me; Of righteousness, because I go to my Father, and ye see me no more [upon earth]; Of judgment, because the prince of this world is judged (John 16:7–11).

The Prince of This World

The term "the prince of this world" has a connotation here: It refers to the spiritual enemy of mankind, Satan; and it also refers to the human who shall be the embodiment of Satan during the last half of the Tribulation period. This human "prince of this world" will be the one of whom it is written in the Book of Daniel:

> . . . and the people of the prince that shall come shall destroy the city and the sanctuary [fulfilled by the Romans in A.D. 70] . . . and unto the end of the war desolations shall be determined. And he [the prince that shall come] shall confirm the covenant with many [the remnant of people now returning to Israel, and who dwell in the city of the sanctuary] for one week [one prophetic week is seven years]: and in the midst of the week [after three and a half years] he shall cause the sacrifice and the oblation to cease, and for the overspreading of abominations he shall make it desolate, even until the consummation . . . (Dan. 9:26,27).

This "prince that shall come" is identical with the wicked one referred to by Paul when he wrote about the withholding power of Christ "hindering" until he be "taken out of the way."

Thus, when Christ removes the spiritual temple of the Holy Spirit (i.e., the church is taken out of this world), the Holy Spirit shall no longer hinder the working of Satan's plans by any activity of the body of Christ.

The unrestrained world, in all of its "freedom" and in all of its apostasy, shall once again worship "the queen of heaven" even as it did in the days of ancient Babylon, and "the prince that shall come," whom Daniel referred to, shall be revealed in accordance with the prophecy recorded by Paul when he wrote:

> Even him, whose coming is after the working of Satan with all power and signs and lying wonders, And with all deceivableness in them that perish; because they received not the love of the truth, that they might be saved (2 Thess. 2:9,10).

Therefore, since it is written that "the people of the prince that shall come shall destroy the city and the sanctuary"; and that the Roman people did indeed fulfill that prophecy in A.D. 70, then it is absolutely correct to state that the end-time "prince," or "the king" as he is called when he actually comes into his power, shall indeed be the head or the leader of the ten-nation Western European segment of the old Roman Empire (the Eastern European nations referred to as "Gomer and his hordes" being aligned with Russia and its leader, "the chief prince of Meshech [Moscow] and Tubal [Tobolsk]," the capital of Siberia, recorded in Ezekiel 38).

The Biblical Verification of the "Partnership" of the Western European Powers

In the portrayal of the end-time "prince," "king," "wicked one," "beast" (Rev. 13:1,2), and "the scarlet colored beast" (Rev. 17:3–18), we again see identity with the Western European ten-nation empire.

The scarlet-colored beast is depicted as having seven heads and ten horns, and as having on its back "Mystery, Babylon the Great, the Mother of Harlots and Abominations of the Earth" which is representative of the base and adulterous false world–church of the end time, which is to have its headquarters in Rome (at that time). Being a conglomerate of religions, and as such, accepting all religions (except the truth), it will be a "world church" that shall have a vile and worldly form of "worship" like that of the first false religion ever organized. This occurred at Babylon where, with all of its astrology, mysticism, and occultism, it promulgated the licentious worship of Asherah (Astarte), "queen of heaven." She was said to be the consort of Bel (Baal), the sun-god. The Tower of Babel was built for the use of the high priests as they sought to "reach unto heaven" with their zodiac astrology.

Revelation 17:9,18 read:

> And here is the mind which hath wisdom. The seven heads are seven mountains, on which the woman sitteth . . . And the woman which thou sawest is that great city which reigneth over the kings of the earth.

Both of the above statements, you will note, are written in the present tense. When the Book of Revelation was written by the apostle John in A.D. 95, Rome was still in its original power "over the kings of the earth." His wording, therefore, is correct. Furthermore, it portrays that the seat of the false religious body of the end time will be, at the beginning of the Tribulation period, in Rome.

(To forestall any jumping at conclusions, be it here understood that every Roman Catholic person who truly believes in Jesus Christ as the One who was delivered for our offenses and raised again for our justification (Rom. 4:25), and has placed his or her faith in Jesus Christ as Redeemer and Savior, not one of them will be left behind when He comes for His body, the church. Those who remain, therefore, whether they be in Rome or elsewhere, will be the ungodly, the hypocrites, and the unbelieving ones, regardless of any church "membership.")

The Woman and the Beast

Our concern in this book is more with the political and military leader of the end-time than it is with the ecclesiastical power. So specific, however, is the Bible statement relative to "the woman" riding on the back of the scarlet-colored beast which has the seven heads and ten horns that it cannot be ignored. There will be a definite cooperation between the apostate end-time church, referred to as "the woman," and the powerful "beast." That the term "apostate," as used in this writing, is proper is verified by the description in the following quotation:

> . . . and I saw a woman sit upon a scarlet-colored beast, full of names of blasphemy, having seven heads and ten horns. And the woman was arrayed in purple and scarlet color, and decked with gold and precious stones and pearls, having a golden cup in her hand full of abominations and filthiness of her fornication: . . . And I saw the woman drunken with the blood of the saints, and with the blood of the martyrs of Jesus: . . . (Rev. 17:3,4,6).

Truly, the end-time "co-op" of "the woman" and "the beast" and "the ten-nation empire" is destined to be the greatest conglomerate of infamy ever known!

Further Identification of the Beast

Turning from the portrayal of the vileness of the antichrist "world-church" entity, the Apostle John then wrote of what he was told concerning "the beast":

> And, there are seven kings: five are fallen, and one is, and the other is not yet come; and when he cometh, he must continue a short space. And the beast that was, and is not, even he is the eighth, and is of the seven, and goeth into perdition. And the ten horns which thou sawest are ten kings, which have received no kingdom as yet; but receive power as kings one hour with the beast. These have one mind, and shall give their power and strength unto the beast (Rev. 17:10–13).

The seven kings of verse ten, where it is written that "five are fallen, and one is, and the other is not yet come," refer to the seven world empires shown in the world empire image described by Daniel.

The five empires that have "fallen" would be Babylon, Media, Persia, Greece, and Egypt. The empire that "is" would be the Roman Empire that took control of the ancient empire areas with the conquest of Egypt in 30 B.C.. The old Roman Empire was in full control when John wrote the Book of Revelation in A.D. 95; hence, the statement, "and one is."

The last of the empires is described in Revelation 17:10: ". . . and the other is not yet come; and when he cometh, he must continue a short space." Whereas the old Roman Empire existed for seven centuries, the revived Roman Empire shall exist but the "short space" of seven years: the total time of the Tribulation period.

"The beast that was, and is not," is descriptive of the ruler of this seventh and last empire, for the Bible prophecy states specifically: ". . . even he is the eighth, and is of the seven . . ." (Rev. 17:11).

In the spiritual realm, it is written in both 2 Thessalonians 2:9 and also in Revelation 13:2 that "the beast" who represents the earthly and human ruler of the seventh Gentile empire will receive his power from him who is described in Revelations 12:9 and also in Revelations 20:1,2 as "the dragon, that old serpent, which is the devil, and Satan."

In the earthly realm, however, as far as mankind of that time is concerned, it will be the ten kings (rulers) of the ten-nation entity of Western Europe that shall, according to Revelation 17:13, ". . . have one mind, and shall give their power and strength unto the beast."

The Abiding Influence of the Ten Nations

It is worthy of note that, although the primary "strength of the iron" shall be in the hands of the "beast," that end-time

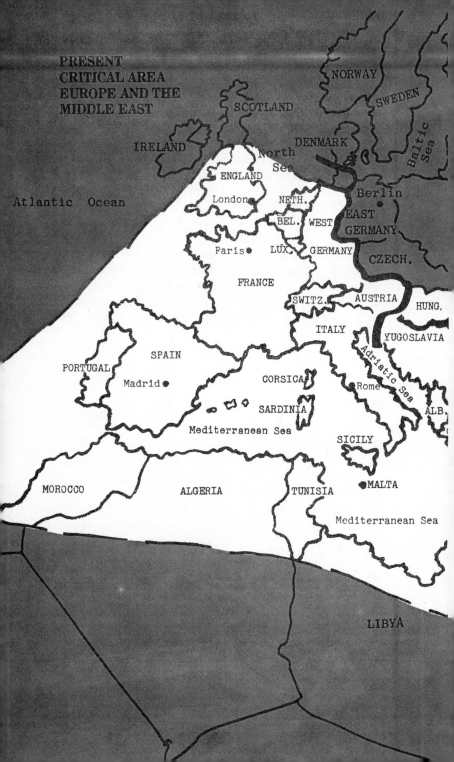

PRESENT
CRITICAL AREA
EUROPE AND THE
MIDDLE EAST

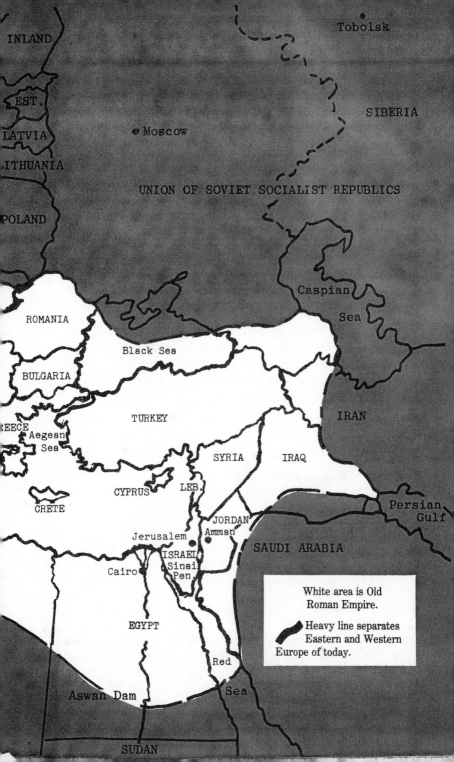

FINLAND

EST.

LATVIA

LITHUANIA

POLAND

Tobolsk

SIBERIA

Moscow

UNION OF SOVIET SOCIALIST REPUBLICS

ROMANIA

Black Sea

Caspian

Sea

BULGARIA

GREECE

Aegean
Sea

TURKEY

IRAN

CYPRUS

LEB.

SYRIA

IRAQ

CRETE

Persian
Gulf

JORDAN

Jerusalem

Amman

SAUDI ARABIA

Cairo

ISRAEL
Sinai
Pen.

EGYPT

White area is Old
Roman Empire.

Heavy line separates
Eastern and Western
Europe of today.

Red

Aswan Dam

Sea

SUDAN

despot "king" who is often referred to as "the Antichrist," the ten rulers of the Western European union (or whatever may be the name by which that region is to be known during the Tribulation period) will continue as a separate entity even up to the time of the battle of Armageddon. This is easily verified by the wording of Revelation 17:13–17. According to Revelation 17:13, these ten nations ". . . shall give their power and strength [military support] unto the beast." Verse 14, however, refers to a battle that shall occur nearly seven years after the holocaust of World War III for it is definitely descriptive of the battle of Armageddon:

> These shall make war with the Lamb, and the Lamb shall overcome them: for he is Lord of lords and King of kings: and they that are with him are called, and chosen, and faithful (Rev. 17:14).

The Lamb of God is the Lord Jesus Christ, and this is a description of what will happen when He returns to earth with His saints and in power, even as it is fully depicted in Revelation 19:11–21; and as stated, that war will not occur until the very close of the Tribulation period, for the end result of it will be the overthrow and disposition of "the beast."

When the Kings Turn Against the Apostasy

So great will become the influence of "the beast," and so vile will become the unrestrained wretchedness of the end-time Babylonian type lascivious "worship" that,

> . . . the ten horns which thou sawest upon the beast, these shall hate the whore, and shall make her desolate and naked, and shall eat her flesh, and burn her with fire. For God hath put in their hearts to fulfill his will, and to agree [Note the continuous unanimity of agreement of "the ten."], and give their kingdom unto the beast, until the words of God shall be fulfilled (Rev. 17:16,17).

The "ten-nation empire" of the Western European nations of the old Roman Empire area certainly fits the allegorical status of the group of ten nations portrayed as the ten toes of the empire image described by Daniel, and also that of the ten horns depicted as being on "the beast" in the Revelation account. Their separate entity is acknowledged, but, like the "miry clay" of the image, they are broken in power and have no individual strength of their own, for they commit it all to "the beast."

The fact remains, however, that "the king," also referred to as "the beast," is to be given his power by these ten rulers at the instigation of Satan's influence.

It is also true that his coming is associated with the then accepted unified apostate world-church system referred to as "Mystery, Babylon the Great," for that apostate worship system and "the beast" are seen as coming in together.

When the millions of Bible-believing and Christ-honoring people suddenly disappear from the face of the earth, many "adjustments" will necessarily be made very rapidly; and all of these entities will come forth as a result.

Prelude to the Scenario of World War III

How this all fits together so perfectly is a marvel of the ages, but it is the plan of God, and it shall all come to pass in great precision—in spite of the efforts of Satan to cause it to fail.

If we recognize the "one hour" during which the ten kings shall rule "with the beast" before they "agree, and give their power and strength unto the beast" as being on the same time basis as the proven historical record of the seventy weeks of Daniel's prophetic account—wherein each week equals seven years—then one day would equal one year, and thus one hour would be equal to 1/24th of one year. This would be just two weeks of time in accordance with the Hebrew lunar calendar year of 360 days. In simple terminology, this would mean that in just two weeks time from the day that the true believers are "caught up to meet the Lord in the air," the wicked "king" of the

235

end-time will be given his authority to carry out that which God has ordained that he shall do.

The greatest service that I can do by correlating Scripture with documented news information of today is to set before you a step-by-step scenario of the events to come, placing them in their proper chronological order to the nearest possible determination in accordance with all of the material that we have at hand.

Inasmuch as no human being can know for a certainty any thing that might happen even one day in advance, there is but one immutable source: that is the historically proven Book of all books, the Bible. Modern archaeological findings have verified its record. Hundreds of fulfilled prophecies have proven its amazing authenticity.

Out of the hundreds of specific prophecies that have been fulfilled and which can be verified by reading accounts in many books, consider just one example:

> In the third year of the reign of king Belshazzar a vision appeared unto me, even unto me Daniel, . . . behold, an he goat came from the west on the face of the whole earth, and touched not the ground: and the goat had a notable horn between his eyes. And he came to the ram that had two horns, which I had seen standing before the river, and ran unto him in the fury of his power. And I saw him come close unto the ram, and he was moved with choler against him, and smote the ram, and brake his two horns: and there was no power in the ram to stand before him, . . . and there was none that could deliver the ram out of his hand. Therefore the he goat waxed very great: and when he was strong, the great horn was broken; and for it came up four notable ones toward the four winds of heaven.
>
> And I heard a man's voice . . . Gabriel, make this man to understand the vision.
>
> The ram which thou sawest having two horns are the kings of Media and Persia.
>
> . . . the rough goat is the king of Grecia; and the great horn that is between his eyes is the first king. Now that being broken, whereas four stood up for it, four kingdoms shall stand up out of the nation, but not in his power (Dan. 8:1,5–8,16,20–22).

a) Daniel, as a young man, had been taken to Babylon from Jerusalem when that city was first conquered by Nebuchadnezzar in 604 B.C. He had the above vision "in the third year of Belshazzar" which would date it at 554 B.C.

b) In the vision he saw the rise of the Medo-Persian Empire as "the ram with the two horns," and he saw the defeat of that Medo-Persian Empire by the first King of Greece depicted as "the great horn" between the eyes of "the rough goat" that "smote the ram, and brake his two horns." He also saw depicted that "when the he goat waxed very great . . . and was strong, the great horn was broken, and for it came up four notable ones toward the four winds of heaven."

c) The remarkable factor is that Daniel not only foresaw the future rulers, but he also foresaw the destiny of each, and was even given to know the name of the nation which was to conquer Media and Persia, and that it would be by the first king thereof. Also, his kingdom was to be divided four ways.

d) Daniel died about 530 B.C..

e) Greece, named in Daniel's vision, conquered the Medes and Persians in 334 B.C., and its first king, Alexander the Great, died in Babylon in 323 B.C. which was over 200 years after the death of Daniel. Also, in 323 B.C. the Greek Empire was divided into four kingdoms as prophesied over two hundred years previously. The divisions were Macedonia, Egypt, Syria, and Asia Minor.

Only by the omnipotent foreknowledge and power of the living Lord God could such precise prophecies be written and then come to pass exactly as prophesied and recorded over 200 years in advance. This is positive proof.

f) Bible prophecy gives the pattern; documented history and current events give the verification.

"The scenario" can now be given. Bible prophecies, written for centuries and thus unalterable, shall be placed in their proper chronological order and will be compared with and/or verified with the news of today. The vision accounts of George Washington and of the evangelist will be taken into full account, but it must be fully understood that whereas their visions do up-date into modern terminology and technology certain relative phases of the prophecies, only the Bible account can be "guaranteed" to occur. The other accounts do, however, agree in every detail; and they do not disagree with the Bible prophecies. They can, therefore, be considered "probable."

Some repetition will be needed to give clarity, but the following "scenario" is hereby submitted trusting that it will alert all who read it to an awareness that "this generation" is, indeed, the generation that "shall not pass, til all these things be fulfilled" (Matt. 24:34).

The destiny of the United States will be unfolded as a part of the final section of this writing.

The Handwriting on the Wall

Like "the handwriting on the wall" which actually appeared as the final decree against the Babylonian rulers, the signs of the times portray today the prophesied events and conditions which are to prevail "at the time of the end."

All of history is the background, but the turning point was the year 1948. It was, indeed, the year of beginning concerning the events of this generation. "The scenario," therefore, shall begin with the events of that crucial year.

Israel's Non-secret Weapon

Israeli ground crewmen load bombs for a mission. Members of Israel's Air Force are carefully selected, superbly trained, and totally dedicated.

20

THE YEAR OF BEGINNINGS: 1948

1. Israel

The year was 1948. Israel was anxiously awaiting its recognition as a nation. It had been waiting for a long time—for more than 2,500 years. Palestine had been freed from the Turks in 1917, but it remained under British authority for the next thirty years. When the British mandate ended in 1947, its disposition had been turned over to the United Nations which in turn had voted on November 29, 1947, to divide the land, giving a portion of it to the Arabs and designating the balance as the State of Israel. The Arabs immediately rejected the plan and attacked the Israelis. A struggle for survival was in progress.

Harry S. Truman, President of the United States at that time, had been the first dignitary to sign the papers of full recognition of the State of Israel, but other signatures were needed. When these were obtained, the Republic of Israel was proclaimed a nation on May 14-15, 1948. It continues to struggle, but it is now a nation recognized by, and a member of, the United Nations.

The Bible contains many prophecies regarding the restoration of the nation of Israel. One prophecy in particular should be noted here as recorded in Ezekiel:

> The word of the LORD came unto me, saying, Moreover, thou son of man, take thee one stick, and write upon it. For Judah, and for the children of Israel his companions: then take another stick, and write

upon it, For Joseph, the stick of Ephraim, and for all the house of Israel his companions: and join them one to another into one stick; and they shall become one in thine hand.

And when the children of thy people shall speak unto thee, saying, Wilt thou not show us what thou meanest by these? . . . say unto them, Thus saith the Lord GOD; Behold, I will take the children of Israel from among the heathen, whither they be gone, and will gather them on every side, and bring them into their own land: . . . they shall be no more two nations, neither shall they be divided into two kingdoms any more at all (Ezek. 37:15–18,21,22).

The Israelis of today are "gathered" together from more than 100 different countries of the world, and they are from every tribe of the children of Israel. They are, therefore, in fulfillment of the prophecy, "one nation in the land." This significant prophecy had its fulfillment in "the year of beginnings: 1948."

2. The Ten-Nation Revived Roman Empire

It was the same year, 1948, that the first step was taken to officially unite the war-torn countries of Western Europe. The "little three" countries of Belgium, The Netherlands, and Luxembourg agreed on June 8, 1948, to unify their efforts toward a basic coordination of domestic, economic, and financial policies. They signed the Benelux Agreement which became the foundation stone for the entity known today as the Common Market, which is, in turn, the beginning of "the ten-nation empire." Its goal of ten is well documented by the following news item.

(August 17, 1970, *Newsweek*) When a relatively obscure Italian Cabinet minister named Franco Maria Malfatti became president of the six-nation European Common Market Commission last spring . . . Malfatti got the job primarily because it was Italy's turn for the Presidency—a two-year stint at European Economic Community (EEC) headquarters in Brussels . . . And during a recent interview in Rome with *Newsweek* Senior Editor Arnaud de Borchgrave, Malfatti expressed his devotion to the cause of European integration. . . . Below, excerpts from the conversation between de Borchgrave and Malfatti:

Q. Once the Common Market countries have agreed to a common currency, haven't they, in effect, agreed to give up their own independent foreign and domestic policies?

A. It's a logical process. Monetary and political union go hand in hand. . . .

Q. What role, if any, do you see for Eastern Europe? Isn't the European movement predicated on the continued division of the Continent?

A. We are building Europe for those who accept the Rome treaty. In other words, for like-minded democratic states. This is the only way we can play an important role of equilibrium in the world. East Europe does not accept the reality of the Common Market.

Q. How many states do you think will be part of this new Europe?

A. At the present time we have six members (France, West Germany, Italy, Belgium, The Netherlands and Luxembourg) and four more, including Britain, have applied to join. Anything beyond that is, to my way of thinking, an abstract concept.

Q. . . . But once Britain and the other three candidates are in, won't this ten-nation organization have to move fairly quickly from unanimous voting to majority voting?

A. . . . Majority voting is . . . already overdue, so naturally it will have to be applied.

Q. When?

A. Certainly before the end of the decade.

Q. Won't this be some form of de facto European confederation?

A. That is a fair description. . . .*

Documented Summary

Progress toward a de facto ten-nation confederation can be summarized as follows:

January 1, 1948: Belgium, The Netherlands, and Luxembourg made the first move toward cooperation in Western Europe. They formed a customs union.

*Condensed from *Newsweek*, Copyright Newsweek, Inc., 1970.

June 8, 1948: The same "little three" nations signed the Benelux Agreement which coordinated their domestic, economic, and financial policies.

May 27, 1952: The European Defense Community (E.D.C.) was created. The E.D.C. Treaty, signed in Paris, called for a combined European army of six nations—West Germany, France, Italy, Belgium, The Netherlands, and Luxembourg; the closest possible liaison of this army with the forces of Great Britain; and full cooperation with the NATO system.

October 23, 1954: The E.D.C. was replaced by a cooperative organization known as "The Western European Union" (W.E.U.). This created, instead of a multi-national armed force, a cooperation of the armed forces of the signatory nations, and it brought in Great Britain as a full member of the European defense system.

March 25, 1957: The Treaty of Rome was signed in Rome, Italy, creating that which is generally known as the Common Market. Its format was largely brought about by the efforts of Jean Monnet, a French economist who had established what was referred to as one of the most potent political pressure groups ever assembled, the Action Committee for a United States of Europe. Monnet, called the "Father of the Common Market," had declared: "Once a Common Market interest has been created, then political union will come naturally." The Common Market Treaty of Rome was actually a 378-page "Declaration of Intent"—first, for the economic integration of Europe; and secondly, for the construction of an entirely new, and revolutionary, political entity. (Note: The information quoted above was taken from *Newsweek* and *Time* reports, and a summary in a *Newsweek* analysis report dated January 7, 1963.)

(October 8, 1962, *Newsweek*) Europe is in the space race. . . . [This article goes on to describe the size and the activities of the following agencies involved] European Space Research Organization (ESRO), European Launcher Development Organization (ELDO), European Space Technology Center (ESTEC), and European Space Data Center (ESDAC). As of October 8, 1962 Eurospace employed over 1,000,000 people in 47 of Europe's biggest corporations.*

(January 15, 1964, *Los Angeles Times*) . . . DeGaulle will call for the European partners to adopt his plan for political union. This will mean the formation of a council of the heads of government to make the decisions—and not a true federal union with a central legislature.

(March 9, 1964, *Newsweek*) . . . Progress was made in Brussels, where the Common Market Council of Ministers voted to merge Western Europe's three most important supra-national institutions: the Coal-Steel Community, the Atomic Energy Community (Eurotom), and the Market. . . . The Brussels agreement fits well with the plans of General Charles DeGaulle. . . . What the General is seeking is greater political cooperation among sovereign states. . . .**

(June 15, 1964, *Newsweek*) Franco believes that DeGaulle's vision of a confederated Europe . . . will emerge triumphant over Washington's fading dream of a vast Atlantic community. DeGaulle, in turn, sees Spain as an essential part of his confederated Europe. . . . Meeting at its Brussels headquarters, the Common Market's Council of Ministers agreed that "exploratory conversations" should be opened with Madrid on the question of Spain's relationship with the Market.†

(March 15, 1965, *Newsweek*) . . . the Common Market members . . . began negotiations aimed at bringing neutral Austria within the Market's tariff structure.‡

(November 7, 1968, *Los Angeles Time*) United Nations—Under the impetus of the Czechoslovak crisis, Italy and Austria are holding intense negotiations here to settle their dispute over the South Tyrol. . . . In the case of the South Tyrol, or Alto Adige, as it is called in Italian, the dispute relates to the rights of German-speaking residents of northern provinces of Italy that formerly were part of Austria. . . . recently Italy vetoed an Austrian application to the Common Market because of the dispute. . . .

(January 1, 1973, *World Almanac*) Great Britain, Ireland and Denmark formally entered into the European Common Market.

(June 13, 1975, *Los Angeles Times*) Greece Thursday asked the nine-nation European Common Market to admit it as a full-fledged member "to consolidate democracy in Greece."

(February 10, 1976, *Los Angeles Times*) The nine governments of the European Common Market unanimously endorsed Greece's membership application. . . .

(March 29, 1977, *Los Angeles Times* [Reuters]) Brussels, Belgium—Portugal, one of Europe's poorest nations, formally applied Monday to enter the European Common Market. . . .

(June 28, 1978, *Baltimore Sun*) . . . Speaking to Spanish television on the eve of his trip, French President Giscard d'Estaing said he was happy to see Spain "affirm its European vocation" . . . now that its application, submitted July 28, 1977, has been "accepted."

(February 9, 1978, *Seattle Intelligencer*) . . . Fernand Spaak, the Common Market's ambassador to this country, yesterday said the Common Market was well under way toward some kind of political unity as a result of the success of the economic union.

For the first time in history, Europe will hold a continental election. . . . "Once a parliament has been legitimized by an election, they tend to grow," said Spaak. "It's very difficult to say what shape the European union will take. . . . But it's clear that we are moving from economic union toward some kind of political unification."

(April 8, 1978, *Los Angeles Times*) Copenhagen, Denmark—Heads of government of the European Common Market countries agreed here Friday to schedule the long-planned direct elections for the nine-country European Parliament for June 7, 8 and 9, 1979. . . .

It was a body of 410 members—81 seats each to Britain, France, West Germany and Italy, 25 for The Netherlands, 24 for Belgium, 16 for Denmark, 15 for Ireland and 6 for Luxembourg . . . to meet monthly 10 months of the year, alternating between assembly halls in Luxembourg and Strasbourg. (The new Palace of Europe is providing facilities for the 410 members of the new European Parliament in Strasbourg, France.)

(December 22, 1978, *San Diego Union*) Paris—Greece completed the details of its entry into the European Economic Community yesterday, agreeing on terms for full membership . . .

Greek Foreign Minister George Rallis termed the agreement "a historic moment in Europe's history." He said it would enable Greece to sign a formal membership treaty with the EEC early next year.

(May 29, 1979, *Los Angeles Herald Examiner*) Athens, Greece—Greece became the 10th member of the European Common Market yesterday, culminating 22 years of efforts by Premier Constantine Caramanlis to join his country economically with Europe.

Greece's active membership is scheduled to start Jan. 1, 1981, after the 10 member parliaments ratify the agreement.

(July 18, 1979, *Los Angeles Times*) Strasbourg, France (AP)— The European Parliament, history's first directly elected multinational assembly, opened its inaugural session Tuesday and elected as its first president Simone Veil, a Jewish Frenchwoman who survived the Auschwitz death camp . . .

It was a measure of how far Europe has evolved democratically from the Hitler years.

Which Ten Nations?

In becoming the tenth nation in the European Community, Greece has paved the way for the revealing of the Antichrist— the military leader of the eleventh nation to join.

Since Greece's *active* membership is to take place January 1,

1981, but the formal treaty was signed in 1979, the *political* union could be considered accomplished at any appropriate moment of time between now and January 1, 1981.

Bible prophecy declares (Dan. 7:8) that three of the first ten will be "plucked up by the roots" and that they will be replaced by three others. This is to be done by the antichrist king:

> The ten horns out of this kingdom are ten kings that shall arise: and another shall rise after them; and he shall be diverse from the first, and he shall subdue three kings (Dan. 7:24).
>
> . . . and he . . . shall divide the land for gain (Dan. 11:39).

The man to watch for, therefore, is the military leader of the eleventh nation!

The European Common Market was established on the premise that it would eventually become a ten-nation entity. Ten flagpoles stand in front of its headquarters in Brussels, Belgium.

3. The King of the Ten-Nation Coalition

It is significant that the European Common Market is established on the premise of a ten-nation entity exactly as prophesied in the Bible. The plans are so predicated on this format that the Common Market headquarters building in Brussels, Belgium, has in front of it *ten* flagpoles.

Also, it is almost startling to realize that as of 1979, there are thirteen nations that have applied for membership. Greece has been approved to become the tenth full member, and the applications for Spain, Portugal, and Austria have been presented and accepted for consideration for full membership.

The Bible declares that three nations will be replaced. Which three?

Bible prophecy states that when the eleventh ruler (king) enters, *after there are ten*, it will be *this* ruler who will be given great authority and strength and will be revealed as the end-time antichrist king. He will be the one who shall "divide the land for gain," determining the final ten-nation entity of the Tribulation period.

The Man With the Potential

The king in Western Europe who has the greatest potential for becoming the antichrist king of the Tribulation period is one who began his training in "the year of beginnings: 1948."

Prince of Spain, Juan Carlos de Borbon, was born in Rome, Italy, the son of Prince Juan de Borbon y Battenberg and Princess Maria de las Mercedes de Borbon y Orleans, on January 5, 1938. His parents being in exile, Juan Carlos spent his early years in Italy and Switzerland.

In 1948, the same year Israel became a nation, his father met with Generalissimo Francisco Franco on the Portuguese border and agreed that Prince Juan Carlos should be educated in Spain. Don Juan remained in Portugal.

For more than a quarter of a century Juan Carlos was in

extensive training. Raised under the tutelage of military genius Generalissimo Francisco Franco, he graduated from Spain's Naval Academy, its Air Force Academy, and from its famed Saragosa Military Academy. Carlos took extra graduate study at Madrid University and served in various governmental positions. He traveled to America and to London (being a direct descendant of Queen Victoria of England).

When Juan Carlos took the oath of succession to the throne in the grand hall of the Cortes, the Spanish Parliament building, he was dressed in the uniform of an army captain. He knelt before a cross and swore his allegiance to his country, the National Movement, and the Catholic faith.

The Prince of Spain: Juan Carlos (in uniform)

The law of Spain required that a king must be of royal blood, at least thirty years of age, a Catholic, and must swear allegiance to the National Movement which is Spain's only legal political organization.

In his acceptance speech before the Cortes on July 24, 1969, when he formally accepted the designation as Spain's next king, Prince Juan Carlos stated: "I am clearly conscious of the responsibilities I am assuming . . . I want to serve my nation publicly, and for our people I want progress, development, unity, justice, liberty and *grandeur* . . . (italics mine).

General Francisco Franco died November 20, 1975, and Juan Carlos became king.

(November 23, 1975, *Los Angeles Times*) Madrid—Juan Carlos de Borbon was sworn in as Spain's first king in 44 years Saturday and immediately pledged to move away from the authoritarian rule of his predecessor as chief of state, Gen. Francisco Franco. . . .

The king, now known as Juan Carlos I, declared, "Today represents the beginning of a new stage in the history of Spain . . . ."

(January 2, 1976, *Los Angeles Herald & Examiner*) Madrid—Spain has taken more steps toward democracy in the six weeks since Gen. Francisco Franco died than it did in nearly four decades under Franco. . . .

(July 5, 1978, *Los Angeles Times*) Madrid—The Congress of Deputies opened formal parliamentary debate Tuesday on a proposed Spanish constitution that would set up a constitutional monarchy giving the king of Spain more power than any other monarch in Europe. . . .

There is no doubt that the politicians want to make the 40-year-old King Juan Carlos more than a figurehead. . . . The proposed constitution . . . makes the king supreme commander of the armed forces. . . . According to the draft, the Cortes (parliament) must submit all legislation to the king for ratification.

(November 1, 1978, *Los Angeles Times*) Madrid (AP)—Parliament voted overwhelming approval Tuesday of a constitution guaranteeing human rights and providing for democracy under King Juan Carlos.

Spain, Carlos, and the Common Market

Spain filed its formal application to join the European Economic Community (Common Market) July 28, 1977. That application was accepted, but joint action awaited the institution of a constitution in Spain that would make that country a qualified democracy. That time now has arrived. How soon will Spain become a member of the Common Market? Probably very shortly after the election of the new European Parliament. Time will tell.

Anticipation

In Daniel 9:26 the Bible refers to the man who is to become the end-time beast-king as "the prince that shall come." For twenty-seven years—from 1948 to 1975—Juan Carlos was in that category waiting for the demise of General Francisco Franco and anticipating the time when he would become king of Spain. That time was devoted to extensive military training as well as diplomatic preparation. Today King Juan Carlos I is the most highly trained military leader in all of Western Europe.

His high qualifications have not gone unnoticed. It seems that many in Europe are aware of his potential for leadership. Note the following:

(July 7, 1978, *The Evening Bulletin*, Philadelphia, Pa.)

As a Philadelphian traveling on vacation through Spain, I cannot but help sense the air of jubilation among Spaniards relative to King Juan Carlos and Queen Sophia stealing the limelight from other crowned heads of Europe upon their return from China. . . .

The momentum is on Spain's side. Europe must now look for leadership from King Carlos. . . .

Many Europeans whom I have spoken to believe, as I do, that

King Juan Carlos is breathing new life into old European principles. . . .

I believe Spaniards and Europeans alike are standing on the threshold of a new era of inter-European understanding and cooperation with Juan Carlos in the driver's seat. And, Latin America is standing in the wings—waiting and listening for her cue, for she too is in need of a new direction.

King Juan Carlos is showing the world much needed spirit with action. . . .

John Paul Paine
Madrid, Spain*

There is speculation that King Juan Carlos I is the man who will become the king of the ten-nation revived Roman Empire of the Tribulation period. He has much potential for that dubious distinction.

Whoever that king shall be, he will be a highly trained military man to whom the ten leaders of the European Common Market will be willing to give great authority.

Revelation 17:12,13 says these ten kings shall rule "one hour with the beast" and that they will "give their power and strength unto the beast." By any standard of measure "one hour" is to be but a very short period of time. Compared with the seventy weeks of years of the ancient prophecies, one hour would be equal to one twenty-fourth of a year which would be about two weeks of time. What would cause so rapid a decision?

Rapture First

According to the prophecies of the Bible, the rapture must take place before the antichrist king, the "man of sin" of 2 Thessalonians 2:3 can be revealed as to his clear identity. The Lord Jesus, functioning in and through the body of Christ, the church universal, will hinder and restrain ". . . until he be taken out of the way" (2 Thess. 2:7).

---

*This letter to the editor reprinted by permission of the *Bulletin* Company, Philadelphia.

Jesus said, ". . . I will build my church; and the gates of hell shall not prevail against it" (Matt. 16:18). If the devil's Antichrist sought to display his great deceptions today in the church age, any truly Spirit-filled saint of God could "bind" him in the name of Jesus and he would be powerless (Matt. 16:19; 18:18).

In seven letters to the seven types of churches which depict seven periods of church history in Revelation 2 and 3, it is repeated seven times, "He that hath an ear, let him hear what the Spirit saith unto the churches." But there is absolutely no instruction or admonition to any church concerning what to do or how to live during any portion of the Tribulation period. It is not deemed essential because the church will not be on the earth during that seven-year period of difficulty and tribulation.

There is, however, a like admonition to the believing saints of that era. It is found in Revelation 13:9. "If any man have an ear, let him hear."

This is an individual admonition only. The church is not on earth.

In the church age, any believer in Christ who dies is immediately ushered into the presence of Christ in the heavenlies. Paul said, "We are confident, I say, and willing rather to be absent from the body, and to be present with the Lord" (2 Cor. 5:8); and in another place he stated, "For me to live is Christ, and to die is gain" (Phil. 1:21). But during the first half of the Tribulation period, this will not be the case. The souls of the slain saints will be detained in what is commonly called "the vestibule of heaven."

And when he had opened the fifth seal [of end-time judgments during the Tribulation period], I saw under the altar the souls of them that were slain for the word of God, and for the testimony which they held [as witnessing Christians during that era]: And they cried with a loud voice, saying, How long, O Lord, holy and true, dost thou not judge and avenge our blood on them that dwell on the earth?

And white robes were given unto every one of them; and it was said unto them, that they should rest yet for a little season, until their fellow servants also and their brethren, that should be killed as they were, should be fulfilled (Rev. 6:9–11).

These are born-again believers in Christ, for the white robes of His righteousness are given unto them, but they are excluded from His presence until "their fellow servants and their brethren" are also slain. Any who believe in Christ as Redeemer and Savior after the Rapture of the church and during the Tribulation period will have to enter heaven through the gate of martyrdom.

There is only one moment in all of history when "we who are alive and remain shall be caught up together . . . in the clouds to meet the Lord in the air" (1 Thess. 4:17). Those who remain can still be saved if they repent and call on the name of the Lord, for His invitation is never withdrawn, but it will cost them their lives, for the enemies of the Lord will kill them. This fact makes it very urgent that every Christian should be a faithful witness to the Lord today in order to win as many to Christ as possible before that great moment.

> For the Lord himself shall descend from heaven with a shout, with the voice of the archangel, and with the trump of God: and the dead in Christ shall rise first: Then we which are alive and remain shall be caught up together with them in the clouds, to meet the Lord in the air: and so shall we ever be with the Lord (1 Thess. 4:16,17).

"The day of Christ (Messiah)" cannot come until the man of sin, the Antichrist, has been revealed and has run his course through seven years of time called the Tribulation period. Then Jesus will come as Messiah of the Jews and King of kings to all people. 2 Thessalonians 2:2 refers to this coming of Christ in power and glory to establish His millennial reign. It has nothing to do with the Rapture of the church.

The False Church

As soon as the true believers in Christ have been "caught up" into heaven, a false worldwide church system will come into prominence. It will be very corrupt and self-centered. Bible prophecy specifies that it will be this false church organization that will kill many saints who try to preach or teach the "old fashioned" gospel. It is likened to a false spouse, a harlot, and it is seen coming on the scene at the same time as the end-time beast-king, the Antichrist. Note the prophecy:

> . . . and I saw a woman sit upon a scarlet–colored beast, full of names of blasphemy, having seven heads and ten horns.
>
> And the woman was arrayed in purple and scarlet color, and decked with gold and precious stones and pearls, having a golden cup in her hand full of abominations and filthiness of her fornication:
>
> And upon her forehead was a name written, MYSTERY, BABYLON THE GREAT, THE MOTHER OF HARLOTS AND ABOMINATIONS OF THE EARTH.
>
> And I saw the woman drunken with the blood of the saints, and with the blood of the martyrs of Jesus! . . . (Rev. 17:3–6).

This wretched "new morality" church system will indeed be an abomination. It will run rampant for the first three and a half years of the Tribulation period, but right after the middle of the Tribulation, the political leaders of the ten–nation empire will ". . . hate the whore, and shall make her desolate and naked, and shall eat her flesh, and burn her with fire" (Rev. 17:16). The graphic description of the burning of Babylon the Great is prophesied in Revelation 18 and it will surely come to pass "in one hour" as stated.

The organizational base of the end-time apostate church system can be traced to the founding of the World Council of Churches (WCC) in "the year of beginnings—1948." This is not "the woman," but it will lead to that entity.

"The Woman" on the Scarlet Colored Beast

In 1948, the first meeting of the World Council of Churches was held in Amsterdam, capital of The Netherlands. The dates were August 22 to September 4. That meeting marked the beginning of an apostate movement that ultimately will become "MYSTERY, BABYLON THE GREAT, THE MOTHER OF HARLOTS AND ABOMINATIONS OF THE EARTH" (Rev. 17:5).

Brief History of the World Council of Churches

An abbreviated history of the World Council of Churches will reveal some very significant factors. Note the following "ten steps downward":

1. August 22 to September 4, 1948: The Founding Assembly of the World Council of Churches in Amsterdam approved and passed along to member churches for study a report entitled "The Church and the Disorder of Society." In that report is the following statement:

> The Christian church should reject the ideologies of both communism and capitalism . . . *Communist* ideology . . . promises that freedom will come automatically after the completion of the revolution. *Capitalism* puts the emphasis on freedom, and promises that justice will follow as a by-product of free enterprise. That, too, is an ideology which has been proved false.
>
> It is the responsibility of Christians to seek new creative solutions which never allow either justice or freedom to destroy the other.
>
> a. (September 5, 1948, Washington D.C. *Sunday Star*) The World Council of Churches' report on communism and capitalism is enough to make one wonder what world its authors have been staying in. . . . To them, evidently there is no choice worth making between communism and the capitalist system. . . . Dr. Bennett said the closest thing to what he had in mind is the democratic socialism of England.

2. (February 1, 1951, The Executive Committee of the World Council of Churches [in a letter sent to all member churches]) . . . All persons in privileged countries, particularly Christians,

must strive to enter sympathetically into the social demands of the needy. "From each according to his ability, to each according to his need. . . ."

3. (March 18, 1952, *New York Herald Tribune*) Dr. O. Frederick Nolde, director of the Commission of the Churches on International Affairs, stated: "Our real enemy is not the Soviet government . . . We must rid ourselves of scare propaganda, iron curtains and insidious loyalty pledges. . . ."

4. (August, 1954, Second Assembly of the World Council of Churches held in Evanston, Illinois.) This Council was mostly organizational. Most notable was the change in the Central Committee which directs the affairs of the Council between assemblies. Communist-dominated ministers on that prime committee doubled—from two to four. A major theme of the assembly was "Living Together in a Divided World."

5. (November 18 to December 6, 1961, New Delhi, India: Third Assembly of the World Council of Churches.) This assembly admitted the Russian Orthodox Church to membership and elected Archbishop Nikodim (at age thirty-two, the youngest archbishop of any church in the world) to serve on the sixteen-member Executive Committee of the WCC.

Dr. Nolde, in a report delivered at the Third Assembly, stated:

> National sovereignty unbridled is the enemy of an inter-related and cooperating world. . . . Nations must progressively relinquish those aspects of sovereignty which are outworn and self-defeating.

6. (February 13, 1966, *Tulsa Daily World*) (Reporting on the meeting of the Central Committee of the World Council of Churches in Geneva, Switzerland) "Dr. Eugene Carson Blake, newly named head of the World Council of Churches, said Saturday an American victory in Vietnam would cause long-range difficulties."

This Central Committee called for the admission of Red China to the U.N.

7. (May 1, 1967, *The New York Times*) Dr. Martin Niemoel-

ler, a president of the W.C.C., has been awarded the Lenin Peace Prize by the Soviet Union. . . .

8. (March 18, 1968, *Milwaukee Journal*) The Russian church, which functions under the strict control of the state, follows the Kremlin line on all matters. . . .

9. (July 4 to July 20, 1968 Fourth Assembly of the World Council of Churches at Uppsalla, Sweden.) For 20 years, since 1948, the World Council of Churches had constantly courted the cooperation of the Eastern Orthodox churches, especially that of the Russian Orthodox church which became a member in 1961. In so doing, the liberal element tended to become more and more socialist and revolutionary in its program. After the entrance of the Russian Orthodox church to its membership, and of Nikodim and other Russians to its Central Committee and its Executive Committee, it not only tended to socialism, but it became more openly contemporary and revolutionary in its activities. Its programming became much more radical.

Uppsala: Updated—Degraded—But Ecumenical

(July 7, 1968, *Los Angeles Times*) Uppsala, Sweden—Pop art and boisterous youth, radical films, striking drama and mild demonstrations—all of these figure in a sometimes exciting way as the World Council of Churches tries to tune in on a turbulent today and an uncertain future.

These areas of popular enthusiasm are encountered by many of the delegates of 240 denominations, representing most of the world's non-Roman Christians, as they gather here for the fourth assembly of the WCC at this ancient university city, 45 miles north of Stockholm. . . .

Unorthodox films, many made in Eastern Europe and some on WCC order, are being shown to illustrate man's technical ability to create incredible miracles and his moral inability to control his intellectual children. . . . All forcefully present the thesis of this WCC assembly—that man in all his activities, lives, moods, passions, projects, accomplishments and undertakings is fair game for the church and for the Christian faith.

Whatever else the WCC may represent, at Uppsala it represents involvement.

Carnality

The ecumenical developments of this fourth assembly will be given; but first, to show the effects of nonevangelical "Christianity" upon carnal mankind, the following news article is quoted:

(June 24, 1968, *The National Observer*) Christians, shocked by the film "The Parable," shown at the Protestant pavilion at the New York World's Fair, have seen nothing yet. In a new film prepared under church auspices for showing at a World Council of Churches (WCC) assembly in Sweden next month, a Protestant minister conducting a worship service removes all his clothes.

The Reverend Alvin Carmines, director of arts at Judson Memorial Church in New York City, wrote "Another Pilgrim" and plays a minor role in it as a bum. . . . The film, commissioned by the WCC and paid for in part by five Protestant denominations, will be distributed to churches in the United States after its premiere in Sweden.

For an expanded view of the trends of the WCC, "The World Council of Churches—Architects of a One World Church," published by Christian Crusade of Tulsa, Oklahoma, gives sixty-three pages of documentation and comment. Following is a quote from page forty-three of that writing:

In its newsletter of October 7, 1968, the Methodist Layman of North Hollywood disclosed some of the extracurricular activities at this WCC assembly: "The WCC established two nightclubs for its delegates. An Associated Press picture, carried in U.S. newspapers, showed an American clergyman in one of the nightclubs enjoying a drink with other clergymen and youths during a floor show at Club '68.' " The Milwaukee *Sentinel* reported: "These bistros, as well as nightly showings of sexy avant-garde films at a local theater, have distinguished the Fourth Assembly as the most 'upbeat,' earthy World Council meeting in its 20 year history."

Time of August 2, 1968, described what was called "touch-and-tell" services conducted at the WCC's Uppsala meeting. . . ."

It is written: "By their fruits ye shall know them" (Matt. 7:20). It also is written: ". . . try the spirits whether they are of God: because many false prophets are gone out into the world" (1 John 4:1).

Ecumenical Expansion at Fourth Assembly

(July 5, 1968, *Los Angeles Times*) Uppsala, Sweden—The Fourth Assembly of the World Council of Churches, the most representative meeting of non-Roman Catholic churches in history, opened Thursday with a striking mixture of the traditional and the contemporary. . . .

The Council includes 232 member churches which have sent nearly 800 delegates to this meeting. . . . Its constituent membership totals about 300 million . . .

(July 12, 1968, *Los Angeles Times*) Uppsala, Sweden—Nine Roman Catholic theologians Thursday were voted in as members of the Faith and Order Commission of the World Council of Churches, the first of their church to become fullfledged members of any part of the WCC.

The Faith and Order Commission is a semi-autonomous agency whose basic purpose is to study and remove those factors of Christian practice which hinder the manifestation of unity.

"It is a matter of great rejoicing that, for the first time in its history, the commission will be representative of all the major Christian confessions," said Dr. Lucas Vischer, director of the Faith and Order Commission.

10. WCC broadens its outreach.

(July 20, 1972, *Christian Beacon*) A conference gathering with a reported attendance of some 50 Muslims and Christians, representing 20 countries on five continents, is being held this week at Broumana near Beirut, Lebanon. The conference is under the sponsorship of the World Council of Churches from its Geneva headquarters. . . . Dr. Eugene Carson Blake, WCC general secretary, gave the welcoming speech. He explained that the World Council already has opened a number of dialogues with "people of living faiths". . . . In this regard, it was said that, with a 1970 general meeting of Hindus, Buddhists, Christians and Muslims, smaller meetings were being convened separately by the WCC with Buddhists and Muslims, and, at present, there is an ongoing consultation program with a representative group of Jews. . . .

Editorial Comment

Dr. Eugene Carson Blake seemed to set a course when he stated in 1967, "The WCC radically challenges each separate church and each separate tradition to lose itself into a single worldwide communion of Word and sacrament."

Bible prophecy, which has been written for nineteen centuries, portrays in allegorical manner the "woman" of church apostasy and of blasphemy coming onto the world scene riding on the scarlet–colored beast which has seven heads. Revelation 17:9 states: "And here is the mind which hath wisdom. The seven heads are seven mountains, on which the woman sitteth."

It has been previously shown in this book that the prophesied "beast" of the end time is to be a military and political leader of the Old Roman Empire area of Western Europe. Rome is literally built on seven hills, or "mountains." It is highly significant, therefore, that the World Council of Churches now should turn its attention so strongly toward the city of Rome.

It is even more significant in the light of developments which have come from the Vatican since the time of the Uppsala WCC meeting. Some very important trends can now be noted.

(October 2, 1968, Exclusive to the *Times* from the *Washington Post*) Rome—The Roman Catholic Church issued an unprecedented, broad call for Catholics and members of other faiths to join in a dialog with atheists.

The appeal was issued in a document prepared by the Vatican's secretariat for nonbelievers, headed by Franziskus Cardinal Koenig of Vienna, who on Monday had a long private audience with Pope Paul VI.

Pope Paul gave the 5,700-word policy-making document, "Dialog With Nonbelievers," his full approval.

The appeal, to make the world "more human," was not intended to convert people but to express "brotherly love" and meet the needs of mankind. . . .

(May 10, 1970, *Los Angeles Times*) A World Conference of Religions for Peace will be held at Kyoto, Japan, Oct. 16 to 22, according to Dr. Maurice N. Eisendrath.

It will be attended by representatives of the world's greatest faiths: Judeo-Christian, Buddhist, Hindu, Shintoist and others, said Dr. Eisendrath, president of the Union of American Hebrew Congregations. . . . It will be the first attempt by the powerful leaders of the great faiths to find a common ground of belief on a matter central to most religions—that of peace for our time.

Message to World Leaders

The conference, the first of its kind, also will send its message for peace, on behalf of most of the world's 3.5 billion people, to global political leaders, in a way that can scarcely be ignored. . . .

"Hardly a religion in the Orient or in the West will not be represented," said Dr. Eisendrath. "The far-reaching geographic representation will include leaders from behind the Iron Curtain, from Africa, and virtually every other corner of the world. It will be unique. Its goal will be to mobilize the religious constituency of the world, and to apply respective teachings of peace to the achievement of peace. . . ."

Broad Dialog for Peace Urged at WCC Meeting

In January 1971, the Central Committee of the World Council of Churches convened in Addis Ababa, Ethiopia. It was composed of 120 members representing about 400 million members of Protestant, Anglican, Orthodox, and Old Catholic churches from around the world. The Central Committee is the principle policy-making body of the WCC. A digest of various reports of the twelve-day meeting reveals the following:

Emporer Haile Selassie urged working for unity of Christian churches and "the welfare of mankind."

The Committee heard messages urging that new approaches be developed to non-Christian faiths . . . Rev. Stanley J. Samartha, a member of the staff in Geneva, stated, "Because Christians cannot claim to have a monopoly of truth, we need to meet men of other faiths and ideologies as part of our trust in and obedience to the promise of Christ."

The Committee was told of new opportunities to widen religious dialog with Marxists, Muslims, Hindus, Buddhists, and other bodies.

Dr. Eugene Carson Blake, general secretary of the WCC, urged that particular attention be given to dialog with Judaism "on the subject of faith in God." He also urged that our times required discussion and collaboration with Judaism in the fields of racial justice and world peace.

2.5 Billion Believers Represented at Ecumenical Service

(May 25, 1975, *Los Angeles Times*) Representatives of faiths embracing 2.5 billion people met for the second of three ecumenical services last Sunday and heard anew a plea for the walls that separate them to come down.

The service sponsored by the Inter-religious Council of Southern California was a Holy Year interfaith affair, in keeping with the "Reconciliation and Renewal" theme of the 26th Roman Catholic Holy Year, and was held at Wilshire United Methodist Church.

Faiths other than Catholic, Orthodox and Protestant Christian believers taking part included the Board of Rabbis of Southern California, the Buddhist Federation of Southern California, the Islamic Foundation of Southern California, the Vedanta Society of Southern California and the Sikh Dharma Brotherhood. . . .

In his message, United Methodist Bishop Charles F. Golden said that "these are great days, when the Light of our world is calling us to live in keeping with the best. . . . It is fitting that we gather in the 26th Holy Year of the Roman Catholic Church to seek unity in our diversity. . . . We meet as representatives of almost every major faith . . . representing considerably more than half the population of the world.

"Conceivably these faiths could change the course of human history. . . ."

Bible Prophecy and Peace

With the World Council of Churches, which has a constituency of over 400 million members, in dialog with other religious bodies whose membership totals more than 1,300,000,000 (Muslim and Hindu religions alone accounting for almost exactly 1 billion), it can be seen that over one half of the population of the world is in conference and "dialog" seeking peace.

In the light of the extent of the search for peace on the part of so many people today, one cannot help but recall the Bible prophecy in that respect:

> For when they shall say, peace and safety, then sudden destruction cometh upon them . . . and they shall not escape (1 Thess. 5:3).

4. Editorial Summary and Analysis

The foregoing pages of this chapter have shown that great and highly significant changes have taken place within this generation.

Israel

Beginning in 1948, Israel again became a recognized nation of the world.

In fulfillment of the prophecy quoted from Ezekiel 37, it is not just a "Jewish" entity, but it is a combined single nation of both Jews and Israelites.

The Ten–Nation Empire

Beginning also in 1948, the ten-nation entity began to come into being in Western Europe. Bible prophecies were quoted to show that Daniel, writing in the 6th century B.C., and also John, writing in A.D. 95, were given specific visions and prophecies concerning this ten–nation empire which was to come into being at the close of earth's history. They also saw that a single leader, or "king," would become the head of it. Tendencies to that end already exist.

When the great chaos period comes, which shall upset many authorities due to the taking up into the heavenlies of all true believers in Jesus Christ, American leadership will be affected more extensively than that of any other nation. While the U.S. is temporarily in a great state of confusion, the Western European nations will very rapidly consolidate into a ten–nation entity and will then give its strategic military power to a European. "He" will become the head of the NATO or Western European Union military alliance. America will still have its great military power and thermonuclear deterrent, but fear will cause Europe to select its own leader in case Russia should strike before America can catch its equilibrium and be able to counteract the very real threat of Communist aggression.

The North Atlantic Treaty will still be in effect, and when Russia does strike, great firepower from both the American and the Western European revived Roman Empire entity will devastate that nation. In the all-out thermonuclear exchange that will take place, however, Russia's vaunted SS-9 and other missiles, its FOBS armed satellites, and everything that she has militarily will be shot primarily at the United States in a first-strike effort to "knock out" this nation.

The Apostate "World Church"

Also in 1948, the World Council of Churches was founded.

As noted within this chapter, "the king" of the revived Roman Empire area will come into his power accompanied by a great conglomerate of religious organizations who shall be advocating peace. Already worldwide symposiums are being held to try to avoid the dreaded confrontation between the super-powers and to find some manner of securing world peace. They advocate disarmament, but it will not happen.

World War III

The much-feared holocaust of World War III will come. It will be one-day, all-out pushbutton warfare. Bible prophecy refers to it as "the day" of which God has spoken (Ezek. 39:8), as "that day" (Ezek. 38:19), as "a day" and "the day" in Joel 1:15 and Joel 2:2, and as "the day of the Lord . . . as a destruction from the Almighty" in Isaiah 13:6. Numerous other prophecies are quoted in Chapter two of this book. "Their faces shall be as flames. . . ." and "the fire hath devoured the pastures of the wilderness, and the flame hath burned all the trees of the field. . . ." and "therefore are many men burned. . . ." These are but a few of the prophecies concerning the holocaust of the "battle by fire" referred to herein as World War III. The end result of such an all-out confrontation will be that most of the great arsenals of horrendous nuclear weapons will be exhausted. Russia and America will both be greatly devastated. This, also, is prophesied.

With Russia and America virtually in ashes, the sly "king" of the revived Roman Empire will lay claim to the victory, having guaranteed Israel's security. The Arab nations will be under his control in fulfillment of many prophecies, especially those of Isaiah 19. Israel will be given title to the temple-site in Jerusalem, and "he" will allow them to build their temple and renew the altar worship as in days of old (Dan. 9:27).

With great deception and "lying wonders" (2 Thess. 2:9), he shall advocate "peace" while he goes forth to consolidate his power. He shall also allow the conglomerate "World Church" to proclaim its "brotherly love" theories of mysticism, astrology, and sensuous free love until he is ready to demand that they worship him as God.

How Soon?

When shall these things come to pass?

The climaxing generation of this era of time had its beginning in 1948.

1948 saw the establishing of the nation of Israel.

1948 saw the beginning of "The Ten–Nation Empire."

1948 saw the beginning of organized worldwide ecumenity among the churches through the founding of the World Council of Churches. Orthodox Church addition brought changes, and the including of Roman Catholicism eliminated "Protestantism" as such. "Dialogs" with non-Christian religions have brought, and will bring more, oriental mysticism, astrology, and Babylonian occult practices and "liberty."

Matthew, Mark, and Luke all recorded that Jesus proclaimed:

> Now learn a parable of the fig tree; When his branch is yet tender, and it putteth forth leaves, ye know that summer is nigh: So likewise ye, when ye shall see all these things, know that it is near, even at the doors (Matt. 24:32,33).

21

COMING EVENTS

It is evident that the world is in crisis—and time is running out.

I have no fear for myself nor for the true believers in Christ, for very soon we shall all hear "the sound of the trumpet" and shall be taken out of this world and into the presence of our wonderful Lord.

My concern is for those who know not the Lord as their personal Redeemer. Terrible times are ahead for those who remain upon this earth. May this writing serve as a warning—and as a guide to survival.

The Status

God's mercy is not withdrawn. Personal salvation, after the true Christians have been "caught up to be with the Lord," will still be possible. But it will probably require martyrdom.

That which is before us now is the order of events from today until that moment—that "twinkling of an eye"—wherein the Christians will simply disappear from the earth; and from today until that same moment when chaos shall strike this world.

Today

1. "The land" of Israel has been, indeed, "brought back from the sword," and it has now become "the land of unwalled

villages" consisting of hundreds of unwalled kibbutzim (farm colonies) "upon the desolate places that are now inhabited," in exact fulfillment of the prophecies of Ezekiel 38:8, 11, and 12.

In further fulfillment of these same verses, its populace "today" consists of a great conglomeration of Jews, Israelites, Anglo-Saxons, Americans, Edomites, Khazars, Ethiopians, and Hebrews of all sorts "gathered out of many peoples." They are "the people that are gathered out of the nations." The official language of Israel today is Hebrew.

2. The Arabs of "Persia, Ethiopia, and Libya" are in full allegiance with the leaders of Meshech (Moscow) which have become "a guard unto them" in exact fulfillment of Ezekiel 38:3–7, today.

3. The nations of Western Europe which were a part of the old Roman Empire are now formulating that which will soon become the prophesied "revived Roman Empire." It shall, as a ten–nation entity, "rule for one hour" (two weeks of actual time in proportion to the 70 weeks of years recorded in the prophecies of Jeremiah and of Daniel) "with the beast" (the end–time despotic ruler of that region which is to be ruled from Rome). The heads of the ten nations which will make up the ten–nation empire will cooperate with this "king" from Rome and will, in the face of the soon-coming emergency, "have one mind, and shall give their power and strength (militarily) unto the beast" in fulfillment of Revelation 17:13.

4. Exactly one third of the land area of the world (see Chapter five of this book) is in battle array on one side or the other of the Middle East crisis over the Arab-Israeli confrontation regarding the "land" of Israel today.

5. The whole world is breathlessly awaiting the earthshaking assault which it seeks to avert with "peace talks," but which it feels sure will soon result in the total all–out thermonuclear exchange of World War III.

6. Today we stand at the brink of the fulfillment of the many prophecies concerning the "Battle by Fire" (see Chapter two of this book for the details).

7. A summarizing prophetic chronology can now be presented, and one special chapter in the Bible lends itself well to a full coordination of all of the prophecies.

Whereas the destiny of the United States was primarily portrayed in Isaiah 18, Isaiah 19 is a prophecy of the events which shall occur from the time of the translation (rapture) of the church until the ultimate reign of the Lord of hosts, the Messiah, over all the earth.

The Theme of Isaiah 19

The theme of Isaiah 19 is the destiny of the Arab nations, referred to as Egypt. The events cover the last seven years of "the times of the Gentiles"—that era which is commonly called the Tribulation period. Through the disclosure of the course of the events of those days shall unfold the destinies of all nations.

That the time is in the future is proven by the prophecy of Isaiah 19:5–10 wherein it is proclaimed that "the river shall be wasted and dried up." The river referred to is the Nile River, the longest river in the world. On its fertile banks and in the irrigated areas of the Nile Valley live 95 percent of the people of Egypt. It has never been dry, historically, but the largest man-made project in the world, the Aswan High Dam located 600 miles upriver from Cairo, now makes that prophecy feasible; for if that dam were to be closed it could most certainly cause "the river" to be "wasted and dried up." Even the very means of its becoming empty is portrayed within the prophecy of Isaiah 19, as follows:

> They shall turn the rivers far away; and the brooks of defence [irrigation canals] shall be emptied and dried up: the reeds and the flags shall wither . . . every thing sown by the brooks shall wither, . . . The fishers also shall mourn . . . And they shall be broken in the purposes thereof, all that make sluices and ponds for fish (Isa. 19:6–10).

"The rivers" referred to in this passage are the two great sources of the Nile: the Blue Nile from Ethiopia and the White Nile which originates in Uganda, 3,000 miles from the Nile delta at the Mediterranean Sea. These two rivers converge at Khartoum, the capital of Sudan, and flow on down into Egypt as "the" Nile River. The Aswan High Dam, located below the junction, is in the southern area of Egypt.

Egypt's Folly

God forewarned Egypt concerning the error of making a foolish alliance, such as with Russia. That warning is, in fact, the very next portion of Scripture after the prophecy concerning the drying up of the Nile River:

> Surely the princes of Zoan [ancient dwelling place of the Pharaohs in the days of Joseph and of Moses] are fools, the counsel of the wise counselors of Pharaoh is become brutish: how say ye unto Pharaoh, I am the son of the wise, the son [descendant] of ancient kings?
>
> Where are they? where are thy wise men? and let them tell thee now, and let them know what the LORD of hosts hath purposed upon Egypt. [Note that it is not by chance, but by the decree of God.]
>
> The princes of Zoan are become fools, the princes of Noph [Hebrew for Memphis, a later capital of Egypt until destroyed by Cambyses, when Egypt fell to the Persian Empire. It was situated near present Cairo] are deceived; they have also seduced Egypt, even they that are the stay of the tribes thereof (Isa. 19:11–13).

The Russian Bear Moves In

That Russia is the "stay" of the tribes of Egypt and of the Arab nations there is no question or need for documentation. It is constantly in the news of today.

Ezekiel lived 200 years after Isaiah. In Ezekiel 38, the "chief prince of Meshech" (Moscow) is stipulated as being "a guard unto them." Since 1960 the U.S.S.R. has poured billions of dollars into the Arab world in both economic and military aid.

The New Strong Man of Syria

(February 24, 1971, *Daily Breeze*, Torrance, Calif.) [Copley News Service] Beirut—The new strongman of Syria, Lt. Gen. Hafez Assad . . . of the ruling Arab Baath Socialist Party, is carving a new image for himself and his country. . . .

Gen. Assad has improved the general political conditions by cooperating with other Arab nationalist and left-wing forces, such as the Nasserites and Communists. . . .

(February 26, 1971, *Daily Breeze*, Torrance, Calif.) Beirut—The Soviet Union has agreed to extend economic and military assistance to the new Syria regime in the hope of boosting Soviet influence in that key Arab country.

A joint communique issued at the end of talks held in Moscow between Soviet leaders and Syrian strongman and Premier Lt. Gen. Hafez Assad said the USSR and Syria have agreed to increase their cooperation in order to eliminate the consequences of the Middle East war of June, 1967. . . .

Trained Cuban Troops in Syria and Lebanon

(December 28, 1978, San Gabriel Valley *Daily Tribune*) The Carter administration is trying to keep this very quiet—but there are now Cuban troops not only in Syria but also in Lebanon.

Trained by Moscow and battle hardened in Angola and Ethiopia, the presence of these troops explains the jitters in Israel and the refusal of Prime Minister Menachem Begin to bow to Egypt's escalation demands. . . .

What are these troops doing?

In Syria, they are bolstering an anti-peace government as surrogates for the Kremlin. Syrian President Assad, whose interventionist policies in Lebanon are eroding his support at home, desperately needs them if he is not to be overthrown.

In Lebanon, Cubans are backing up the Syrian army in its efforts to liquidate Christian Arabs. . . .

The Cubans are also working with Yassir Arafat's Palestine Liberation Organization, supplying arms and training to terrorists intent on destroying Israel.

The Cuban mercenaries are, of course, the new cutting edge of Soviet imperialism. There can be no peace in the Middle East as long as they remain in Lebanon—and this is what the Kremlin wants. As long as they remain, the Camp David "frameworks" are merely scraps of paper.

Syria and Iraq Plan Merger

(January 20, 1979, *Jerusalem Post*) Damascus (Reuter)—Syria and Iraq are planning to merge into a single state under one leader with command over combined armies on Israel's northeast border, Arab diplomatic sources reported Sunday. Between them, Syria and Iraq can muster an estimated 415,000 men, 750 warplanes and 4,400 tanks.

U.S.S.R. Arms Its Allies

(March 22, 1971, *Newsweek*) . . . The most important new factor has been the installation of an estimated 60 new missile sites. All told, the Egyptians now have some 180 Soviet-installed SAM-2 ground-to-air missiles and 240 of the more advanced SAM-3s. Egypt's air defense has been further bolstered by a Soviet radar system along the Mediterranean coast and by the addition of 50 new MIG-21s, giving Cairo an air force of 450 Soviet jets.

Howitzers

Beneath this air umbrella, the Russians have armed the 100,000 Egyptian troops along the canal with a vast array of modern weapons. This includes 750 Soviet-built tanks, 350 Czechoslovakian amphibious craft and perhaps as many as 1,000 artillery pieces. (Three dozen of these are the mighty Russian 203-millimeter howitzers, which can lob a 200-pound warhead on to Israel's Bar Lev line from 18 miles inside Egyptian lines.) There are also reports that the Egyptians have received Russian "Frog" ground-to-ground missiles which can fire 800-pound warheads 30 to 40 miles. And stiffening the Egyptian ranks, there are some 12,000 Russians— half of them operational troops manning SAM-3 sites and the MIG-21s. . . .*

Concerning Egypt's folly, we read the following:

. . . they have also seduced Egypt, even they that are the stay of the tribes thereof. The LORD hath mingled a perverse spirit in the midst thereof and they have caused Egypt to err in every work thereof, as a drunken man staggereth. . . (Isa. 19:13,14).

U.S. Reacts to the Soviet Threat

(February 25, 1971, *Daily Breeze*, Torrance, Calif.) Washington (UPI)—President Nixon said today the greatest danger of nuclear conflict lies in the Middle East where Soviet attempts to dominate the area "must and will be resisted."

Carter Says "Forever"

(May 2, 1978, *Jerusalem Post*) Washington—President Jimmy Carter yesterday told Prime Minister Menachem Begin that the U.S. will "never waiver" in its "absolute commitment to Israel's security," even though "we may, from time to time, have a transient difference with the leaders of Israel."

At a White House reception marking Israel's 30th anniversary of independence, the president declared that "the establishment of the nation of Israel was a fulfillment of Biblical prophecy," and he thanked God that Israel is strong today. . . .

Carter said he was proud that the U.S. was the first country to recognize Israel in 1948 and that the U.S. has since remained deeply committed to Israel's security.

"I can say, without reservation, as the President of the United

---

*Condensed from *Newsweek*, copyright Newsweek, Inc., 1971.

States of America, that we will continue to do so, not just for another 30 years, but forever," Carter said.

U.S. Strategy Defined

(March 28, 1971, *Daily Breeze*, Torrance, Calif.) (The Eaker Report)—. . . President Nixon, in his report to Congress February 25, in his State of the World message, introduced a new security label, "realistic deterrence." His secretary of defense, Melvin Laird, has now defined this new strategic term in his testimony March 9 before the Armed Services Committee of the House. . . .

Currently, according to this defense posture review, the United States and the U.S.S.R. have a rough parity in strategic-force nuclear capability. In general purpose forces, the U.S.S.R. greatly exceeds the United States in land forces, and its naval strength, although presently inferior to our Navy numerically, is increasing at an ominously rapid rate.

"Realistic deterrence" is dedicated to the proposition that we shall never allow the Russians to gain preponderant strategic superiority. We shall not now, however, attempt to match the present rate of Red strategic force buildup, relying for the time being upon the hope that SALT may reach agreements to insure strategic force parity. . . .

Hope Shattered by Reality

The hope of a SALT agreement retention of parity slipped in the Nixon administration, slid in the Ford administration, and disappeared in the Carter administration.

(June 12, 1978, *Newsweek*) The Soviet Union's powerful military buildup in recent years is often viewed solely in terms of a threat to Western Europe. NATO now finds itself badly outgunned, and many Western officials fear that the Russians mean either to launch a nuclear war or to crush Western Europe with a conventional attack. But the Soviets' new arsenal has also given them a new ability to project their military power to distant corners of the globe. . . .

B-52 in Flight

Equipped with two Hound Dog missiles, the intercontinental range B-52 heavy bomber can fly faster than 650 m.p.h. and either "on the deck" or at altitudes above 50,000 feet. With the air-launched missiles plus weapons carried in its bomb compartments, a B-52 can hit several targets hundreds of miles apart on one mission. (U.S. Air Force photo)

The Russians are now able to challenge the West in a way they were unable to do for lack of global reach during the Cuban missile crisis in 1962.*

(October 30, 1978, *U.S. News and World Report*) Even as Jimmy Carter and Leonid Brezhnev prepare to bolster détente through a new superpower arms agreement, strategic analysts are sounding this warning:

The U.S. faces a period of heightened danger rather than greater tranquility in its relations with Moscow, at least until the mid-1980s. . . .

By 1983, most analysts predict, Russia will achieve an unprecedented, but probably temporary, strategic advantage over the U.S. . . .

In this situation, strategic analysts warn, the Soviets will be tempted to exploit their military advantage before the U.S. can reverse the balance. . . .

In the words of one of the major contributors to this study, Prof. Samuel P. Huntington, director of Harvard University's Center for International Affairs: "Historically—and we can cite Hitler as an example—crises and conflicts occur when one power has gotten a lead and the other party wakes up and attempts to catch up. . . ."

The Russians in a decade have overcome a 2-to-1 American lead in strategic nuclear forces. They now are superior in overall numbers of launchers and in throwweight—the power of their missiles to carry nuclear warheads to a distant target. The U.S. still retains a significant advantage in accuracy and in the number of warheads that it can fire at individual targets.

But by 1983, the Pentagon calculates that the Soviets will add enough warheads and improve the accuracy of their ICBMs to the point where they could destroy America's land-based missile force of 1,000 Minutemen and 54 Titans in a single blow. . . . In military manpower, the Soviets now outnumber the U.S. by more than 2 to 1, or 4.4 million against 2.1 million. . . . There have been comparable increases in hardware. The Soviet tank inventory, for example, has grown from 35,000 to more than 50,000 while the artillery strength has gone up from 12,000 to 20,000 guns in a decade. . . .

What American strategists view as potentially most ominous is Russia's newly acquired capacity to project military power into areas far from its borders. . . . A Pentagon specialist points out that Soviet military literature and training manuals now devote increasing space to possible operations in distant parts of the world. He explains: "Soviet troops are being inculcated with the notion that they may be asked to go abroad to protect the coming world order. This contrasts with past emphasis on defense of the Soviet homeland. If this trend continues, it will have major significance for us."*

Summary of the Status of "Today"

The Soviets are at the brink of achieving, temporarily, strategic superiority over the U.S. and NATO forces. Their military literature portrays that they have worldwide visions and ambitions concerning "the coming world order." Their optimum time to achieve this goal is either now or soon!

Intervention in the Middle East crisis could give the Soviets the excuse to launch the strategic nuclear war we call World War III. The fate of the entire world is contingent on Soviet action in regard to the Arab-Israeli confrontation.

Israel, although confident of America's deterrent strength, is apprehensive, feeling that political factors may not allow the United States to move fast enough at the crucial moment. Israel's leaders know that when the moment of truth comes, the Arab-Russian thrust will be sudden, powerful, and all-out. It will be total war.

The worldwide stage is at flashpoint. Even now the moment of decision is being held back only by the hand of God. The next big move will be one of immense proportion.

*Copyright 1978, U.S. News and World Report, Inc.

22

THE SCENARIO

Amazing as it may seem, all prophecies pertaining to the destinies of the nations adjust to the declarations contained in Isaiah 19. It becomes a scenario of the coordinated order of events of "the time of the end."

"The burden of Egypt." This is the first phrase in the first verse of this chapter. Its message is, first of all, one of woe. It is a total portrayal of the soon-coming Tribulation period as seen by Isaiah, a prophet of Israel who lived over 2,500 years ago, in the 8th century B.C.

"Behold, The Lord Rideth"

Inasmuch as Isaiah lived 800 years before the church ever came into being, he could not conceive of its being "caught up" to be with the Lord. He did, however, describe that event which closes the church age: the translation, or rapture, of the church. He portrayed it in relation to his subject at hand: the destiny of Egypt—and he did so in a language that the Egyptians would understand.

Approximately 700 years before Isaiah walked upon the earth, Moses stood before Pharaoh and declared that the children of Israel should be released from their bondage to Egypt and that they should be allowed to return to their homeland of Canaan, now known as Palestine. Before Pharaoh was fully convinced, ten great plagues came upon the Egyptians. The most severe was the tenth and last one, for the decree of that plague was that the firstborn throughout all of the land of Egypt should die. It even took the life of the first born son of Pharaoh. The only ones spared were those who believed the message of Moses and who obeyed the specific direction of God that the blood of a sacrificed lamb should be applied to the doorposts and over the lintel (doorway) of their homes. God told Moses to instruct the children of Israel concerning this manner of protection, and that, wherever the blood was applied, he would "pass over" that house and spare the lives therein. This was the origin of the "Passover." Note the actual decree:

> For the LORD will pass through to smite the Egyptians; and when he seeth the blood upon the lintel, and on the two side posts, the LORD will pass over the door, and will not suffer the destroyer to come in unto your houses to smite you (Exod. 12:23).

That great smiting of the Egyptians has never been forgotten, even though it took place so long ago, for Exodus 12:30 records, ". . . and there was a great cry in Egypt; for there was not a house where there was not one dead."

Writing by the inspiration of God, Isaiah declared: "Behold, the LORD rideth upon a swift cloud" (Isa. 19:1). This shall be the first "burden" of Egypt.

The definition is that it coincides exactly with the New Testament prophecies concerning the Lord's coming again to receive His body, the church, unto Himself. Four Scripture quotations will verify this.

The loss of their infants will startle the Egyptians and cause "a great cry" to again be heard in that land.

1. Luke recorded the miraculous prophecy to the disciples of Christ at the time of His ascension into heaven (forty days after His bodily resurrection from the dead, as specified in Acts 1:3), as follows:

> And . . . while they beheld, he was taken up; and a cloud received

280

him out of their sight. And while they looked steadfastly toward heaven as he went up, behold, two men stood by them in white apparel; Which also said, Ye men of Galilee, why stand ye gazing up into heaven? this same Jesus, which is taken up from you into heaven, shall so come in like manner as ye have seen him go into heaven (Acts 1:9–11).

2. Paul, the apostle, wrote unto the church:

For this we say unto you by the word of the Lord, that we which are alive and remain unto the coming of the Lord shall not prevent them which are asleep [those who have died].

For the Lord himself shall descend from heaven with a shout, with the voice of the archangel, and with the trump of God: and the dead in Christ shall rise first:

Then we which are alive and remain shall be caught up together with them in the clouds, to meet the Lord in the air: and so shall we ever be with the Lord (1 Thess. 4:15–17).

3. As to the acceptance into heaven of innocent babes, this is clarified by Paul's inspired statement,

For I was alive without [Greek *choris* "apart from"] the law once: but when the commandment came [indicating an older child's willful, rebellious, and sinful breaking of a commandment of God], sin revived, and I died. For sin, taking occasion by the commandment, deceived me, and by it slew me [spiritually—necessitating forgiveness and the experience of being redeemed by faith in the atoning sacrifice of Christ—the Lamb of God—and being thusly, by a willful action of faith, "born again"] (Rom. 7:9,11).

4. Jesus spoke the following concerning little children:

. . . Suffer the little children to come unto me, and forbid them not: for of such is the kingdom of God. Verily I say unto you, Whosoever shall not receive [the Gospel of] the kingdom of God as a little child, he shall not enter therein (Mark 10:14,15).

The return of Christ just prior to the Tribulation period shall be an actual event, for at that time he shall take from this earth all of the innocent babes and all who are true believers in Him: "For God hath not appointed us unto wrath, but to obtain salvation by our Lord Jesus Christ" (1 Thess. 5:9); "and none of the wicked shall understand" (Dan. 12:10).

The disappearance of the believers and babes shall be worldwide and instantaneous, but Isaiah was led to drive the point home to the Egyptians to whom he was writing:

> . . . Behold, the LORD rideth upon a swift cloud, and shall come into Egypt: and the idols of Egypt shall be moved [shaken] at his presence, and the heart of Egypt shall melt in the midst of it (Isa. 19:1).

Egyptians Against the Egyptians

One of the reasons for the lack of solidarity among the Arab (Egyptian) nations is that the vast majority of them are Muslim in religion. They do not accept Jesus as Savior, but they do acknowledge him as a great teacher. They follow, however, the teachings of their prophet Mohammed concerning whom it is their creed that "There is one God, and Mohammed is his prophet." They do believe in God.

Russian advisers have been sent by the thousands into most of the Arab countries to proclaim Marxist atheism wherever they go. Seeking to win the young people to socialism, atheism, and communism, they have caused even more division and strife than the more passive Christian missionaries.

Thus it will be that when the Egyptians' infants disappear from the earth when they join the rest of the body of Christ "to meet the Lord in the air" when He comes to receive His body unto Himself, "the heart of Egypt shall melt in the midst of it. The confused Muslims shall turn against all others, bringing about the fulfillment of the next prophecy recorded in Isaiah 19:

> And I [God] will set the Egyptians against the Egyptians: and they shall fight every one against his brother, and every one against

his neighbor; city against city, and kingdom against kingdom. And the spirit of Egypt shall fail in the midst thereof, and I [God] will destroy the counsel thereof: and they shall seek to the idols, and to the charmers, and to them that have familiar spirits and to the wizards (Isa. 19:2–3).

Chaotic Conditions Elsewhere

The chaotic conditions of "brother against brother, neighbor against neighbor, etc." shall be but the momentary reaction of panic caused by the "disappearance" of the Christians and the infants. The Isaiah 19 prophecy applies it to "Egypt," but each nation on earth will have a crisis and panic conditions.

Western Europe to Receive a Leader

The main international developments will be in Western Europe, for all other alignments are already in their exact prophesied order.

As soon as the influence of the believers in Christ is removed by the divine act of their being "caught up" into heaven, a man of great prominence shall step forth from some portion of the old Roman Empire area of Western Europe. Jesus prophesied concerning this man when he stated: "I am come in my Father's name, and ye receive me not; if another shall come in his own name, him ye will receive" (John 5:43).

This man shall exalt himself and shall be greatly admired. "With all power and signs and lying wonders, and with all deceivableness," in fulfillment of 2 Thessalonians 2:8–12, he shall delude the people and their leaders to the extent that he shall be placed in high authority as "the king" of the ten-nation empire of Western Europe.

Proclaiming the message of "peace and safety," in fulfillment of 1 Thessalonians 5:3, the apostate end–time church of the world will lend its blessing, for these two entities are depicted as coming on the scene together. "He" shall then proceed to guarantee the security of Israel, and the preparation for World War III will be complete. When the Arabs and the Russians strike against Israel, America—being already committed to its assistance unilaterally—will join the fray. The "king" of the revived Roman Empire will be ready also, for he, according to the prophecies of the Scriptures, shall have made a covenant with Israel to assure its "peace and safety" for seven years.

The Starting Time of World War III

The total Tribulation period, referred to in the Scriptures as "the time of Jacob's trouble," shall consist of but one week of years (seven years), it being the 70th week of prophetic years referred to by Jeremiah and explained in Daniel 9. Of this final seven years of "the times of the Gentiles," it is stated in Revelation 17:12,13 that the ". . . ten kings, who have received no kingdom as yet . . . receive power as kings one hour with the beast. These have one mind and shall give their power and strength unto the beast" (the end-time "king").

On the historically proven basis of one week representing seven years and thus one day equalling one year, one hour would represent one twenty-fourth of one year—a period of two weeks.

Most likely, therefore, within two weeks of time from the translation of the saints into heaven, all basic adjustments will have been made and the long-sought-for "guarantee" of Israel's security will be a signed agreement, the covenant prophesied in Daniel 9:27. When this takes place, earth's history will be at the point referred to in the key verse of Daniel 11:40—"at the time of the end"—meaning literally, at the beginning of the time of the end.

Section VII

CORRELATED SCENARIO OF WORLD WAR III

Brezhnev poses with Soviet military leaders.

23

THE FIRST BATTLE
OF WORLD WAR III

The first battle—the starting gun of World War III—will be
that of the renewal of the Egyptian thrust, in force, against
Israel. This will take place only when ordered by the Kremlin,
for the Russians are to make the next move.

Grechko on the Go

(October 1970, *Reader's Digest*) From his office at the Soviet
Defense Ministry in Moscow, ramrod-straight, impeccably uni-
formed Marshal of the Soviet Union Andrei Antonovich Grechko,
76, minister of defense of the U.S.S.R. . . . commands an efficient,
modern armed force of 3,320,000 men and oversees the Soviet's
swift nuclear-arms buildup. He also has charge of the military side of
the Warsaw Pact, where forces of the Soviet satellites, together
with Soviet forces, make up the world's most powerful and well-
coordinated assembly of conventional military might. . . .

(April 3, 1971, *Los Angeles Times*) Moscow (UPI)—Defense
Minister Andrei A. Grechko said Friday "the forces of reaction are
preparing to unleash terrible war," but the Soviet Union would win
with nuclear missiles that can hit any target on earth.
   Grechko delivered his hypothetical scenario for nuclear war in an
address to the 5,000 delegates . . . to the Communist Party Congress
. . . Grechko's words were blunt. . . . "We are strengthening our

army, not for attack but for defense. However, our armed forces are always ready to chastise the aggressor and right on that territory from which he dares violate our borders," he said. "Our army is equipped with weapons of great destructive force and capable of reaching any point on the globe, on land, sea, and air."

Western studies of the Soviet missile arsenal say their biggest long-range punch is the SS-9 Scarp rocket, estimated to be able to hurl a 35-megaton warhead about 6,600 miles. The Russians are also believed to have orbiting space bombs. . . .

Grechko singled out the United States for condemnation in a related portion of his address. "American imperialism has never stopped preparations for aggression," he said.

From Bluster to Boast

Former Russian Defense Minister Andrei A. Grechko and former Premier Nikita Khrushchev were the sabre rattlers and outstanding spokesmen in the early days of the Soviet arms buildup. They talked tough when the Russian strategic strength was tender (but growing). Khrushchev proclaimed on numerous occasions: "We will bury you!"

After the demise of these two militarists, however, it became more expedient for Russia to try to hide its fast-growing military power. Braggadocio gave way to Dimitry Z. Manuilski's ploy of "peace movements" and Leonid I. Brezhnev's deceitful détente. The Soviets did not want the West to know how strong they were becoming. Manuilski's plans were bearing fruit: The capitalist countries were "stupid and decadent" and the Russians were preparing "the element of surprise."

At about the time the Western powers realized the dangerous extent of the Soviet strategic buildup, Communist boss Leonid I. Brezhnev broke the silence of the years of "peace overtures and unheard of concessions." Russia was achieving "temporary" strategic advantage!

In 1973, at a meeting of top East European Communists, Leonid I. Brezhnev admitted that détente was a hoax on the West—a smokescreen to hide the fact that Russia is building immense, world-threatening power. "Furthermore," he said, "the trick is working. By 1985, Soviet power will be so irresistable that Russia will be able to do as it wishes anywhere on the globe."

In addition, Soviet civil defense has been preparing at a fever pitch, *knowing* that a nuclear war is coming.

(February 15, 1978, *Daily News Digest*, Phoenix, Ariz.) The Soviets have deployed and developed the most intensive system of nuclear shelters for its military leadership, its civilian leadership, its industrial factory workers and its civilian population ever deployed or built in history, and the result of that is that if the Soviets attacked today, and I have no reason to think they would try that, but if they did attack today, about 160,000,000 Americans would die, and probably no more than 5,000,000 Russians. . . .

Our communications resources, by and large, are all soft and unprotected, and basically we've done nothing to shelter the American people. In the beltway around Moscow, we discovered that the Soviets have built 75 giant underground command posts for their military and civil defense leaders. These are buildings that are the size of the White House, dug down in the earth several hundred feet deep, covered by 200, or 300 or 400 feet of earth and as much as 75 feet of reinforced concrete. They have protected water. They have protected power generators and communications and the cost of building just one of these was assessed here in the US at somewhere around $500 million. We found 75, all complete. . . . And then in looking around the Soviet Union we found an additional 1,500, all the way from Vladivostok westward, all complete and ready to go to war. . . .

My friends, *it is later than you think!*

Nasser's Successor Chosen by Kremlin

(October 13, 1970, *Daily Breeze*, Torrance, Calif.) Beirut, Lebanon (AP)—President Gamal Abdel Nasser named his successor shortly before he died, but his nominee is under house arrest because he is unacceptable to the Soviet Union, reliable diplomatic informants reported today.

The sources said Nassar's deathbed choice to lead Egypt was Zakaria Mohieddin, a relatively liberal former prime minister who at times embarrassed his chief by opposing the growing Soviet penetration of Egypt. Nasser reportedly expressed his last wish to Information Minister Mohammed Heikal, one of his closest friends, who was at his bedside when the president died of heart failure Sept. 28. The information reached the foreign diplomats from some of Heikal's associates.

The Arab Socialist Union, Egypt's only political party, nominated Vice President Anwar Sadat to succeed Nasser, and he will be elected Thursday in a nationwide referendum in which he is the only candidate . . .

The diplomats said Soviet Premier Alexei Kosygin, when he came to Cairo for Nassar's funeral, told the Egyptian leaders the Soviet government would have no confidence in a government headed by Mohieddin. . . .

Heikal, long-time editor of the semi-official newspaper *Al Ahram* and Nasser's mouthpiece for many years, tried to convince the other Egyptian leaders to honor Nasser's last wish despite the Soviet veto of Mohieddin, the informant said.

(October 18, 1970, *Los Angeles Times*) Cairo—Anwar Sadat was sworn in Saturday as president of the United Arab Republic, succeeding the late Gamal Abdel Nasser. . . .

The ceremony completed his move to the top. A colleague of Nasser for 32 years, Sadat had been interim president since the former's death Sept. 28. Then in a national referendum Thursday, Sadat was formally elected president by 90.04 per cent of the vote.

Sadat Establishes His Regime

(June 3, 1971, *Copley News Service*) Beirut—Throughout the reign of the late Gamal Abdel Nasser, there was not a single power struggle as sharp, decisive and intriguing as the one which shook Egypt recently under Nasser's successor, 52-year-old Anwar Sadat. . . .

In a bold stroke, he dismissed Sabry from the vice presidency on

May 2. Eleven days later, he took all powers into his own hands when he announced to the nation in a dramatic speech that a plot against him had been foiled. All those involved in it, including six ministers, three top leaders of Egypt's only political organization, the Arab Socialist Union (ASU), and several members of the ASU Central Committee and National Assembly, were arrested pending their trial. The war minister, Lt. Gen. Mohammed Fawzi, was placed under house arrest.

Sadat also announced his decision to dissolve the present structure of the ASU in order to hold new elections from the base to the top. The purge has affected nearly all the political institutions in the country, leaving the Egyptian leader all the powers of a dictator. . . .

Sadat and the Russians

Anwar Sadat became president of Egypt with the nod of approval from the Kremlin. He continued in their apparent favor and accepted thousands of Russians into Egypt as technicians and advisers. Much war equipment was supplied and more Russians came, but Sadat was not pleased. He asked for the best equipment and was ignored.

During the times Sadat went to Moscow from March of 1971 until June 1, 1972, he tried in vain to get sophisticated weaponry. On the latter date, according to a special report in *Newsweek*, he said, "I sent Brezhnev a seven-point questionnaire and made very clear that the future policy of Egypt would hinge on his answers."

On July 7, 1972, Russian ambassador Vinogradov called on President Sadat with the reply. Again it was negative. Sadat's reaction follows:

(August 7, 1972, *Newsweek*) Two weeks ago, Egypt's President Anwar Sadat startled the world by announcing that he had ordered thousands of Soviet military men stationed in his country to pack up and go home.

In a private meeting with a select group of Egyptian newspaper publishers, he divulged the dramatic story behind his decision. Last week, from talks with participants, *Newsweek* Senior Editor Arnaud de Borchgrave reconstructed Sadat's speech. Below, excerpts:

"You cannot imagine what my life has been like since I became President. There has hardly been a quiet day without some quarrel with the Russians. They never trusted me. They said I was pro-American and convinced (former Egyptian Vice President) Aly Sabry that I was selling Egypt out to the Americans. My tongue went dry arguing with them.

"When I went to Moscow in March 1971 and made our first request for MIG-23s, which we needed to counter the Phantoms the Americans were giving the Israelis, I was told (that the advanced Soviet fighters) were so complicated to fly it would take five years to train our Egyptian pilots. I knew this was nonsense, as my own experts had told me it would only take six months to convert a pilot from MIG-21s to MIG-23s. The Russians said they could only supply these planes with Soviet pilots and that they would have to remain under Russian command. I told them this was an unacceptable breach of Egyptian sovereignty. But they would not relent. . . .

"I visited the Soviet Union two more times. . . . More empty and broken promises. I then decided the time had come to clarify our relations once and for all. On June 1 (1972), I sent Brezhnev a seven-point questionnaire and made very clear that the future policy of Egypt would hinge on his answers. I wanted to know whether—yes or no—they planned to supply the weaponry we had repeatedly requested. . . .

"On July 7, I was informed that Vinogradov wanted to see me right away. Hafez Ismail and another assistant were present when the ambassador walked into the room. He said he had received Moscow's reply. . . .

"The first page was a reminder of the warm and friendly relations that had governed Soviet-Egyptian relations and so on. The second page was an attack against (Mohammed Hassanein) Heikal (the powerful editor of Al Ahram and Sadat's confidant) as the man allegedly responsible for the deterioration in these good relations. The third page was only a continuation of the attack against Heikal. And then nothing. Silence. I looked up and said, 'What about my answers?' Vinogradov, visibly embarrassed, said that was all he received from Moscow.

"I got very angry and immediately dictated my orders—in front of Vinogradov: (1) All Soviet advisers in the Egyptian armed forces were to leave within ten days, beginning July 17; (2) All Soviet military installations were to be handed over to Egyptian control; (3) All Soviet equipment must be sold to Egypt or taken out of the country; (4) All further negotiations between Egypt and the Soviet Union are to be conducted in Cairo and nowhere else.

"Vinogradov left for Moscow immediately. The next thing I knew was the arrival of (Syrian) President Assad, direct from Moscow. He asked how I could do such a thing when he had just signed a long-term agreement with the Soviet Union for $700 million worth of arms. I told him not to worry about us and to do what he thought was good for Syria. . . ."*

From that moment on, President Anwar Sadat was prepared to go it alone. Since help was not forthcoming, his only alternative seemed to be some form of Arab action apart from Soviet military assistance. Soviet arms, however, continued to flow into Egypt as well as into Syria.

(July 9, 1973, *Newsweek*) Syria has attained most–favored–nation status for Soviet arms. So far this year, Damascus has received $185 million worth of Russian armament, including planes, tanks and the Strela shoulder-fired anti-aircraft missile (a most successful weapon for the communists in Vietnam). The total for Syria during all of 1972 was $150 million. More than 1,400 Soviet technicians are also in Syria to help with the new material.**

(July 5, 1973, *Daily Breeze*, Torrance, Calif.) Cairo (UPI)—Hafez Ismail, an adviser to Egyptian president Anwar Sadat, returned from a three-day visit to Moscow Saturday and said the Soviet Union and Egypt are in total accord on their future relationship and the Middle East crisis.

Ismail told newsmen the Soviet Union is determined to strengthen the Egyptian and Arab capability to confront the Zionist occupation, which is backed by imperialism, until this aggression is liquidated and the aspirations of the Palestinian people are realized.

"The two sides are in total accord in their assessment of the Middle East situation," Ismail said. "They are also in agreement on future steps they will take . . ."

(September 11, 1973, *Jerusalem Post*) Beersheba—"Egypt is still receiving huge quantities of arms from the U.S.S.R. though this fact gets no publicity," Defense Minister Moshe Dayan said here Sunday.

The vast supply of arms to Syria and Egypt (and to other Arab nations) was not without its intent. On October 6, 1973, the Arabs launched the Yom Kippur War.

The Yom Kippur War

On the Jewish holy day of Atonement, Yom Kippur, October 6, 1973, the Arabs of Syria and Egypt attacked Israel simultaneously.

The Syrians, with help from Iraq and Jordan, launched a fierce tank attack against Israeli positions on the Golan Heights, while Egypt sent a massive attack force against the Israeli Bar Lev line along the Suez Canal.

Fighting a delaying action on the Egyptian front, the Israelis concentrated their air power and tank forces in an all-out effort to stop the invasion from the north. They gained the upper hand in fierce fighting there, and by October 12 Israeli armored divisions were within eighteen miles of Damascus.

In the meantime, Egyptian forces had broken the vaunted Bar Lev line of defense on the east bank of the Suez, and by October 11 there were 60,000 Egyptian troops in the Sinai.

The Israelis, by this time being in command on the northern front, dug in for a holding position half way to Damascus and rumbled all the tanks they could spare south to the Sinai. Also, U.S. military replacement equipment began arriving in Israel.

(October 13, 1973, *Los Angeles Times*) Washington—The United States has begun an extensive airlift to replace military equipment, including F-4 Phantom jets, lost by Israel in the Middle East war, according to informed sources.

"The U.S. decision to replace heavy Israeli losses counters a Soviet move three days ago to airlift military supplies to Egypt and Syria," the sources said. . . .

The United States now intends to resupply Israel "with whatever it needs," one source said.

The two most critical areas of Israeli losses are in jet aircraft and tanks. U.S. intelligence reports indicate that Israel has lost some 95 combat planes in less than a week of fighting. The intelligence figure for Israeli tanks knocked out of action stands at about 600, about one-third of its tank force.

(October 17, 1973, *Los Angeles Times*) The United States has shipped about 500 tons of military equipment to Israel since the weekend, according to U.S. officials. The equipment arrived aboard the first 30 American transport planes to land in Israel. The Administration figures do not include supplies ferried to Israel by Israeli and chartered aircraft, as well as other equipment on the way to that country on ships. . . .

U.S. officials said the Soviet Union has flown more than 300 cargo flights with 5,000 tons of military equipment to the Arabs in the first six days of the airlift.

(October 23, 1973, *Jerusalem Post*) The American airlift to Israel was described by the Defense Department Monday as so big that U.S. civilian airlines have been pressed into service.

U.S. and Soviet ships squared off in the Mediterranean, the Soviets totaling 71 ships, including 16 submarines there by Oct. 20. The U.S. Sixth Fleet had 49 ships including two aircraft carriers, their support ships and submarines. Each fleet nervously watched the other.

On land, the Israelis were turning the tide.

(October 23, 1973, *Jerusalem Post*) Tel Aviv—An Israeli armoured unit Monday routed the remnants of the Iraqi division in Syria. The Iraqi force no longer exists as a fighting unit, according to military sources.

The Air Force, which on Monday provided cover for the Israeli operation against the Iraqis and also bombed targets deep inside

Syria and Egypt, is now for the first time in this war, able to strike where and when it wants to on either front, the sources said.

In a bold thrust, an Israeli tank column crossed the Suez Canal near Bitter Lake and fanned out in both directions, silencing Egyptian tanks and overrunning SAM missile sites.

(October 23, 1973, *Jerusalem Post*) Washington (AP)—U.S. military sources report that at least 12,000 Israeli troops and 200 tanks have poured across the Suez Canal. . . .

In short order, Israel controlled over 500 square miles of African Egypt, coming within 12 miles of Cairo.

Sending a curt note to Washington, and acting unilaterally, the Soviet Union put seven airborne divisions on high alert, relocated much of its air transport planes to bases near the airborne divisions—apparently to move troops if necessary—and sent several amphibious ships steaming toward Egypt, according to U.S. intelligence sources.

This information reportedly led Pres. Nixon, at a 3 a.m. emergency session of the National Security Council, to order a full alert of U.S. strategic forces worldwide.

(October 28, 1973, *Daily Breeze*, Torrance, Calif.) The "precautionary alert" of U.S. forces this week around the world served its purpose and served it well. . . .

The Soviet Union was testing us by alerting its own armed forces and announcing plans to send a "peacekeeping" force to the Middle East whether the United States liked it or not.

After President Nixon's response, Moscow dropped its plan and joined in urging the United Nations to pursue what was really the only realistic course—to try to supervise an Arab-Israeli truce with a force excluding any of the nuclear powers, especially the two superpowers.

(October 24, 1973, *Los Angeles Times*) A second Mideast cease-fire—after renewed fighting had broken an earlier truce called by the United Nations—was agreed to by Israel and Egypt early today, an Israeli military communique said. . . . Syria Tuesday night accepted the initial U.N. cease-fire resolution.

(October 27, 1973, *Daily Breeze*, Torrance, Calif.) Washington (UPI)—President Nixon relaxed the worldwide alert of 2.3 million U.S. servicemen and nuclear bombers Friday and declared the outlook for permanent peace in the Mideast is the best in 20 years.

Arab Audacity

Arab rationale is amazing.

Israeli forces were 18 miles from Damascus; the Egyptian 3rd Army was trapped and cut off in the Sinai, and Israeli advance forces were occupying 500 square miles of Egyptian territory between the Suez Canal and Cairo. In addition, U.S. military forces had been put on worldwide "precautionary alert" to offset any possible Soviet intervention.

Ignoring all these preposterous odds, Egyptian President Anwar Sadat announced that "Egypt would accept the cease-fire if Israeli forces withdrew from all territories occupied since the 1967 Arab-Israeli war"—as though he had won the war!

He knew the superpowers did not want a war of extinction and that the U.S. was not likely to fight the U.S.S.R. to force his hand. He virtually turned the tables and claimed the victory. U.S. and U.N. pressure caused the Israeli army to back off and sign the cease-fire that established U.N. forces along the Suez Canal. International pressure continued and Israel withdrew to the 1974-negotiated cease-fire line east of the Mitla and Gidda mountain passes in the Sinai.

Sadat's Peace Initiative

On November 19, 1977, Egyptian President Anwar Sadat made his historic pilgrimage for peace by going to Jerusalem. He spoke to Prime Minister Menachem Begin and brought a public address to the Israeli Knesset (parliament). In so doing, he granted de facto recognition of a legal State of Israel. In exchange, he asked for the return of all Arab territories occupied by Israel and for the establishment of an independent Palestinian state—the latter a condition Israel rejects.

(The Egyptian-Israeli peace talks began at that point and have proceeded to date, Camp David being the summit of summits. President Sadat, President Carter, and Prime Minister Begin, together with the appointed associates of each, met at Camp David, Maryland, September 5 to September 17, 1978. At the close of that marathon session the three leaders gathered at the White House in Washington Sunday night, September 17, and signed the historic "Framework For Peace in the Middle East" and a separate "Framework For Conclusion of a Peace Treaty Between Egypt and Israel." Shuttle diplomacy concerning these "framework" treaties brought about several changes, but the founding principle, that of U.N. resolution 242, remained as the core of the negotiations for peace.)

Arab Reaction

Morocco and Sudan rather quickly approved Sadat's peace initiative and called on other Arab states to do likewise. Saudi Arabia and Jordan adopted a wait-and-see attitude of caution and moderation. But while some Arab entities were passive, five others met in Algiers on February 4, 1978, and formed a "resistance front" to oppose Sadat. The five consisted of Algiers, Libya, Syria, South Yemen, and the Palestine Liberation Organization (PLO). An article in the *Los Angeles Times*, February 5, 1978, stated:

> The declaration said the five members were seeking the support of Moslem, non-aligned and Socialist countries "with the U.S.S.R. at their head."

They established a $1 billion fund to overthrow Sadat and to torpedo the Camp David-inspired peace talks.

The Arab League
The twenty one–nation Arab League (minus Egypt and plus the PLO) met in Baghdad, Iraq, November 5, 1978, voted a $3.5

Sadat, Carter, and Begin celebrate the Camp David peace "frameworks" at the White House.

billion war fund "to continue the armed confrontation with the Jewish state," and reaffirmed that "the Palestine Liberation Organization (PLO) is the sole representative of the Palestinian people." The league set only very minor political and economic sanctions against Sadat's Egypt.

Of the $3.5 billion war fund, $1.85 billion went to Syria, $1.2 to Jordan, and 450 million to the PLO. Yasser Arafat, leader of the PLO, praised the conference as a "huge success."

Not So Peaceful Sadat: Cautious and Wily

In March, 1975, President Anwar Sadat said, "If we are attacked, or if the enemy continues to procrastinate and deny our rights or the rights of our brothers, then we have only one plan, from which we will not deviate, which is jihad (Moslem Holy War)."

(June 28, 1977, *Los Angeles Times*) Moses Well, Egyptian Sinai— Apparently alarmed over increasingly hard-line remarks from the Israeli government of Menachem Begin, Egypt has begun stressing a new readiness to fight another Mideast war, if necessary, to regain Arab land lost in the Arab-Israeli wars of 1967 and 1973. . . .

"Sadat bought support for his peace strategy by promising his officers and some reluctant Arab governments that if the talk failed he would resort again to the military option," said one diplomatic observer.

(December 5, 1977, *Los Angeles Times*) Cairo—President Anwar Sadat of Egypt said Sunday that Israeli leaders must be willing to make concessions if they want to safeguard the mutual nonaggression pledge that capped his mission to Jerusalem. If Israel does not, Sadat said, "they will have to face the consequences. . . . We will have a new situation."

(December 13, 1977, *Jerusalem Post*) President Sadat, interviewed shortly after meeting with U.S. Secretary of State Cyrus Vance, said he had agreed to no more war in return for an Israeli agreement "to put everything on the table and to talk like civilized people. If this does not happen, we shall return to being barbarians."

(June 7, 1978, *Los Angeles Times*) Cairo (AP)—President Anwar Sadat told troops stationed at the Suez Canal Tuesday to brace for a continued "battle of liberation" if Israel does not respond satisfactorily to his peace overtures.

"You are carrying out your duties every day for the defense of Egypt and for the completion of the battle of liberation if there is no alternative," Sadat told the 2nd Army soldiers.

Egypt: A Military Powerhouse?

Two news items from October and November, 1977, convey

an important point. Sadat is not negotiating from a position of weakness, but of military power:

> (October 7, 1977, *Los Angeles Times*) Western military observers say there are numerous signs that the Egyptian military machine may be even stronger today than it was when Sadat launched the 1973 war. Logistical capabilities reportedly have been substantially improved with the addition of a large number of Mercedes transport trucks.
>
> Armored equipment remains in good enough shape for the military to run full-scale desert maneuvers every two months or so. "That tells you something," a military source said. "An army that can maneuver as often as this one isn't hurting for spare parts or equipment on the ground." He added that the maneuvers have been extremely well planned and executed.

> (November 23, 1977, *Jerusalem Post*) What could have prompted Chief of Staff Mordechai Gur into making his public statement that Egypt was preparing for war? In his interview, he himself cited the fact that the Egyptian army was conducting military offensive maneuvers on an unprecedented level. He claimed as well that the Egyptians have built 350 outposts as part of two large-scale entrenchment systems along the east side of the Suez Canal that could absorb five Egyptian divisions simultaneously. . . .
>
> But what Gur did not mention was a report in the American "Armed Forces Journal" that a two-year $6 billion arms modernization plan has just been launched by the Egyptians.
>
> The "Journal" quotes one Western observer as claiming that the plan will make Egypt "a military powerhouse. . . ."
>
> Points covered by the plan include:
> *Purchase of 200 Alpha Jets from Britain. . . .
> *Transfer of 36 Mirage 111E and 40 Mirage F-1 fighters to Egypt from Saudi Arabia.
> *Overhaul of all of Egypt's 200 Mig-21 fighters and installation of new navigational and attack systems.
> *Purchase of 400 British-made Lynx helicopters.
> *Modernization of 12 Hawker-Siddeley 748 short-field transports.
> *Purchase of 21,000 Swingfire anti-tank missiles mounted on new landrovers.
> *Overhaul of Egypt's missile-boat fleet. . . .

*Refurbishing all Egypt's Soviet T-55 tanks. . . .
*New and highly improved fuses for all 122mm and 130mm artillery shells.
*Purchase of 12 Teledyne Ryan pilotless aircraft from the U.S.
*Another 14 Lockheed C-130 transports—also from the U.S.

Egypt in Retrospect

A rather lengthy resume has been given concerning the recent history of Egypt. It has been presented to reveal a paradox: talks of peace, but very extensive preparations for war.

Sadat is more shrewd than most. He turned Israel's almost sure victory of October 1973, into a negotiated compromise. He held a hard negotiating stance and gained control of virtually all he had lost militarily. He talked peace. A hint of his long-range intent, however, is seen in the following:

> (January 2, 1978, *Los Angeles Times*) . . . "We should renounce the policy of either getting everything or rejecting everything," Sadat said in remarks published in the weekly Cairo magazine "October." "We should get what we can get until we can get all that we want."

President Anwar Sadat of Egypt still wants "the whole thing." He will side with the rejectionist states and the Soviet Union when the time comes for the showdown fight with Israel.

Bible Prophecy

Current events are not just random happenings. The nations of one third of the world are in the exact and precise alignments that the inspired writers of the Scriptures declared that they would be "at the time of the end" and "in the latter days"; and these declarations were permanently recorded many centuries ago. It is important to remember this fact, for just as surely as the alignments are set, even so are the actions and conflicts of those alignments—and the end results thereof. This is all by divine foreknowledge. God knows the thoughts and intents of the hearts of men, and He directs their destinies in full accordance therewith, for we are accountable to God. A direct quotation of this fact is recorded in the Bible as follows:

> For the word of God is quick, and powerful, and sharper than any two-edged sword, piercing even to the dividing asunder of soul and spirit, and of the joints and marrow, and is a discerner of the thoughts and intents of the heart.
> Neither is there any creature that is not manifest in his sight: but all things are naked and opened unto the eyes of him with whom we have to do (Heb. 4:12,13).

It might be well to point out at this point, also, that "God is not the author of confusion, but of peace," as stated in 1 Corinthians 14:33, and in the ultimate end of it all,

> . . . God shall wipe away all tears from their eyes; and there shall be no more death, neither sorrow, nor crying, neither shall there be any more pain: for the former things are passed away.
> And he that sat upon the throne said, Behold, I make all things new. And he said unto me, Write: for these words are true and faithful (Rev. 21:4,5).

It is because a sinful world must be judged by a righteous God that the events which are immediately before us must and will come to pass; and then will come peace.

Atheistic Russia Attacks "God's Land"

It is written in Ezekiel 38 that God is against the primary leader of the U.S.S.R. referred to as "Gog, the chief prince of Meshech and Tubal." This Scripture portion declares also that the Arab nations of ancient "Persia, Ethiopia and Libya" will be in league with Russia and the Warsaw Pact nations, and, likewise, that a Russian ruler "will be a guard unto them," and will be "the chief prince."

Ezekiel 38:8 declares that "in the latter years" this combina-

tion of powers will "come into the land that is brought back from
the sword, and is gathered out of many people, against the
mountains of Israel, . . ."

It is further said of Russia:

> Thou shalt ascend and come like a storm . . . like a cloud to cover
> the land, thou, and all thy bands, and many people with thee. Thus
> saith the Lord God: It shall also come to pass . . . thou shalt think an
> evil thought; and thou shalt say, I will go up to the land of unwalled
> villages [kibbutzim] . . . to take a spoil, and to take a prey; to turn
> thine hand upon the desolate places that are now inhabited, and
> upon the people that are gathered out of the nations, . . . (Ezek.
> 38:9–12).

Whereas, according to this prophecy, the "chief prince" of the
U.S.S.R. is to "think an evil thought," etc., it is specified that
God is fully aware of that thought and intent, and we find the
following decree:

> Thou shalt come from thy place out of the north parts, thou, and
> many people with thee, . . . a mighty army: and thou shalt come up
> against my people of Israel, as a cloud to cover the land; it shall be in
> the latter days, and I will bring thee against my land, . . . and it shall
> come to pass at the same time when Gog shall come against the land
> of Israel, saith the Lord GOD, that my fury will come up in my face.
>
> Surely in that day there shall be a great shaking in the land of
> Israel; . . . and all the men that are upon the face of the earth, shall
> shake at my presence, and the mountains shall be thrown down, and
> the steep places shall fall, and every wall shall fall to the ground.
>
> And I will call for a sword against him [Gog] throughout all my
> mountains, saith the Lord GOD: every man's sword shall be against
> his brother (Ezek. 38:15–21).

The Order of the Attack

The fact of the attack against Israel has been documented
above. For correlation, we now turn to the Book of Daniel to
find the precise time and manner of that attack. The key verse

of Daniel 11:40 gives us this information, specifying that it shall be "at the time of the end":

> And at the time of the end shall the king of the south push at him: and the king of the north shall come against him like a whirlwind, . . . (Dan. 11:40).

Four major factors are brought out in the first portion of this verse:

1. It is the initial action of the war—"at the time of the end."

2. The attack is specified, even though the context shows that it is directed against the land of Israel, as being "against him"; indicating thereby that "the king" of the revived Roman Empire area has already signed or otherwise given his "covenant" with Israel, assuring Israel of his military "guarantee" of its security.

3. Although Russia is known to be "the guard" and "the stay" of the Egyptians as specified in Ezekiel 38:8 and in Isaiah 19:13, it is declared that the first attack shall occur when "the king of the south" shall "push at him."

4. After the "Egyptians" make the initial thrust, the mighty Russian military colossus "shall come against him like a whirlwind. . . ."

Egypt's Compliance in Spite of Fears

Egypt's President Anwar Sadat declared to Russian President Nikolai V. Podgorny, on the occasion of Podgorny's visit to inaugurate the official opening of the Aswan High Dam, "Egypt will be a faithful friend because we can never forget your help. . . ."

Thus it shall be, that when the Kremlin's leader (or military leader, whichever one is to be the prophesied "Gog" of "the time of the end") gives the order—in spite of the fact that Egypt may still be in turmoil due to the various reactions of the Muslims, agnostics, socialists, and atheists as a result of the "disappearance" of the babes (and of the adult Christians) when the Lord takes out His own; and also very possibly because the worldwide broadcasts will have brought news of the deluding "lie" which will be proclaimed from Rome as being the so-called reason for the disappearance of so many people from every country on the face of the earth—the Egyptian army, led by, or at least influenced by Russian "advisers," and with the promise of Russian military intervention from "out of the north parts," will open up the massive military move against the land of Israel.

The accompanying cartoon, published in the *Los Angeles Times* on August 1, 1970, may well depict the inner fears of the Egyptians, for it was at the Red Sea in 1447 B.C. that Egypt's army was destroyed when it sought to recapture Moses and the children of Israel.

The Bible account is as follows:

> And Moses stretched forth his hand over the sea, and the sea returned to his strength when the morning appeared; and the Egyptians fled against it; and the Lord overthrew the Egyptians in the midst of the sea.
>
> And the waters returned, and covered the chariots, and the horsemen, and all the host of Pharaoh that came into the sea . . . there remained not so much as one of them. . . .
>
> Thus the Lord saved Israel that day out of the hand of the Egyptians (Exod. 14:27–30).

When Egypt Strikes!

When Egypt strikes at Israel, in spite of the Western assurances of aid to the Israelis, it would be because Egypt's leaders have been given "confidential" information that America will be so devastated by the Soviet first–strike thermonuclear attack that it will be unable to respond with a nuclear counterattack against them.

Most conspicuous is the total absence of any reference anywhere in the Bible of any assistance to Israel from anyone other than from "the king" of the ten–nation revived Roman Empire. There just is no other prophecy in this regard.

The Egyptians will be given to understand that they shall

"Yes, this is the way to Israel . . . why?"
(May 28, 1971, *Daily Breeze*, Torrance, Calif.)

only have Israel itself to contend with, for the strategic arsenal of the U.S.S.R. will be directed against its primary foe, America. If it were to be directed against the land of Israel, which is no larger than the state of Massachusetts, there would be no Israel left to contend with nor to acquire.

Almost Simultaneously: "From the Ends of Heaven"

Russia is fully aware of the U.S. commitment to help Israel. It knows that a renewed Egyptian advance in force against the Israelis automatically calls for that aid. Therefore, when Egypt strikes as "the king of the south," Russia's "whirlwind" attack must be poised and ready to obliterate the massive power of the U.S.

There can thusly be only one logical answer—and it is in exact compliance with the various prophecies—Russia will launch its first strike against the people "terrible from their beginning hitherto," to quote the Isaiah 18:2 description of the U.S., at virtually the same moment that Egypt leads the Arab assault against Israel.

Within fifteen minutes of the launching of the Soviet missile assault against the U.S., the American military will retaliate. In this age of computerized millisecond phase-array radar and of watch-dog satellites, no decision of Congress will be needed. The response will be automatic and swift and profound. Then will come to pass the fulfillment:

> The noise of a multitude in the mountains, like as of a great people; a tumultuous noise of the kingdoms of nations gathered together: the LORD of hosts mustereth the host of the battle.
>
> They come from a far country, from the [opposite] end of heaven, even the LORD, and the weapons of his indignation, to destroy the whole land.
>
> Howl ye; for the day of the LORD is at hand; it shall come as a destruction from the Almighty (Isa. 13:4–6).

The Multitude in the Mountains

Anticipating a complete devastation of America from so mighty an attack, the Kremlin leader, "Gog," shall have ordered the mighty land army of the U.S.S.R. and of the Warsaw Pact region into position to attack Israel "out of the north parts," from the Syrian and Lebanese mountain area. (Recall that Lebanon was formed September 1, 1920, as a haven for the Christians of the Arab states, its president always to be a Christian, and its premier always a Moslem.) Today Lebanon is considered one-half Christian. This has been a major reason for Lebanon's resistance to the Arab guerrilla movement. When the prophesied "translation" of the church takes place, however, those Christians will be "caught up" with the rest of us, which will leave the way clear for the Russian-Warsaw Pact army to gather there in readiness to "come from thy place out of the north parts" in fulfillment of Ezekiel 38:15.

The "multitude in the mountains" of Isaiah 13:4 is seen to be identical with the "mighty army" of Ezekiel 38:15, and is a part of "the host" mustered to the battle.

Russia's Error

Russia's great error is in its atheism and in not taking into consideration the power and judgments of the Lord God. This it shall learn—to its sorrow. God's decree against the army of "Gog" and against his home base of "the land of Magog" is given in Ezekiel 38 and 39. It starts as follows:

> . . . Thus saith the LORD GOD; Behold, I am against thee, O Gog, the chief prince of Meshech [Moscow] and Tubal [Tobolsk]: and I will turn thee back. . . (Ezek. 38:3).

After giving the alignment of the nations that are to accompany the U.S.S.R. in its "evil thought" referred to in Ezekiel 38:10, and after mentioning the futile efforts of the United

Nations described in Ezekiel 38:13 as "Sheba, and Dedan, and the merchants of Tarshish, with all the young lions [nations] thereof" wherein they say, "Art thou come to take a spoil? . . . and to take a prey?" but are without power or authority to stop him, God instructs Ezekiel to make the fateful proclamation:

> Therefore, son of man, prophesy and say unto Gog, Thus saith the LORD GOD; In that day when my people of Israel dwelleth safely, shalt thou not know it?
> And thou shalt come from thy place out of the north parts, thou, and many peoples with thee, . . . a mighty army: and thou shalt come up against my people of Israel, as a cloud to cover the land; it shall be in the latter days, and I will bring thee against my land, that the heathen [nations] may know me, when I shall be sanctified [Hebrew: *qadesh*—to be set apart] in thee, O Gog, before their eyes [When the atheistic heathen see the furious judgment of the Lord God actually "set in motion" against their vaunted leader and his "mighty army."].
> . . . my servants the prophets of Israel, . . . prophesied . . . that I would bring thee against them. . . .
> And it shall come to pass at the same time when Gog shall come against the land of Israel, saith the LORD GOD, that my fury shall come up in my face.
> For in my jealousy and in the fire of my wrath have I spoken, Surely in that day there shall be a great shaking in the land of Israel; so that the fishes of the sea, and the fowls of the heaven, and the beasts of the field, and all creeping things that creep upon the earth, and all the men that are upon the face of the earth, shall shake at my presence [Remember this statement, for other correlations will be given later.], and the mountains shall be thrown down, and the steep places shall fall, and every wall shall fall to the ground [including the "Dome of the Rock" Mosque of Omar in Jerusalem] (Ezek. 38:14–20).

Russia's defeat is positively prophesied, and it shall be brought about in several ways. (America shall also be greatly devastated, "pruned," "cut," and "burned." The all-out thermonuclear exchange between these two "super-powers" shall be extremely destructive.)

Order of Events "at the Time of the End"

The cataclysmic events to take place "at the time of the end" are to be so vast, so worldwide in scope, so rapid in occurrence, and so varied in action that words are simply inadequate to describe it all in any one sentence or paragraph. It can only be described topic by topic and in basic chronological order, for many things shall occur in many places at the same time. This has been a major reason for variations of thought, and of rather considerable confusion on the part of some theologians, as to the order of the events "at the time of the end." Only by a correlation of the prophecies can there be a proper event sequence established. That has been the reason for the rather extensive background in this writing before a presentation of a "scenario" of the end–time events.

The following timetable is given in summary and with brief excerpts from the Scripture passages and/or other prophecies which have credence.

Timetable of Events

1. "The Rapture," wherein all true believers shall be "caught up" together with all of the resurrected believers who have passed away previous to that moment and also together with all of the innocent babes of all time up to that moment, shall take place, when "the Lord himself shall descend from heaven with a shout, with the voice of the archangel, and with the trump of God" (1 Thess. 4:13–18; 1 Cor. 15:51–58; Isa. 19:1). This is the "translation" of the church which is the body of Christ:

> And he [Christ Jesus] is the head of the body, the church: who is the beginning, the firstborn from the dead; that in all things he might have the pre-eminence (Col. 1:18).

The saints of the Tribulation period (those who accept the message of salvation by grace through faith in Jesus Christ after the Rapture of the church), who are slain, or are killed in any manner, shall be resurrected later and shall become, in unison with (but not as a part of the distinct "church which is the body of Christ of which He is the Head thereof") the church "the bride of Christ." This uniting of all of the saints of all of the ages will take place at the close of the Tribulation period. It is recorded as follows:

> And after these things [all of the Tribulation judgments *previous* to the return of Christ as "KING OF KINGS AND LORD OF LORDS," when he shall come back to the earth with his saints] I heard a great voice of much people in heaven, saying
>
>> Allelujah; Salvation, . . . and honor, and power, unto the Lord, our God. . . .
>
> And I heard as it were the voice of a great multitude . . . saying . . .
>
>> Let us be glad and rejoice, and give honor to him: for the marriage of the Lamb is come, and his wife hath made herself ready. And to her was granted that she should be arrayed in fine linen, clean and white for the fine linen is the righteousness of saints.
>
> And he said unto me, Write, Blessed are they who are called unto the marriage supper of the Lamb. And he saith unto me, These are the true sayings of God (Rev. 19:1,6–9).

No saints are slain from this moment on throughout all of eternity; that is, not after the marriage supper of the Lamb, when the saints of all of the ages shall be forever united with their Lord, at the end of the Tribulation period.

2. As a result of the initial removal from this world of all of the true believers in Christ, there shall be a brief time of adjustment and chaos. Turmoil shall prevail in the nations. Out of this turmoil, certain definite developments shall take place according to the Word of God.

a. The first specific event to occur upon the earth after the removal of the saints of God will be the revealing of the identity of the "wicked" referred to in 2 Thessalonians 2:8 and 9. He is identical with "the king" of Daniel 11:36, "the beast" of Revelation 13:1, "the scarlet-colored beast" of Revelation 17:3, "the prince that shall come" of Daniel 9:26, and the one depicted as riding upon the "white horse" in Revelation 6:2. In that reference we have the beginning of the chronology of the tribulation judgments. Chapters six and eight of the Book of Revelation cover the time period of the events of World War III. Chapter seven is parenthetic, and has to do with the gospel of the kingdom which shall be preached during the first three and a half years of the Tribulation period. Only by the writing of another book can the chronology of the Book of Revelation be given, together with the other correlating passages required to properly explain that chronology.

The "Wicked" shall immediately proceed to delude the leaders of the Western European nations "and shall divide the land for gain," as prophesied in Daniel 11:39. He shall succeed "with all power and signs and lying wonders," as portrayed in 2 Thessalonians 2:9, in convincing the "ten kings, which have received no kingdom as yet; but receive power as kings one hour [prophetically—two weeks in actuality—] with the beast," that he, "the prince that shall come," is the one who can lead them to victory and that he is the one who can save Israel from the very ominous threat of "Gog," the chief prince of Moscow. Then shall come to pass the fulfillment of the prophecy:

> These have one mind, and shall give their power and strength
> unto the beast (Rev. 17:13).

This coordination of the prophecies reveals the prophesied strategy of the one revealed as the rider of the "white horse" of Revelation 6:2 who "had a bow [as of a bow and arrow—military strength]; and a crown was given unto him: and he went forth conquering, and to conquer." (Since it is stipulated that he "had" the military capability, only the legal authority was needed to be "given.")

b. The movements of the "mighty army" of the Russian and Warsaw Pact nations into their place "in the north parts" in preparation for their coming against the land of Israel "like a whirlwind," and the simultaneous "mustering" of the Arab nations under the leadership of "the king of the ,south" (prophesied in Daniel 11:40), shall be incentive enough to cause Israel to cry for help (Note Joel 1:14,15) and for a covenant of assistance to be entered into by them with the new and very powerful "king" of the newly created ten–nation empire of the old Roman Empire area of Western Europe. It shall come to pass, for it is prophesied that:

> . . . he ["the prince that shall come"] shall confirm the covenant with many ["the people that are gathered out of the nations"—the Israelis] . . . (Dan. 9:27).

The moment that this "covenant" is made, all is in readiness for World War III.

"Peace" Removed: the Mighty Conflict

3. "Peace" shall be removed from the earth by the second rider of "the four horsemen of the Apocalypse." The Bible prophecy reads as follows:

> And there went out another horse that was red: and power was given to him that sat thereon to take peace from the earth, and that they should kill one another: and there was given unto him a great sword (Rev. 6:4).

"Red" Russia, led by "Gog, the chief prince of Meshech [Moscow]," shall be the nation that shall institute the tremendously destructive World War III which is "the Battle by Fire." The holocaust which shall occur will be far greater than the world has ever known before—thermonuclear devastation. The Bible prophecies relative to the battle are quoted in Chapter two of this book. They need not be repeated here except to give the following specifics:

> . . . and the third part of trees was burnt up, and all green grass was burnt up.

. . . the third part of the sea became blood; and the third part of the creatures [including the men in the ships and submarines] which were in the sea, and had life, died; and the third part of the ships were destroyed.

. . . and the third part of the [fresh] waters became wormwood; and many men died of the waters, because they were made bitter [most likely by radioactivity].

. . . and the day shone not for a third part of it, and the night likewise [evidence of tremendous atomic clouds covering one third of the face of the earth] (Rev. 8:7–12).

"Gog," the leader of the Kremlin's mighty strategic arms and military colossus, seeking self-preservation, shall endeavor to "knock out" its only super-power rival, the United States, by the "great sword" arsenal referred to in the prophecy of Revelation 6:4. He also will attack Western Europe, but not with such fury. His hope is to conquer Europe intact so he can dominate it. Instead, the antichrist king will become the victor and ruler of all Europe, the Middle East, and northern Africa—all of which was in the ancient Roman Empire.

God's Judgment Upon Russia

The prophet Ezekiel, living in the 6th century B.C., was instructed to write the following proclamation against the instigator of World War III:

THEREFORE, thou son of man, prophesy against Gog and say, Thus saith the Lord GOD; Behold, I am against thee, O Gog . . . And I will turn thee back, and leave but the sixth part of thee, and will cause thee to come up from the north parts, and will bring thee upon the mountains of Israel. . . .

Thou shalt fall upon the mountains of Israel, thou, and all thy bands, and the people that is with thee: I will give thee unto the ravenous birds of every sort, and to the beasts of the field, . . . for I have spoken it, saith the Lord GOD.

And I will send a fire on Magog [the land of Russia] . . .

Behold, it is come, and it is done, saith the Lord GOD; this is the day of which I have spoken (Ezek. 39:1–8).

A careful analysis will reveal here that there are different locations involved and also different destructive forces utilized.

It is a matter of specific prophecy that "a fire" will be sent upon Magog, which is the land of Russia. This is the location of virtually all of its missile launching sites and of most of its industrial complex and therefore a prime target of the U.S. strategic forces in its massive counter-attack. This will come to pass.

A different fate, however, is decreed against the military leader "Gog" and the "mighty army" which he is to assemble "in the north parts." They are to "fall upon the mountains of Israel." Note the prophecy as God led Ezekiel to write it:

> . . . I am against thee, O Gog, the chief prince of Meshech and Tubal: and I will turn thee back, and leave but the sixth part of thee [Five sixths of that vaunted army shall die, and not in Russia] . . . Thou shalt fall upon the mountains of Israel, thou, and all thy bands, and the people that is with thee: I will give thee unto the ravenous birds of every sort, and to the beasts of the field to be devoured.
>
> Thou shalt fall upon the open field: for I have spoken it, saith the Lord GOD (Ezek. 39:1–6).

In order for this phase of the prophecy to come to pass, the manner of destruction of this "chief prince" and of his "mighty army" must be other than that of nuclear devastation, for in that case there would not be the remains to be devoured by the birds and by the beasts.

In Revelation 6:5–8 it is portrayed that the last two of "the four horsemen of the Apocalypse" are Famine and double-riders Death and Hell. The end result of World War III, wherein one third of the trees and all green grass shall be burnt up, will be the fulfillment of the prophecy of Joel:

> Alas for the day! For the day of the LORD is at hand, and as a destruction from the Almighty shall it come. Is not the meat cut off before our eyes . . . the barns are broken down; for the corn is withered.

How do the beasts groan! the herds of cattle are perplexed, because they have no pasture; yea, the flocks of sheep are made desolate.

O LORD, to thee will I cry; for the fire hath devoured the pastures of the wilderness, and the flame hath burned all the trees of the field (Joel 1:15–19).

Famine is bound to follow the tremendous burning and flames that shall devour the fields of the greatest grain-producing countries on earth, the U.S.A. and the U.S.S.R. With the flocks largely slain by flame, by depleted and contaminated (radioactive) water supply, and by famine, the carnivorous beasts shall have no alternative but to turn upon mankind, for it is also written, that one fourth of mankind will be slain as the over-all result of World War III. Note the description of the fourth horse—the pale horse—of the Apocalypse:

And I looked, and behold a pale horse: and his name that sat on him was Death, and Hell followed with him. And power was given unto them over the fourth part of the earth, to kill with sword [warfare], and with hunger [famine], and with death [by pestilence, by CBW, by radioactivity, etc.], and with the beasts of the earth (Rev. 6:8).

That the destruction of the massive "great army" is not by fire is proven as follows:

And they that dwell in the cities of Israel shall go forth, and shall set on fire and burn the weapons [evidently of lignostone content] . . . and they shall burn them with fire seven years: So that they shall take no wood out of the field, neither cut down any out of the forests; for they shall burn the weapons with fire: and they shall spoil those that spoiled them, and rob those that robbed them, saith the Lord GOD (Ezek. 39:9,10).

If the vast invading army had been slain by nuclear weapons, the intense blast heat and the fire-storms that follow would have burned the weapons also.

Two Alternatives to "Fire" Destruction

There are two alternatives seen in the prophecies concerning this matter:

1. Nerve gas. Brimstone (sulphur), used in nerve gas, is mentioned in Ezekiel 38:22; and in Revelation 8:7 it is written: "there followed hail and fire mingled with blood." In Chapter three of this book it was established that the lungs of the victims of the nerve gas attacks in Yemen were scorched with this brimstone causing an issuance of blood. The Red Cross investigating team reported that "the victims suffered headaches, difficulty in breathing, coughing of blood and nose bleeding, and died in 10 to 30 minutes."

There is an interesting report in my files relative to this factor. It states that the St. Louis *Post-Dispatch* said Saturday (June 17, 1967) it had learned that large quantities of deadly nerve gas were stockpiled by the Egyptians in the Sinai Peninsula prior to the Arab-Israeli War. The report stated further that "the gas was contained in artillery shells ready for firing."

It is worthy of note that these field pieces and their deadly nerve gas artillery shells were part of the $1 billion worth of supplies captured by the Israelis in the Six Day War and it can logically be assumed that Israel now possesses that equipment, and may also have duplicated much more of the same.

2. "Overflowing rain and great hailstones" are predicted in Ezekiel 38:22; and, likewise, "hail" is predicted in Revelation 8:7.

Apart from the fact that the omnipotent Lord God can add His "hail and fire mingled with blood" as an added part to any World War III, two additional reports in my files are worthy of note:

On October 14, 1966, Dr. Walter Orr Roberts, the director of the National Center for Atmospheric Research, forecast that "man would be able to achieve major control over the weather in this century."

That same month, in a private interview with U.S. intelligence authorities, a Polish scientist warned that the Russians were planning a "weather changing" experiment designed to "electrify the world." This scientist further stated that the Soviets were dealing with forces "almost beyond imagination." Many of the Russian scientists, he said, were concerned that their tinkering might touch off a catastrophic reaction.

Thus it is that the potentials for all of the Bible prophecy forces relative to World War III are basically within the grasp of mankind. Even "overflowing rain and great hailstones" can be produced, either intentionally or otherwise.

"Gog" to be Buried, Not "Burned"

For verification, we need only read the specific prophecies:

> And it shall come to pass in that day, that I will give unto Gog a place there of graves in Israel, the valley of the passengers [travellers] on the east of the [Mediterranean] sea . . . and there shall they bury Gog and all his multitude; and they shall call it The Valley of Hamom-gog. And seven months shall the house of Israel be burying of them, that they may cleanse the land (Ezek. 39:11,12).

"Gog and Magog"

The terminology is used once more, in the closing portion of Revelation 20, but a glance at the context of that reference shows clearly that it refers to Satan and to all who rebel with him after the thousand years of the reign of Christ upon the earth. "Magog" in that reference refers to "the nations that are in the four quarters (all of) the earth," and "Gog" is an obvious sub-title for Satan. They gather "together to battle," but there is no struggle.

> And fire came down from God out of heaven, and devoured them (Rev. 20:9).

That will be the concluding act of Satan, also, for the very next verse reads:

> And the devil that deceived them was cast into the lake of fire and brimstone, where the beast and the false prophet are [by that time], and shall be tormented day and night for ever and ever [for all of the great evil that they have caused] (Rev. 20:10).

Satan will come to his doom at the final battle of "Gog and Magog." Do not confuse that prophecy with the ones concerning Russia in Ezekiel 38 and 39.

God's Earthquake

God's actions are always performed with purpose. In announcing that a great earthquake will occur "at the time of the end" and "in the day of the Lord," He caused Ezekiel to write:

> And it shall come to pass at the same time when Gog shall come against the land of Israel, saith the Lord GOD, that my fury shall come up in my face. For in my jealousy and in the fire of my wrath have I spoken, Surely in that day there shall be a great shaking in the land of Israel . . . and all the men that are upon the face of the earth shall shake at my presence, and the mountains shall be thrown down, and the steep places shall fall, and every wall shall fall to the ground (Ezek. 38:18–20).

The statement, "and all the men that are upon the face of the earth shall shake at my presence," reveals that this earthquake is identical to the one prophesied in Revelation 6. Note the wording:

> And I beheld when he had opened the sixth seal, and, lo, there was a great earthquake, . . . And the stars of heaven fell unto the earth, even as a fig tree casteth her untimely figs, when she is shaken of a mighty wind. . . .
> And the kings of the earth, and the great men, and the rich men, and the chief captains, and the mighty men, and every bondman, and every free man, hid themselves in the dens and in the rocks of

the mountains; And said unto the mountains and rocks, Fall on us, and hide us from the face of him that sitteth on the throne, and from the wrath of the [resurrected] Lamb: For the great day of his wrath is come; and who shall be able to stand? (Rev. 6:12–17).

Great Fear Throughout the Earth

So great will be the holocaust and the tremendous shock waves from the simultaneous explosions of thousands of multi-megaton thermonuclear warheads over the expanse of one third of the face of the earth in the all-out thermonuclear exchange on "the day of the Lord," that awesomeness and fear and trembling shall come upon all manner of men. The wicked ones shall be filled with great dread, thinking that "the end of the world" has come: and they shall be afraid to face God. Thus the cry, "Fall on us, and hide us from the face of him that sitteth on the throne. . . ."

Those who had trusted in the blood-atonement of the Lamb of God, the Lord Jesus Christ, will have been taken out, "caught up to meet the Lord in the air," previous to that day of which God caused Ezekiel to write:

> Behold it is come, and it is done, saith the Lord GOD; this is the day of whereof I have spoken (Ezek. 39:8).

The ungodly, the unrighteous, the unruly rebellious ones and all those who so boastfully and egotistically said that there is no God, or that "God is dead," shall be the ones who shall now be in great fear before the outpoured wrath of the very God whom they said did not exist. They shall flee into their air-raid shelters and into the caves and the rocks of the mountains to try to hide themselves. It is not in vain that it is written in Hebrews 10:31, "It is a fearful thing to fall into the hands of the living God." The indescribable force of the multiple explosions shall cause the earth to rend and to quake, causing many of the faultlines of the earth's crust to give way, resulting in a great earthquake worldwide.

Some Who Shall "Escape"

There shall be some people (perhaps even some who read this book, consider its message, but do not act upon it at the time) who shall realize, to their sorrow, that the warning was indeed true, and that the saints shall actually be taken out of this world before the Tribulation period. When some of their loved ones "disappear," they shall find themselves to be like the foolish ones in the parable of the ten virgins who had lamps, but had no oil (spiritual life) in them.

> And at midnight there was a cry made, Behold, the bridegroom cometh; go ye out to meet him.
> Then all these virgins arose, and trimmed their lamps. And the foolish said unto the wise, Give us of your oil, for our lamps are gone out. But the wise answered, saying, Not so, lest there be not enough for us and you: but go ye rather to them that sell, and buy for yourselves.
> And while they went to buy, the bridegroom came; and they that were ready went in with him to the marriage: and the door was shut (Matt. 25:6–13).

When the Lord descends "with a shout, the voice of the archangel, and the trump of God . . . and we which are alive and remain shall be caught up" to be forever with Him, any who are not spiritually born-again Christians at that moment will be left behind. Christ is the only "door" (John 10:7–10).

In that moment, the true Christians shall go to be with the Lord.

In that same moment, however, and in the days to follow, there shall be many who have heard (or read) the warning who shall cry unto the Lord for salvation.

Because it is written: "Heaven and earth shall pass away [ultimately], but my words shall not pass away" (Matt. 24:35), the promise that "whosoever shall call upon the name of the Lord shall be saved" (Rom. 10:13) shall still be in effect. It will be too late to become a part of the body of Christ and thus be spared the Tribulation judgments, but it will not be too late to "believe on the Lord Jesus Christ" and thus receive eternal life rather than eternal damnation. Anyone can still be saved, but that person shall have to suffer and to die "for their testimony" (Rev. 6:9–11).

The Opening of the Seals

Let it be understood that the opening of the seven seals depict seven great actions which are to occur between the Rapture of the church and the end of World War III (Rev. 6; 8:1–12) until angelic proclamation of the three "woes" concerning about which it is written in Revelation 8:13 that they "are yet to sound."

The first four seals will reveal the identity of "the four horsemen of the Apocalypse."

The opening of the fifth seal will give a glimpse into heaven where it is revealed that there are souls there who have believed in Jesus Christ as Redeemer, but who did not believe the message until after the Christian body of Christ was "caught up" to be with Him. These suffered martyrdom.

> And when he had opened the fifth seal, I saw under the altar the souls of them that were slain for the word of God, and for the testimony which they held . . . And white robes [of redemption] were given unto every one of them; and it was said unto them that they should rest yet for a little season, until their fellow servants also and their brethren, that should be killed as they were, should be fulfilled (Rev. 6:9–11).

Many people have refused to believe in the translation or Rapture of the church. Others simply have not been able to comprehend so great an event. They shall believe it when they see it happen; but for them, it will be too late to become a part of it. Those who take a stand for Christ then shall be put to death by the enemies of true Christianity.

The Sixth Seal: the Climax

The opening of the first seal on the book of end-time events will reveal the identity of the Antichrist, "the king," who is to covenant to protect the "Promised Land" of Israel.

The opening of the second seal will reveal the rider on the red horse, his "great sword," and his "power to take peace from the earth."

The third seal will reveal the element of famine which is to follow the great holocaust of the thermonuclear World War III.

The fourth seal will reveal the specter of death riding as the companion of hell on earth as World War III comes into its fullness.

The opening of the fifth seal will give a glimpse into heaven and will verify the fact that souls can still be saved even during the Tribulation period.

The opening of the sixth seal will reveal the fury of God and the great earthquake which shall come with and as a result of the tremendous thermonuclear explosions over one third of the land and sea areas of the earth. It shall serve also as a climatic judgment from God and "as a destruction from the Almighty."

The Seventh Seal and First Four Trumpet Judgments

The opening of the seventh seal, recorded in Revelation 8:1, will reveal a period of silence in heaven "for about half an hour." This is generally considered to be a time of prayer before the details are given as to the actual happenings of World War III (and of the great divine judgments which shall follow thereafter).

The sounding of the first four trumpets of Revelation 8 are but a specification of the details of the manner of destruction to be wrought upon one third of the trees and vegetation, one third of the seas, one third of the fresh waters of the earth (they are made bitter, most evidently by radioactive fallout, causing many men to die), and upon one third of the sky which shall become dark (due to vast atomic clouds and vaporized debris). God begins in this chapter to outline the specific judgments which are to befall the earth and the people on it.

The Climax of the War

Revelation 6:12 reads as follows:

> And I beheld, when he had opened the sixth seal, and, lo, there was a great earthquake, and the sun became black as sackcloth of hair, and the moon became like blood.

The specification of the great earthquake at this point, after the stipulation of peace having been taken from the earth and after the depiction of famine, death, and hell having ridden across the face of the earth, indicates again that the "great earthquake" will follow the great thermonuclear exchange of World War III.

The portrayal of the sun becoming "black as sackcloth of hair" cannot be taken as a literal factor due to the fact that such an act of judgment would cause all light to cease from the earth, all heat likewise, the cessation of photosynthesis and thus the end of all oxygen supply and would cause sudden death to all life upon the face of the earth. It can only mean, therefore, that which is described in Revelation 8:12 wherein great clouds of debris shall darken the sun to the extent that sunlight cannot penetrate it until the atomic clouds dissipate. In similar manner, any who have looked at the moon through the density of thick smog realize that it appears reddened; and its appearance through the even denser clouds which would follow nuclear explosions could most certainly cause it to appear "like blood."

> And the stars of heaven fell unto the earth, even as a fig tree casteth her untimely figs, when she is shaken of a mighty wind (Rev. 6:13).

Here, again, ultra-literal interpretation of the statement is impossible due to the fact that actual stars are many, many times the size of the earth; even the falling of one star upon it would completely destroy it. The portrayal, therefore, especially inasmuch as it depicts many stars falling "as a fig tree casteth her untimely figs, when she is shaken of a mighty wind," is a manner of stating (for the scribe of the Revelation knew not of FOBS, ICBMs, SLBMs, etc.) that a great shooting of, or falling of, nuclear-tipped rockets would take place, as indeed it shall.

As to the statements in Revelation 6:14–16, wherein it is declared that "the heaven departed as a scroll when it is rolled together"; and that the men of the earth "hid themselves in the dens and in the rocks of the mountains; and said to the mountains and rocks, Fall on us, and hide us from the face of him that sitteth on the throne, and from the wrath of the Lamb" it is conceivably possible that the wicked (unredeemed) ones of the earth might be given a glimpse of almighty God who is described in Revelation 4 and 5 as sitting upon "the throne," over which is seen the emerald rainbow of grace; but this author is not inclined to agree with such an interpretation. When the unredeemed ones of this earth see God, it will be when he sits upon the "great white throne" of judgment described in Revelation 20:11–15. There will be no grace evidenced there. The rebellious ones have rejected the grace and mercy of God. Only final judgment and condemnation can await them.

The portrayal, therefore, is most likely that of the blasting of the earthly firmament (sky) by nuclear explosions; and the cry of the men is more likely that of fear, knowing that they are totally unprepared to view the countenance of a just and a holy God.

In response to such a cry of terror as depicted at the close of chapter six, it is then that the still merciful God caused John to write the message of chapter seven which reveals that the gospel of the kingdom shall yet be preached upon the earth and that a "great multitude" will be saved thereby, even though it shall be required of them that they shall suffer martyrdom during the era of the Tribulation period.

The end result of World War III, climaxed by the great earthquake, can now be given, starting first with the reaction of the Egyptians as we return to the order of events outlined in Isaiah 19.

Fulfillments of the Prophecies of Isaiah 19

Isaiah 19, like so many other portions of Bible prophecy, is written in topical order rather than in precise chronological order.

Verse 1 proclaims "the burden of Egypt." It also contains the prophecy of the Lord again entering Egypt—this time "upon a swift cloud." In retrospect, the people of that land shall mistakenly consider, evidently, the disappearance of their infant children (and such born again Christians as were there) very much in the same manner as they did the loss of all firstborn children at the time of that great judgment the night before the Israelites left the bondage of Egypt under the leadership of Moses: "and the heart of Egypt shall melt in the midst of it."

In verse 2 is the prophecy that God will "set the Egyptians against the Egyptians: . . . and every one against his neighbor; city against city, and kingdom against kingdom." This shall come to pass in the brief "chaos" period right after the translation of the church wherein all true believers in Christ and all infants shall be "caught up . . . in the clouds, to meet the Lord in the air."

The non-Christians, disillusioned by the atheistic and paganistic Marxists and socialists, shall, according to verse 3, "seek to the idols, and to the charmers, and to spiritists and to the wizards [astrologers]."

Egypt's Foolish Alliance

To pick up the continuity from the first declarations in this Bible chapter, one must look to verse 11 to find the background for the next action which is to take place.

God warns Egypt concerning the making of a foolish alliance, and the danger of trusting "they that are the stay of the tribes thereof," referring to the deceiving of Egypt and its Arab-aligned "tribes thereof" by "those [Russians] who have also seduced Egypt."

Egypt "At the Time of the End"

Isaiah 19:16 and 17, in a tight summary, give the result of the great "push" of "the king of the south" when he follows the direction of the Russian advisers and again moves in strength against the land of Israel.

The rapid momentum of "the day of the Lord" is seen here also, in that when Egypt makes the first move, which shall "trigger" World War III, by attacking Israel, "Gog" of the U.S.S.R. will almost simultaneously "cut" and "prune" the U.S. with its all-out thermonuclear attack and will at the same time follow Egypt's action by also coming "from the north parts" and "like a whirlwind" in a pincer thrust against Israel.

That this is the order of the action is verified by Daniel's prophecy wherein it is proclaimed:

And at the time of the end shall the king of the south push . . . and the king of the north shall come . . . like a whirlwind . . . (Dan. 11:40).

That this is a virtually simultaneous action is also verified by the declaration of God through His prophet Ezekiel:

And it shall come to pass at the same time when Gog shall come against the land of Israel, saith the Lord God . . . Surely in that day there shall be a great shaking in the land of Israel; . . . and all the men that are upon the face of the earth shall shake at my presence, and the mountains shall be thrown down, and the steep places shall fall, and every wall shall fall to the ground (Ezek. 38:18–20).

Note now the initial proclamation against Egypt for its part in World War III:

> In that day shall Egypt be like unto women: and it shall be afraid and fear because of the shaking of the hand of the LORD of hosts, which he shaketh over it.
>
> And the land of Judah shall be a terror unto Egypt, every one that maketh mention thereof shall be afraid in himself, because of the counsel of the LORD of hosts, which he hath determined against it (Isa. 19:16,17).

Thus it is that we have before us still another purpose of God in the "great earthquake" which shall climax that "day of the Lord."

> The noise of a multitude in the mountains . . . the LORD of hosts mustereth the host of the battle. They come from a far country . . . the weapons of his indignation . . .
>
> Howl ye; for the day of the LORD is at hand; it shall come as a destruction from the Almighty. Therefore shall all hands be faint, and every man's heart shall melt: and they shall be afraid . . . they shall be amazed one at another: their faces shall be as flames.
>
> Behold, the day of the LORD cometh . . . For the stars of heaven and the constellations thereof shall not give their light: the sun shall be darkened in his going forth, and the moon shall not cause her light to shine.
>
> And I will punish the world for their evil, and the wicked for their iniquity; and I will cause the arrogancy of the proud to cease . . .
>
> Therefore I shall shake the heavens, and the earth shall remove out of her place, in the wrath of the LORD of hosts, and in the day of his fierce anger . . .
>
> They shall every man turn to his own people, and flee every one into his own land (Isa. 13:4–14).

When the international "weapons of his indignation" shall go into conflict; when "they shall be amazed one at another" and "their faces shall be as flames"; when, in the day of the Lord, the earth shall so quake that it shall "remove out of its place"; in fear and trembling the Egyptians (and others) shall "flee every one into his own land." Thus will be the terror of "the day of the LORD" at the very beginning of the seven-year Tribulation period.

"The Beast" Begins to Take Over

"The beast" of Revelation 13:1, elsewhere identified as "the king" of the end time, shall come mightily into the conflict over Israel. Daniel wrote:

> He shall enter into the countries, and shall overflow . . . He shall enter also into the glorious land [Israel] and many countries shall be overthrown. . . .
> He shall stretch forth his hand [of rule] also upon the countries; and the land of Egypt shall not escape. . . (Dan. 11:40–43).

Egypt Under "The King"

In Isaiah 19, chronologically, we return now to verse 4, having seen the foolish alliance of Isaiah 19:11–14 broken in its purpose and having seen Egypt defeated and afraid as depicted in verses 16 and 17. The next prophecy reads:

> And the Egyptians will I give over into the hand of a cruel lord; and a fierce king shall rule over them, saith the Lord, the LORD of hosts (Isa. 19:4).

Insurrection in Egypt will be rendered impossible by the fact that the "king" will hold them cruelly under subjection by cutting off the only water supply: The Nile River controlled now by the locks of the Aswan High Dam. The control of "the king" shall be absolute, as verified by the following:

And the waters shall fail from the sea [the fertile delta], and the river shall be wasted and dried up . . . and everything sown by the brooks, shall wither, be driven away, and be no more . . . (Isa. 19:5–7).

Verse 15 enlarges upon their plight: "Neither shall there be any work for Egypt."

God's Purposes Exemplified

Although other references have been used to expound the events relative to "the time of the end" and concerning the "Tribulation period," I have chosen to use Isaiah 19 as the framework for the exposition of "the scenario" of this book. The reasons can now be made evident:

1. It contains a prophecy as to the initial factor: "The coming of the Lord."

2. It contains a prophecy of the Russian-Arab alliance.

3. It contains a prophecy of the foolishness and failure of that alliance.

4. It contains a prophecy as to the effect on mankind of the "Great Earthquake."

5. It contains a prophecy of the end-time control to be seized by "the king."

6. It contains a prophecy as to Egypt, a land portrayed throughout the Scriptures as an example of bondage to sin, as suffering for its error.

7. It contains a prophecy of God's mercy, even upon Egypt, when, in sincerity, it cries unto the Lord for deliverance.

The seventh item listed above is contained in the following quotation:

In that day shall there be an altar to the LORD in the midst of the land of Egypt, and a pillar [the ancient sign of a peace covenant] at the border thereof to the LORD. And it shall be for a sign and for a witness unto the LORD of hosts in the land of Egypt: for they shall cry unto the LORD because of the oppressors, and he shall send them a savior, and a great one, and he shall deliver them (Isa. 19:19,20).

In the above brief statement are prophecies of tremendous importance!

1. It shows the ultimate humbling of the great arrogance of the stubborn and proud Egyptians who have avowed their own strength from the ancient days of the building of the pyramids even unto the last foolish "push" against the land of Israel.

2. It shows that even the most independent and proud ones, when they come to the point of utter helplessness, will "cry unto the Lord"; and, of even greater significance, it reveals that the Lord God will hear the penitent cry of even such as these.

3. It shows that God can, and will, deliver any people—if, and when, they heed His provisional promise to

> . . . humble themselves, and pray, and seek my face, and turn from their wicked ways, then will I hear from heaven; and will forgive their sin, and will heal their land (2 Chron. 7:14).

The Scriptures, the eternally existent words of the living God, record the following:

> God is no respecter of persons; but in every nation he that feareth him, and worketh righteousness, is accepted with him; . . . To him give all the prophets witness, that through his name whosoever believeth in him shall receive remission of sins (Acts 10:34,35,43).

Therein is the importance of the message of Isaiah 19.

God Responds to Their Cry

The Isaiah 19 prophecy moves progressively forward from "the coming of the Lord," unto "the day of the Lord," unto the Tribulation period time of oppression, and on to "that day" in which "he shall send them a savior, and a great one, and he shall deliver them."

And the LORD shall be known to Egypt, and the Egyptians shall know the LORD in that day, and shall do sacrifice and oblation; yea, they shall vow unto the LORD, and perform it.

And the LORD shall smite Egypt: he shall smite and heal it: and they shall return even to the LORD, and he shall be intreated of them, and shall heal them (Isa. 19:21,22).

Egypt's Destiny Revealed

The theme of this book now comes before us: "The Destiny."

In the closing verses of Isaiah 19 we find a monumental statement. It not only reveals the destiny of Egypt, but, in its total framework, it contains the outline of the destiny of all peoples of the world.

1. "Egypt," in the manner of the terminology utilized here, represents the nation of Egypt; but more, it represents all of the people who have been historically opposed to, by disposition, the people of God, but who have in the ultimate end accepted both the Lord God and His people.

2. "Assyria," mentioned in this closing prophecy of this passage of Scripture, represents not just those of the ancient land of Assyria, but it represents the "mixed people": the peoples of the nations of the world, and, more specifically, those people of the world who have responded to the call of God and the message of the gospel, whether it be the gospel of grace as preached during the church age or the gospel of the kingdom as preached during the first three and a half years of the Tribulation period or the everlasting gospel preached by an angel during the last three and a half years of that which is the Tribulation period (Rev. 14:6–13).

3. "Israel, mine inheritance," as used in the last sentence of the prophecy, represents those who are "Israelites indeed," not by blood lineage or national heritage, but those descendants of Jacob (whose name was changed to Israel by a decree of God) who have believed in and trusted in the Lord God and who have recognized the Lord Jesus Christ as their Messiah and Redeemer during the time of their existence upon the earth and

333

before their death, or else they lived through "the time of Jacob's trouble" and thusly beheld the Lord when he came to earth as their Messiah, Savior, and King in ultimate fulfillment of many prophecies, and particularly those of Zechariah 12 and 13:

> And it shall come to pass in that day, that I will seek to destroy all the nations that come against Jerusalem [at the battle of Armageddon] . . . I will pour upon the house of David [of Judah] and upon the inhabitants of all Jerusalem [all of the hoping and trusting descendants of Jacob-Israel], the spirit of grace and of supplications: and they shall look upon me whom they have pierced, and they shall mourn for him, as one mourneth for his only son . . . (Zech. 12:9, 10).

In that day there shall be a fountain opened to the house of David and to the inhabitants of Jerusalem for sin, and for uncleanness—

> And it shall come to pass in that day, saith the LORD of hosts, that I will cut off the names of the idols out of the land, and they shall no more be remembered: and also I will cause the [false] prophets and the unclean spirit to pass out of the land . . . (Zech. 13:1,2).
> They shall call on my name, and I will hear them: I will say, It is my people: and they shall say, The LORD is my God (Zech. 13:9).

Such is the magnitude and the magnificence of the definitions of the categories of the peoples mentioned in the last two verses of Isaiah 19, which reads:

> In that day shall Israel be the third with Egypt and with Assyria, even a blessing in the midst of the land:
> Whom the LORD of hosts shall bless, saying, Blessed be Egypt my people, and Assyria the work of my hands, and Israel mine inheritance (Isa. 19:24,25).

24

THE DESTINY OF AMERICA

The fact of World War III has been established.

The fact that the primary powers—the "super-powers"—involved therein are to be the U.S. and the U.S.S.R. has also been explained in detail.

The fact that Egypt, the lesser ally of Russia, shall "be afraid and fear because of the great shaking" in the land of Judah (Israel), when God causes his great earthquake to be felt in the land, has also been verified as well as the fact that "the king" of the revived Roman Empire area shall "stretch forth his hand . . . and the land of Egypt shall not escape."

Egypt shall come under the iron hand of the "cruel" king, and that "fierce king" shall rule over them. He shall cut off their lifeline of the water resource of the Nile River, and the Egyptians "shall cry unto the Lord because of the oppressors."

"Gog," of the land of Russia and his mighty army shall fall "upon the mountains of Israel" and upon the open fields thereof, and it shall take the men of Israel seven months to bury Gog and his army "that they may cleanse the land."

Russia, itself, "the land of Magog," shall be destroyed by the thermonuclear counter-attack of the U.S.—this nation being used of God as "a weapon of his indignation" against that land. The all-out thermonuclear exchange on "the day of the Lord" shall cancel out Russia's vaunted strategic nuclear strength.

Russia shall deplete itself and exhaust itself against America on the same day that God shall "send a fire on Magog [the land of

Russia]," according to Ezekiel 39:6, and will ". . . plead against him ["Gog" of Russia] with pestilence . . . and with blood; and . . . rain upon him, and upon his bands, and upon the many people that are with him, an overflowing rain, and great hailstones, fire, and brimstone" (Ezek. 38:22).

America in the Bible

The Bible record deals in a specific manner only with those nations which come in direct contact with the "Promised Land"—Israel. America does so only in a secondary sense: by destroying Israel's assailant, Russia. Thus it is that only one chapter in the Bible is devoted to America, which is described:

> . . . the land shadowing with wings, which is beyond the rivers of Ethiopia: that sendeth ambassadors by the sea. . . .
> . . . a nation scattered and peeled [highly developed] . . . a people terrible [tenacious] from their beginning hitherto; a nation meted out and trodden down [travelled upon], whose land the rivers have spoiled [traversed]!
> All ye inhabitants of the world and dwellers on the earth, see ye, when he lifteth up an ensign on the mountains; and when he bloweth a trumpet, [they are admonished] hear ye (Isa. 18:1–3).

The Bible prophets did not otherwise write of it specifically. Only by the above description is America mentioned in the Bible.

The manner of the attack against the United States is not given in the Bible except that, after the very thorough description of this land and its people is given in the early verses of Isaiah 18, it states that an individual who is simply referred to as "he" shall "both cut off the sprigs with pruning hooks, and cut down the branches" of this affluent country "when the bud is perfect, and the sour [developing] grape is ripening in the flower." When this country is still in the process of developing its strength, America is to be greatly "cut."

America on the Brink

It takes no imagination today to foresee the manner in which this nation can be very severely damaged.

Mr. Stewart Alsop, reporting from Washington D.C., in summarizing a series of cold, hard facts concerning Russia's strategic capability, stated in an article which appeared on the last page of *Newsweek* Magazine May 10, 1971:

> They have probably achieved the capability [which we lack against them] to blind our intelligence satellites [with their already tested and proven hunter-killer nonnuclear satellites]. And the experts are betting 2 to 1 that they are also on the way to achieving the capability to knock out, with very powerful multi-MIRVed missiles, our land-based nuclear deterrent.
>
> In short, the available clues suggest that the Russians are now going all-out to achieve in the near future a really decisive nuclear-strategic superiority.*

Documentations throughout this book have shown that the Soviets now are within reach of that goal. One report, dated October 30, 1978, reads in part: "By 1983, the Pentagon calculates that the Soviets will add enough warheads and improve the accuracy of their ICBMs to the point where they could destroy America's land-based missile force . . . in a single blow." Another report states that existing Soviet missile accuracies are capable of destroying ninety percent of our ICBMs with a single strike by firing only twenty percent of their multiple warhead missiles. The latter article, from the *Detroit News*, also states that "the new generation of Soviet missiles can hit within 200 yards of their target from a distance of over 6,000 miles."

The day of destiny for the United States is very near! Any observant reader of the news of today—censored though it may be—can see warnings of this kind almost every day. Let us not

---

*Condensed from *Newsweek*. Copyright Newsweek, Inc., 1971.

be blind or naive. The Russians plan to be in a position to demand "surrender—or else," and that, very soon.

Biblically, we have only the consolation of the first line of Isaiah 18:6 (in that chapter which pertains to the destiny of the United States): "They shall be left together. . . ."

The Trigger of the Attack

Russia's intelligence information is not complete.

The factor that shall cause Russia's Kremlin leadership "at the same time" to "think an evil thought," as predicted in Ezekiel 38:10, shall be that great event of which she has so little, if any, knowledge: the translation into heaven of all of the truly born-again children of God—"the Rapture of the church."

When that great event takes place, and it shall, "in a moment, in the twinkling of an eye" (1 Cor. 15:52), tremendous adjustments will transpire in rapid succession all over the world. Multitudes will be missing. In the so-called "Christian countries," even though there are millions of people who are not spiritually born-again Christians, there are other millions who are; and many of the top leaders of these nations, including many of the military as well as of the legislative leaders in the United States, are still believers in the Bible and in the Lord Jesus Christ whom they love and serve and look for. They shall suddenly disappear from this earth, having been "caught up together . . . to meet the Lord in the air, and so shall we ever be with the Lord" (1 Thess. 4:17).

The situation which will result will be parallel to a sign which I saw by the side of the road in Alaska a few years ago. It read: "Grizzly bear country. Take your pictures from the road. Grizzlies are vegetarians, but they are also opportunists."

When the wily Russian Bear sees America in temporary turmoil due to God's great "air-lift," she shall move up her target date "at the same time" and shall seek to "strike while the iron is hot," anticipating that America will be totally off-guard and therefore be easy prey. This will be Russia's fatal mistake.

By the time the Kremlin leadership can adjust itself to the shocking news of that which has happened around the world and can order its "mighty army" of the Warsaw Pact nations together with its own immense military forces into their places of position "in the north parts" of the Middle East in anticipation of the concerted Arab-Russian thrust against Israel (and also to get its forces away from their usual places to avoid their destruction in the fast counterattack that they know will come, but hopefully not too swiftly or strongly), two events will have already taken place.

1. "The king," who shall immediately emerge as the military leader of the Western European forces, will already have "divided the land for gain" and will have secured the support of the ten-nation entity of Western Europe. He will have "guaranteed" Israel's protection against the Arab-Russian Confederacy and be poised and ready—probably as a newly authorized head of the already highly efficient NATO forces.

2. America's "Emergency Regulations" (probably) will have been put into effect by presidential order; the top-secret chain of command of the U.S. strategic forces will have automatically made any adjustments needed in accordance with NMCA—National Military Command Authorities—authorizing the top person in command from the President on down to the Joint Chiefs of Staff to use the "cryptographic key" to the mighty U.S. nuclear trigger; in NORAD headquarters and in the Looking Glass Command Planes the top-secret SIOP—Single Integrated Operations Plan—papers in the red emergency boxes will be "at the ready" to most strategically release the land, sea, and air-positioned thermonuclear holocaust according to the top-secret NSTL—Nuclear Strategic Target List. America will not strike first, but it will be ready to retaliate unmercifully at a moment's notice.

Uncle Sam knows that Communist Russia's strike will be secret, sudden, and a full scale all-out strategic arsenal attack of multitudes of thermonuclear and possibly CBW weapons coming from all directions possible, and this nation, "terrible from its beginning hitherto," has a fantastically automatic retaliatory response so ready that even the taking out of all of the spiritually born-again Christians will not alter its operations but momentarily.

Then will come to pass the fulfillment of Ezekiel 39:6 wherein America, as a weapon of God's indignation, will "send a fire on Magog [Russia]," even as Russia's military leader referred to as "Gog" will function first as another weapon of God's indignation to "prune" and to "cut" this nation when that horrible all-out thermonuclear exchange takes place and the rockets, like falling stars, shall be, in fulfillment of the many Bible prophecies, the source of "flames" and "burning" sent "from the [opposite] end of heaven" upon one third of the earth as a destruction from the Almighty "for the day of the Lord is at hand," concerning which it is written in Ezekiel:

> Behold, it is come, and it is done, saith the Lord GOD; this is the day of which I have spoken . . . And it shall come to pass in that day, that I will give unto Gog a place of graves there in Israel. . . (Ezek. 39:8,11).

USS Sam Rayburn at Newport News Shipyard

(U.S. Navy photo)

". . . Polaris subs carry only four torpedoes for self protection. They carry enough nuclear missiles to char a continent." (July 19, 1970, *Daily Breeze*, Torrance, Calif.)

25

AMERICA'S DARKEST DAYS

The Bible prophecies establish the FACT of the devastation of America. But ultimate victory is assured for the faithful ones and for those who can exist through the seven years of tribulation which shall follow. All will do well, however, to heed the last words spoken to General George Washington on that eventful day in the winter of 1777:

> Let every child of the republic learn to live for his God, his land and Union.

A Chronology of the Destiny of America

America shall be horribly damaged. In spite of the preparations and counter-measures taken by the U.S., the "first-strike" of the Soviets will be a terrific one. Russia has FOBS and huge ICBMs with multi-MIRV warheads capable of travelling at tremendous speeds and with deadly accuracy and destructibility.

Following on the wake of that attack will be rampant "survival-of-the-fittest" actions on the part of the insurrectionists and anarchists and of the desperate ones. It falls under the category of a fulfillment of the just declaration of a holy God who caused his prophet Isaiah to write:

> . . . they shall be afraid: pangs and sorrows shall take hold of them . . . they shall be amazed one at another; their faces shall be as flames.

Behold, the day of the LORD cometh . . . and he shall destroy the sinners out of it . . . And I will punish the world for their evil, and the wicked for their iniquity; and I will cause the arrogancy of the proud to cease, and will lay low the haughtiness of the terrible.

They shall every man turn to his own people, and flee every one to his own land. Every one that is found shall be thrust through, and every one that is joined unto them shall fall by the sword.

Their children also shall be dashed to pieces before their eyes; their houses shall be spoiled, and their wives ravished (Isa. 13:8–16).

Let us start the chronology, "the scenario," with a statement from the vision of the Evangelist:

1. MIRV-Missile CBW Attack

As I saw the horrible black cloud in the form of a skeleton bending toward America, I knew its one intent was to destroy the multitudes.

As I watched in horror . . . out of the horrible mouth and nostrils came great puffs of white vapors. . . .

One could see readily by the painful coughing that these white vapors had seared her lungs . . . What were these white vapors?

The context of the evangelist's vision, as outlined earlier, portrays the strong evidence that the first attack shall be a "brimstone" type of nerve gas attack in an effort to immobilize the populace—to prevent, if possible, the capability of anyone "pushing the button" or "turning the key" that would initiate the counter-attack.

In view of the computerized war games "played on miles and miles of tape" at the Pentagon, and the findings there that Russia would win in a war because of its unrestrained use of chemical and biological warfare (CBW), it is very likely that this phase of the vision will come to pass, even though it is not a Bible prophecy.

2. Thermonuclear Attack

Then suddenly I saw from the Atlantic and from the Pacific, and out of the Gulf, rocket-like objects that seemed to come up like fish leaping out of the water. . . . Then suddenly the rockets . . . all exploded at once. The explosion was earsplitting.

The next thing which I saw was a huge ball of fire . . . and I viewed the widespread desolation brought about by the terrific explosions.

In Isaiah 18, the chapter concerning the destiny of this nation, are the words:

For so the LORD said unto me . . . I will consider . . . like a clear heat upon herbs, and like a cloud of dew in the heat of harvest [Both illustrating destructive elements] . . . afore the harvest, when the bud is perfect . . . he shall both cut off the sprigs with pruning hooks, and take away and cut down the branches (Isa. 18:4,5).

The destructive forces illustrated here are explained in many passages of Scripture which are quoted for you in Chapter two of this book. The desolation of the lands of the two "super-powers" shall be almost beyond description. And that shall be only the beginning of the "woes" to befall the people of the earth during the seven-year Tribulation period. Coming woes in general are described from Revelation 6 to 19. Our concern now is with America, for a correlation of the prophecies in this book indicate that, in addition to the many plagues and "woes" which will be worldwide, this beloved country shall be in a state of constant strife and warfare until the very end of the Tribulation.

3. Continual Warfare

Russia's power will have been broken by the immensity of the U.S. counter-attack plus whatever punishment it shall have received from the NATO forces and/or by the direct intervention of the fury of almighty God.

For America, however, there is an indication of extra trouble and even of an invasion of this nation by foreign armed forces.

Consider the fact that at the close of the prophecy recorded in the eleventh chapter of Daniel is the following statement:

But tidings out of the east and out of the north shall trouble him ["the king"]; therefore he shall go forth with great fury to destroy and utterly to make away [with] many (Dan. 11:44).

After "the king" of the end time has claimed the credit for the victory of the end of World War III and has "entered into Egypt also," already having stretched forth his hand "also" upon the countries, as recorded in Daniel 11:42, it is then that the above statement is made.

Who said that during the first three and a half years of the Tribulation period there would be peace? Some men have stated this, but not the written Word of God!

The only nation assured of even relative peace during that time is Israel, and that is by covenant with "the beast," the end-time king who shall break his seven-year covenant with them "in the midst of the week"—at the end of the first three and a half years.

Revelation 6:2 portrays "the king" as the rider upon the white horse who "had a bow; and a crown was given unto him: and he went forth conquering and to conquer."

Daniel 11:41 states that "many countries shall be overthrown," and after the statements about the conquest of Egypt, and the Ethiopians and Libyans, and after the statement concerning the tidings out of the east and out of the north, then it is stated that "he shall go forth with great fury to destroy and utterly to make away many."

Since there is no absolute statement that can be documented in this regard, the one I am about to make can only be considered an assumption, but in consideration of the facts that are documentable, I believe it to be fair and just.

Russia and China?

With five sixths of the Soviet armed forces destroyed, as specifically stated in Ezekiel 39:2, Russia's only recourse will be to turn all of its technical know-how, and such other resources as it may have remaining, over to Red China to secure a Communist control over as much territory as possible.

This shall most likely be the "tidings out of the east" that shall "trouble" the proud "head" of the revived Roman Empire— "the king" of the end time.

Correlation with the Visions

In his vision concerning the destiny of America, the very first Scripture reference which the evangelist heard proclaimed from heaven was a direct quotation as follows:

> . . . the eyes of the LORD run to and fro throughout the whole earth, to show himself strong in behalf of them whose heart is perfect toward him. Herein thou hast done foolishly: therefore, from henceforth, thou shalt have wars (2 Chron. 16:9).

In the latter part of George Washington's vision is the statement: "Then my eyes beheld a fearful scene." He proceeded to describe it as follows:

> From each of these continents [previously identified as Europe, Asia and Africa] arose thick black clouds that were soon joined into one. And through this mass there gleamed a dark red light by which I saw hordes of armed men. These men, moving with the cloud, marched by land and sailed by sea to America, which country was enveloped in the volume of the cloud. And I dimly saw these vast armies devastate the whole country and burn the villages, towns and cities which I had seen springing up . . . my ears listened to the thundering of the cannon, clashing of swords, and the shouts and cries of millions in mortal combat. . . .

The first statement concerning the dark clouds from the continents merging into one, and with a red light gleaming through the total mass, is an unmistakable indication of the thermonuclear exchange with the Soviets during the holocaust of World War III, being similar to the black skeleton-shaped

cloud which the evangelist saw and which was immediately
followed by the all-out rocket attack.

Ingredients for Anarchy

Nikolai Lenin, in 1905, wrote *Instructions to Revolutionaries*. The pattern is the same today. He said:

> Go to the youth. Form fighting squads everywhere of 3, 10, 30
> persons. Let them arm themselves at once as best they can, be it
> with a revolver, a knife, a rag soaked in kerosene to start fires. . . .
> Some may undertake to kill a spy or blow up a police station,
> others to raid a bank . . . for the insurrection.
> Let every group learn, if only by beating up a policeman; this will
> train hundreds of experienced fighters who tomorrow will be
> leading hundreds of thousands. . . .

In 1919, Allied Forces secured advanced copies of *Communist Rules For Revolution* at Dusseldorf, Germany. The
basic instructions were the same, summarized as follows:

> A. Get the youth corrupted, get them away from religion.
> Get them interested in sex . . . Destroy their ruggedness.
> B. Get control of all publicity. . . . Divide the people into hostile
> groups by constantly harping on controversial matters.
> Destroy the people's faith in their leaders.
> Always preach true democracy, but seize power as fast and as
> ruthlessly as possible.
> Encourage government extravagance. Destroy its credit.
> Incite unnecessary strikes and civil disobedience. . . .
> C. Cause the registration of firearms on some pretext, with the
> view to confiscate them and leaving the population helpless.

Activities of Revolutionaries

Revolutionaries preach democracy and freedom, but they
practice sedition and insurrection—and get paid handsomely

for it. This is proven by government records that from 1967 to 1969, Black Panther speakers (rated militant and potentially dangerous seditionists by the FBI) made more than five hundred appearances on college campuses and received fees as high as $4,000 per appearance.

Their effectiveness is evidenced by the following:

(July 16, 1970, *Los Angeles Times*) Washington—Alarmed senators were told Wednesday that college campuses were the targets of more than half of the 40,934 bombings, attempted bombings and bomb threats in the United States during a recent 15-month study period. . . . Nonstudents have been responsible for many campus bombings. . . .

(April 22, 1970, *Daily Breeze*, Torrance, Calif.) [Hemisphere Report by William Giandoni, Copley News Service] Havana–based Reds have started distributing what is described as a "Minimanual of the Urban Guerrilla." To judge by the digest of the 20,000-word booklet being circulated in the United States, Havana again is attempting to take the lead in popularizing the·latest in revolutionary tactics.

The "Minimanual" . . . amounts to a basic terrorism textbook. . . . The pamphlet affirms that terrorism "is an action the urban guerrilla must execute with the greatest cold-bloodedness, calmness and decision." And it suggests that students, particularly drop-outs who have little to do . . . make good terrorist recruits.

(November 23, 1970, *Newsweek*) Washington experts are impressed—and worried—by a 45-page booklet on building home-made explosives, compiled and published by the Black Panthers. They rate it the best guide for saboteurs ever prepared outside the Pentagon. Moreover, it has turned up in places as widely scattered as Berkeley, Calif., Houston, Texas and the Panama Canal Zone.*

(January 31, 1971, *Christian Crusade Weekly*) According to wire service reports, a New York City publishing firm disclosed that

*Copyright, Newsweek, Inc., 1970.

it is publishing a manual for revolutionaries which contains instructions ranging from assembling bombs to murder.

"The Anarchist Cookbook" . . . will be available to university bookshops. The author is William Powell, a student at Windham College, Putnam, Vt. He wrote in his foreword that his book will serve as a useful handbook for the silent majority. . . .

The truth is, of course, that it's not members of the silent majority that are blowing up ROTC buildings or plotting kidnappings of government officials. Despite his smoke screen, his book is intended for novice revolutionaries who may learn guerrilla warfare in a few easy lessons.

The book instructs in explosives, lethal gases, wiretapping, electronic jamming, use of guns and knives, garroting, and booby-trapping. . . .

(March 16, 1971, *Daily Breeze*, Torrance, Calif.) Washington (UPI)—A Senate subcommittee today released secret accounts telling how the White Panther Party allegedly used a rock band to lure young people into a common life of drugs and sex.

"The party's aim," two Michigan state police detectives said, "was to cause a Mao Tse-Tung style revolution in this country. . . ."

An Associated Press dispatch in my files states that "the White Panthers are an all-white organization whose stand is similar to that of the Black Panthers. There are chapters in several states."

Californians Arming Themselves

(July 17, 1970, *Los Angeles Times*) More Californians are arming themselves out of fear, distrust and hatred than at any time in this nation's history. A statewide survey by *The Times* reveals that:

—Militants on the political left as well as the right are stockpiling enough weapons to equip private armies, although no one knows for sure how many militants or how many weapons . . .

Fear over radicals and the high crime rate has compelled many to buy guns for the first time, not for sports purposes, but for protection. The sale of handguns through licensed dealers in California (alone) increased steadily from 81,709 in 1967 to a peak of 190,724 in 1968 . . . the rate is climbing up again in 1970. . . .

Revolution in the Making

Documentations of revolutionary and activist efforts abound, as any newspaper will reveal. Murder, arson, kidnappings, and rapes are reported constantly.

In Cuba, Fidel Castro is known to have forty-three camps where some 10,000 terrorists are being trained in guerrilla warfare, sabotage, and subversion. This was revealed in 1970 after extensive investigation by agents of the U.S. government.

In documenting these facts, it is not my intention to try to pinpoint the organizations or to show any vast cloak-and-dagger international intrigue—though it may very well exist. What I am seeking to convey is that the spirit of revolution and of anarchy (and the potential power for it) abounds in the United States.

It is stirred in the minds of the youth by seditious activists using the power of the pen as well as by example. One book used to instigate riotous and rebellious actions is *Do It*, written by Jerry Rubin, one of the Chicago Seven. A few of the final statements in that book:

DO IT

People want to be for, not against. We don't need an anti-war movement; we need an Amerikan Liberation Movement. . . . Amerika is trapped with its own contradictions. . . . The thousands of young people in Amerika beginning to ask "why" and finding out that their elders have no answers; they have only power and age. . . .

We've got Amerika on the run. We've combined youth, music, sex, drugs and rebellion with treason—and that's a combination hard to beat.

Life is theater and we are the guerrillas attacking the shrines of authority. . . . We must get middle-class Amerika all whipped up emotionally. . . .

Mr. Amerika. The War is at home.

The State Department will find its ranks infested with the yippies. . . .

High school students will seize radio, TV and newspaper offices across the land.

Police stations will blow up.

Revolutionaries will break into jails and free all prisoners.

Yippee helicopter pilots will bomb police positions with LSD-gas.

The Youth International Revolution will begin with mass breakdown of authority, mass rebellion, total anarchy in every institution in the Western World. . . .

Student Susceptibility

By radical teachers within and by revolutionary activists without, the students of the schools of America have been bombarded with thoughts of violence and rebellion. It has taken its toll in many areas as evidenced by the following:

(January 7, 1978, *Los Angeles Times*) Washington (UPI)—More than 5,000 teachers are attacked each month and 1,000 of them sustain injuries serious enough to require medical attention, a study by the National Institute of Education reports. . . .

Released by Secretary Joseph A. Califano of the Health, Education and Welfare Department, the study concluded:

—About 5,200 teachers are physically attacked in a month. . . .

--About 1.3% of all students — 282,000 — are attacked in a month. . . .

About 11% of secondary school children—2.4 million out of 21 million—have something stolen from them in a given month. . . .

—About 12% of all teachers—12,000—have something stolen in a given month. About 6,000 teachers have something taken by force, weapons or threats.

—More than one-fourth of all schools are subject to vandalism in a given month. . . . About 10% of the schools are burglarized each month, at an average cost of $183 per burglary.

"Schools that should be centers of teaching and learning basic skills and functional literacy have become centers of danger and violence for teachers and students," Califano said.

In checking the record close to home, I found that in the Los Angeles Unified School district, three hundred teachers were assaulted in the 1976-77 school year. According to cases on record, in the course of a year teachers face the possibility of being stabbed, raped, strangled, or robbed—mostly by students, but sometimes by off-campus intruders.

They may have their bones broken, their eyes blackened, their teeth knocked out, and their nerves shattered. They may be hit with anything from rocks, eggs, and books to Molotov cocktails, tear gas canisters, trash cans, and chairs. (So far, although there has been at least one reported attempt, no teacher has been shot or killed at school.)

Yes, many students are responding to the revolutionary agitation.

Tribulation in the Making

When you put all of these ingredients for anarchy together, realize that there is a common goal of them all—the forceful overthrow of all authority and of the government of the United States—add anger and malice, and then add an abundance of weapons and of guerrilla warfare training by subversives. When you subtract the factor of parental delinquency which has resulted in disregard and disrespect for parents because of lack of parental self-discipline and therefore of parental guidance—which has disrupted the American home heritage; subtract also faith in God, which infiltrated atheistic professors and teachers have tried their utmost to break down by teaching the *theory* of evolution as fact so that the youth of today consider themselves but educated animals; add alcoholism, dope addiction, gross homosexuality, and flagrant sex orgies, nudity, coeducational dorms, and love-ins; add the fear of thermonuclear obliteration and the frustrations of this pleasure-mad American "society" which drives itself half crazy with "speed," the "weed," and a mixture of witchcraft, satanism, and Babylonian zodiac astrology, and what do you get? Rebellion, revolution, frustration, suicide, and the "any-way-out" anarchy which can only lead to disruption and to a "do-it-yourself" kit of tribulation.

A Look Into the Future

The destiny of the United States is a part of the total destiny of all of the nations and peoples of the world. That which is happening in this country is happening, in one degree or another, in nearly every country on earth.

As of the present moment, the evil and subversive powers are being held in check by the greater strength of the spiritual power of the universal church.

The final events of the church age are transpiring at the moment of this writing. Spiritually, great evangelistic campaigns are taking place in the nations of the world. The press reveals almost nothing of the fact that multiplied millions of souls are being won to a saving knowledge of the atonement of Jesus Christ. Mass evangelism by gospel literature distribution (which reaches even into Russia and China and other non-Christian countries), gospel radio broadcasting (likewise reaching everywhere), gospel recording teams and linguistic missionary teams that are carrying the message of salvation to the last of "the uttermost" tribes, and spontaneous Holy Spirit revivals in Indonesia, South Korea, India, Congo, South Africa, and even the United States are resulting in untold numbers of conversions.

The church is getting ready to meet the Lord, for the next great event to happen is the translation of the church which is the body of Christ into the heavenlies. The Lord is going to remove the true Christians bodily from the face of the earth, and then the prophesied events of the closing years of sinful man's rule upon the earth will begin to be fulfilled.

Chaos in the Adjustment Period

The fact of the translation or "Rapture" of the church will bring about the first element of great change. Millions of people will suddenly disappear "in a moment, in the twinkling of an eye" (1 Cor. 15:52).

Of those who remain, there shall be many who will immediately be aware of what has happened. They shall mourn exceedingly, knowing that they have been left behind primarily because of their own neglect. They were just too busy or were too stubborn or proud to acknowledge that they needed the Lord as their Savior.

Others, who knew not of the prophecies, shall be bewildered and in great shock at the loss of loved ones because of what has happened.

In addition, a chaotic rubble will result as many of the Christians "caught up" shall be taken from positions of traffic control, industrial production control, and from all walks of life: many of them taken while driving their cars, or even while piloting aircraft—and accidents of all sorts will occur. Communications will be disrupted and broken in many areas, and police and fire control will also be affected greatly.

The revolutionary activists referred to earlier in this chapter will grasp the opportunity to cause further chaos and terror by looting, rioting, and disrupting governmental procedures wherever possible. Many insurgents are waiting for such conditions as shall prevail under those circumstances so that they can step in and take over by force whatever they can conceivably control. Murders, pillage, rape, and terrorist activities of all kinds shall certainly abound.

Reports of this type of turmoil in America and elsewhere will spur atheistic Russia to seek to cash in on the situation—"to think an evil thought" as Ezekiel prophesied, and thusly, "at the time of the end" (actually, "at the beginning of the time of the end")—to order its mighty military forces into action.

World War III

The Kremlin will order the planned onslaught: The combined Arab-U.S.S.R. thrust against the land of Israel synchronized with an all-out CBW and thermonuclear bombardment of the U.S.A.

All fulfillments of Bible and other authentic prophecies as to "the battle by fire" will take place.

America will retaliate against Russia with great and all-out fury.

One third of the sea and land areas of the earth will be involved in the great attack and counter-attack as the holocaust of World War III becomes reality.

Then shall come to pass the sayings of Joel and of Isaiah when they prophesied:

> . . . the flame hath burned all the trees of the field. The beasts of the field cry also unto thee: for the rivers of waters are dried up, and the fire hath devoured the pastures of the wilderness.
>
> . . . a great people and a strong; there hath not been ever the like . . . A fire devoureth before them, and behind them a flame burneth: the land is as the garden of Eden before them, and behind them a desolate wilderness . . . (Joel 1:19–2:3).
>
> Howl ye, for the day of the LORD is at hand; it shall come as a destruction from the Almighty. Therefore shall all hands be faint, and every man's heart shall melt: And they shall be afraid: pangs and sorrows shall take hold of them . . . they shall be amazed one at another; their faces shall be as flames (Isa. 13:6–8).
>
> Therefore hath the curse devoured the earth, and they that dwell therein are desolate: therefore, the inhabitants of the earth are burned, and few men left (Isa. 24:6).

After World War III

Desolation shall be great in America. As a major "super-power" involved in the immensity of the holocaust of World War III, this land shall feel much of the effects of the "whirlwind" prophecy of Jeremiah who proclaimed:

> Thus saith the LORD of hosts, Behold, evil shall go forth from nation to nation, and a great whirlwind [fire-storm] shall be raised up from the coasts of the earth.
>
> And the slain of the LORD shall be at that day from one end of the earth even unto the other end of the earth: they shall not be lamented, neither gathered, nor buried; they shall be dung upon the ground (Jer. 25:32,33).

The war, itself, will be all-out; and it shall last but one day, but the devastation shall defy description. So many shall die that those who remain shall be dazed, shocked, and desolate. And many more shall die from radioactivity exposure.

The Defense Department of the U.S. government has warned, from time to time, that America should be prepared for 150 megadeaths—150 million deaths in one day. It is small wonder then, that "they shall not be buried, but shall be as refuse left upon the ground."

Subsequently, survival shall be a first concern. The vast assault shall burn much of the food supplies, and they will be at a premium. The Bible proclaims that famine shall follow; and so shall, inevitably, "survival of the fittest."

Again, the reactionaries shall be bound to seek control. Remaining authorities shall more than have their hands full trying to maintain control and to prevent raids such as occurred in so many areas after the Civil War.

But "Mr. Amerika," to quote Jerry Rubin's term, shall not be the docile "Mr. Milquetoast" that he was before. Reality will be too stark, and liberty will be held too dear to give it all up without a struggle. It was not in vain that, even as the people of California armed themselves with hundreds of thousands of weapons, others across this nation did likewise. Note the following news item:

(August 17, 1970, *Newsweek*) The private arsenal in U.S. homes now totals 90 million weapons, according to an estimate by the FBI. Family gun racks in the 63 million U.S. households boast 35 million rifles and 31 million shotguns. Add to that 24 million hand guns. The small-arms inventory for the U.S. armed forces: 4.8 million guns.*

Whatever forces shall seek to gain control, they will find that "the people" of this nation, of whom it is written in Isaiah 18:2 and 7 that they are "terrible from their beginning hitherto," are still a force to be reckoned with.

A Foreign Invasion?

Whether America shall go through the experience of actual invasion by some foreign enemy we cannot be sure, for the Bible does not indicate either way. George Washington's vision, however, seems to imply that foreign armies shall, indeed, invade this land.

After giving his description of the great black cloud with its red gleam, note Washington's next statement:

I saw hordes of armed men. These men, moving with the cloud, marched by land and sailed by sea to America, which country was [already] enveloped in the cloud. And I dimly saw these vast armies devastate the whole country and burn the villages, towns and cities which I had seen springing up.

Whence and When?

Russia's navy shall most likely be destroyed in World War III, and China has no navy worthy of mention. Who then is to

*Copyright, Newsweek Inc., 1970.

invade this country? There is a clue given in the last statement of the "mysterious visitor" who revealed the vision unto Washington. Note:

> As my ears listened to the thundering of the cannon, clashing of swords, and the shouts of millions in mortal combat, I again heard the mysterious voice saying, "Son of the Republic, look and learn." When this voice had ceased, the dark shadowy angel placed his trumpet once more to his mouth, and blew a long and fearful blast.
>
> Instantly a light as of a thousand suns shone down from above me, and pierced and broke into fragments the dark cloud which enveloped America. At the same moment the angel upon whose head still shown the word "Union," and who bore our national flag in one hand and a sword in the other, descended from the heavens attended by legions of white spirits. These immediately joined the inhabitants of America, who I perceived were well-nigh overcome, but who immediately taking courage again, closed up their broken ranks and renewed the battle.
>
> Again, amid the fearful noise of the conflict I heard the mysterious voice saying, "Son of the Republic, look and learn." As the voice ceased, the shadowy angel for the last time dipped water from the ocean and sprinkled it upon America. Instantly the dark cloud rolled back, together with the armies it had brought, leaving the inhabitants of the land victorious . . .
>
> The scene instantly began to fade and dissolve, and I at last saw nothing but the rising, curling vapor I at first beheld. This also disappeared, and I found myself once more gazing upon the mysterious visitor, who, in the same voice I had heard before, said, "Son of the Republic, what you have just seen is thus interpreted. Three great perils will come upon the Republic. The most fearful for her is the third. But the whole world united shall not prevail against her. Let every child of the Republic learn to live for his God, his land and Union." With these words the vision vanished, and I started from my seat and felt that I had seen a vision wherein had been shown me the birth, the progress, and destiny of the United States.

Who is it that is to gain control of "the whole world," as such? Only the Antichrist, "the beast," the one referred to as "the king" of the end time shall have that dubious distinction, according to the Word of God.

O America! America!

Is this land to become a battleground whereupon the forces of evil shall fight for the spoils? As the deeply infiltrated communist elements seek to take over, and are being resisted by the patriots of America, will the satanic "king" of the revived Roman Empire area covet this land also?

Who is to help whom? And who is to fight against whom? The Scriptures do not tell. They are silent, as far as the Tribulation period history of America is concerned.

It is the vision that was revealed to the man who was to become the first President of the United States that gives to us the only detail available. In order to understand it properly, however, another factor must first be clarified; and then America's destiny can be defined.

The spiritual aspects of the Tribulation period must be discussed, because spiritual factors do enter into the end-time history of the United States.

Ministers of the Tribulation Period

It has been stipulated that, according to the Scriptures, a "great multitude" shall be "saved" during the Tribulation period.

Since it has also been stipulated that, according to the Scriptures, all true Christians are to be "caught up together in the clouds to meet the Lord in the air" before the seven-year Tribulation period begins, who, then, are to be the preachers of the gospel during that time?

The answer is specifically recorded in Revelation 7, 11, 13 and 14; all of these chapters must be taken into consideration to properly portray the matter. Other chapters are also relevant, but this must necessarily be a summary. Consider, therefore, the following statements, and verify them with your Bible.

A. God's Two Witnesses

In Jerusalem there shall appear two men, of whom it is written:

> And I will give power unto my two witnesses, and they shall prophesy a thousand two hundred and three score days [1,260 days], clothed in sackcloth (Rev. 11:3).
>
> And when they shall have finished their testimony, the beast that ascendeth out of the bottomless pit shall make war against them, and shall overcome them, and kill them.
>
> And their dead bodies shall lie in the street of that great city . . . where also our LORD was crucified [thusly, Jerusalem].
>
> And they . . . shall not suffer their dead bodies to be put in graves. And they that dwell upon the earth shall rejoice over them, and make merry, and shall send gifts one to another; because these two prophets tormented them that dwelt on the earth.
>
> And after three days and a half the spirit of life from God entered into them, and they stood upon their feet, and great fear fell upon them that saw them.
>
> And they heard a great voice from heaven saying unto them, Come up hither. And they ascended up to heaven in a cloud, and their enemies beheld them (Rev. 11:7–12).

This prophecy is self-explanatory. God's two special witnesses shall testify as did the prophets of old, and shall do so in Jerusalem for 1,260 days (three and a half years, at 360 days to the year, in accordance with the Hebrew calendar).

This must be, and can only be, during the first three and a half years of the Tribulation period. They shall be slain when "the king" breaks his covenant with Israel "in the midst of the week": when he demands that all people worship him, or die.

B. God's 144,000 Witnesses

While God's two special witnesses (generally believed to be Enoch and Elijah) conduct their witness and "testimony" in

Jerusalem, another special "sealed" group of men shall testify all over the world during the same time period. These men are on earth today, but they are not Christians, for in that instance they would be "caught up" with the others of us who are Christians when Christ comes for His own, the body of Christ. The men to be sealed for their protection during the holocaust of World War III, and for their ministry of service for God after that horrible war, are all to be Jewish men: 12,000 out of each of twelve specific tribes of the descendants of Jacob (Israel). The prophecy is as follows:

> And I saw another angel ascending from the east, having the seal of the living God; and he cried with a loud voice to the four angels, to whom it was given to hurt the earth and the sea. [This identifies them as the four angels who are to sound the first four trumpets, as recorded in Rev. 8:7-12, for the first four of the seven "trumpet judgments" are the ones which "hurt the earth and the sea."] Saying, Hurt not the earth, neither the sea, nor the trees, till we have sealed the servants of our God in their foreheads.
> And I heard the number of them which were sealed; and there were sealed a hundred and forty and four thousand of all the tribes of the children of Israel (Rev. 7:2-4).

In the next several verses it is specified that 12,000 were sealed from each of the tribes of Judah, Reuben, Gad, Asher, Naphtali, Manasseh, Simeon, Levi, Issachar, Zebulun, Joseph, and Benjamin. That these twelve particular names are used in this listing is highly significant and shows that the service is to be spiritual (for they are to be the preachers of the "gospel of the kingdom," which is the message that Christ specified would be "preached in all the world for a witness unto all nations; and then shall the end come," as recorded in Matt. 24:14), for the names of Ephraim and Dan are omitted, being replaced by Joseph (the spiritually faithful father of Ephraim) and by Levi (the father of the priestly tribe).

It is written in Hosea 4:17, "Ephraim is joined to idols, let him alone." Also, Israel, in his prophecy concerning his sons, stated:

"Dan shall be a serpent by the way, an adder in the path . . ." (Gen. 49:17).

When Jeroboam the Ephraimite rebelled against Rehoboam and set up the ten-tribe kingdom of Israel, the city of Bethel, which was originally a part of the territory of Benjamin, became a southern border citadel of Ephraim. It was at Bethel and at Dan, the southern and the northernmost strongholds of the new kingdom of Israel, that Jeroboam set up two golden calves for the apostate Israelites to worship as their gods so that they would not need to go to the great temple in Jerusalem to worship the true and living God; and it is recorded in 1 Kings 12:25–32 that "this thing became a sin." It was the first spiritually rebellious act of the Israelite kingdom and it showed that their course was set for an earthly kingdom apart from God. That seed of Zionism germinated into the International Zionism of today which seeks not after God, but seeks only an earthly "kingdom."

The followers after British-Israelism, which seeks ever to identify itself with the northern kingdom of Israel, would do well to read the notoriously vile and wicked history of that kingdom as recorded in 1 Kings 12:26 to 2 Kings 17:23. Of every king of northern Israel it was written, "And he did that which was evil in the sight of the Lord: he departed not from the sins of Jeroboam the son of Nebat [of Ephraim], who made Israel to sin." Many of their kings were murdered. There is no blood-line of the heirs thereof!

Since Jeroboam had set up the golden calves in Bethel of Ephraim and in Dan, "and caused Israel to sin," it is no wonder that the living God omitted representatives from Ephraim and Dan at the beginning of the end time when the 144,000 "servants of God" were sealed as His messengers to proclaim the gospel of the kingdom from the close of World War III until the time of their martyrdom "in the midst of the week" when the satanic "beast" of Revelation 13:1–6 was given power to make war with the saints "and to overcome them." These have a special reward in heaven. It is recorded in Revelation 14:1–5, where it is stated that they are very close to Jesus, for "they follow the Lamb whithersoever he goeth. These were re-deemed from among men [resurrected], being the first fruits [among many blood-washed and born-again ones] unto God and to the Lamb." Verses 2 and 3 specify that they are in heaven.

C. God's Preaching Angel

The deaths of the two witnesses, of the 144,000 of God's sealed servants, and of all saints who have been converted by them whom the satanic "beast" shall be able to slay at that moment shall bring to a close "the mystery of God" mentioned in Revelation 10:7. Additional clarification of the transition is given in Revelation 11:15 wherein it is stated that "The kingdoms of this world are become the kingdoms of our LORD, and of his Christ. . . ."

Immediately after the portrayal of the 144,000 being seen in heaven and the statement that "these were redeemed from among men, the firstfruits unto God and to the Lamb. And in their mouth was found no guile; for they are without fault before the throne of God," the very next verse tells of the angelic messenger and his message:

And I saw another angel fly in the midst of heaven, having the everlasting gospel to preach unto them that dwell on the earth, and to every nation, and kindred, and tongue, and people,
Saying with a loud voice, Fear God, and give glory to him; for the hour of his judgment is come, and worship him that made heaven, and earth, and the sea, and the fountains of waters (Rev. 14:6,7).

This preaching of the everlasting gospel by the angel of heaven shall continue throughout the last half of the Tribulation period. You may read the account in Revelation 14:6–13.

"The King" of the World

During the first three and a half years of the seven-year Tribulation period "the king" shall be going forth "conquering and to conquer"; and, hearing ominous news "out of the east and out of the north," as stated in Daniel 11:44, he shall redouble his efforts and shall "go forth with great fury to destroy, and utterly to make away many," apparently seeking to grasp "the whole world" before the Communists can reorganize and "take over."

This being the case, and also in consideration of the fact that he will probably anticipate that more people in America (who remain after the destructions of World War III) will be apt to respond to the preaching of the gospel of the kingdom which he shall hate exceedingly, for it shall be contrary to him, "the king" of the revived Roman Empire shall very likely "enter into" this country also for two reasons. He shall want to "liberate" it from the communistic radicals, and he shall also desire to have his forces in control as much as possible so that he can have them slay as many of the believers of the gospel of the kingdom as they can when his full power is "given unto him" by Satan at the "middle of the week"—after the first three and a half years of his dominion—when, according to the Scriptures,

> . . . power was given him over all kindreds, and tongues, and nations (Rev. 13:7).

American "Liberty" Falls

Liberty, as America has known it for 350 years, shall evidently come to its end at the very beginning of World War III.

The evangelist, in telling the account of his vision, stated:

> . . . They reached the Statue of Liberty [symbol of American liberty]. . . .
> As the white vapors began to spread around the head of the Statue, she took in but one gasping breath and then began to cough, as though to rid her lungs of the horrid vapors she had inhaled. One could tell readily by the painful coughing that those white vapors had seared her lungs. . . .

As I watched, the coughing grew worse . . . the Statue of Liberty was moaning and groaning. She was in mortal agony . . . then she fell to her knees. In a moment, she gave one final cough, made a last desperate effort to rise, and then fell face forward into the waters. . . . Tears ran down my face as I realized that she was dead!

Following this account of the death of Liberty came "the sound of sirens, sirens that seemed to scream "run for your lives," and he described the sight of vast multitudes falling in agonizing death on the sidewalks and in the streets of America.

If this vision is true, and there is no biblical reason to discount it, from the moment that the first strike of the all-out offensive begins, American liberty will "fall, and be no more," even as that prophecy from Jeremiah 25:27 was quoted in the early portion of the vision account.

The Course of Events

The immensity of the devastating effects of the all-out CBW and thermonuclear attack upon America will leave the remaining people in a state of great shock, confusion, and amazement. All will not be slain. In fact, the Bible specifically states that "power was given . . . over the fourth part of the earth, to kill with sword [warfare], and hunger, and with death [probably from CBW and radioactive fallout], and with the beasts of the earth" (Rev. 6:8). But three fourths will survive.

Those who remain shall be in a state of general fear, not knowing what is to come next. Unfortunately, there are within this country many revolutionary anarchists who are like packs of murderous animals lurking about, watching for the moment when the element of surprise will give them the opportunity to launch out in a "reign of terror" activity which can greatly disrupt "the establishment." Only God knows what manner of organized resistance will be possible. Civil controls will be at a minimum. Many of the conservative and the law-abiding citizens of America are Christians, and, before World War III begins, they will have disappeared, having been translated into heaven "to be with the Lord." But many non-Christian patriots will still remain, and they shall be both willing and ready to fight for their lives and for the cause of freedom. America will not die.

The White Panthers, the Black Panthers, the Students for a Democratic Society, the Red Guard, and any and all others may strike in various areas across this nation, but they will be met with staunch resistance.

The evangelist's portrayal of the aftermath of the great onslaught was by way of a quotation from Joel's prophecy:

> They shall run to and fro in the city; they shall run upon the wall, they shall climb up upon the houses; they shall enter in at the windows like a thief (Joel 2:9).

But the Bible's chapter concerning America contains this statement:

> They shall be left together . . . (Isa. 18:6).

Washington's vision tells of the invasion of armed forces. At just what point in time the invasion shall occur is not specified, except that it will be after the advent of the "dark cloud" which is to envelope this nation.

Considering the total correlation of the portrayal of the destiny of America, it is certain that dark days are ahead for this country. Mass destruction shall come first. Revolution, anarchy, and terror tactics shall follow. Invasion seems also destined to come upon the land. However, it is decreed that:

> The whole world united shall not prevail against her.

26

HOW TO SURVIVE WORLD WAR III

In order for a person to exist through the turmoils and the unforeseeable hardships of the Tribulation period, one must first live through the great devastations of World War III.

If you choose not to accept the extended invitation to believe in Jesus Christ as your own personal Redeemer and Savior, then this information and advice is for you.

A Guide to Survival

1. Move away from all strategic target areas. The Soviets will seek to knock out not only the missile sites, but also the strategic air bases and military areas. They will seek also to destroy all war-potential industries.

The strategic target listing of cities in Chapter three of this book was compiled in 1963, and, as stated, there may have been a few changes since that time. Also, the listing does not include reference to naval bases. These factors need to be taken into consideration in selecting any particular point of refuge.

Great Earthquake Prophesied

Since numerous Bible prophecies refer to a great earthquake in conjunction with the devastations of "the day of the Lord" at the very beginning of the seven-year "time of trouble," this author would personally suggest that it would be most advisable not to locate near any known earthquake fault, and especially not to live west of the San Andreas fault in California. Heavy concentrations of thermonuclear blasts on the West Coast due to the many strategic targets, such as army, navy and marine bases, and also many aircraft and electronic and other war-related industries located there could very easily knock off the entire West Coast shelf causing that area to sink below the sea (as has been repeatedly suggested and proclaimed by many "doomsday prophets").

2. Wherever you go, take a good supply of fresh drinking water with you in sealed containers, for radioactivity is bound to, and it is prophesied that it shall, contaminate "the rivers and fountains of waters."

3. Carry also, or stockpile, a quantity of canned goods and other food stuffs which can be protected from radioactivity.

4. If you want gasoline, store it. It will most likely not be available in most areas after "the battle by fire."

5. Dig in, or build, a heavily protected bomb shelter, and preferably one with a self-contained air filter. You may have to "button-up" for two to four weeks to allow dissipation of radioactive clouds which shall darken the skies over a large part of the earth. (The Bible predicts that one third of the skies shall be darkened.)

6. Be sure that you have adequate weapons and ammunition on hand, for marauding bands of insurgents may be anywhere (especially dangerous if food is scarce).

7. Take a copy of this book with you, and also a Bible. The now-trite statement, "there are no atheists in foxholes," will be even more true when the time comes which shall see the fulfillment of the following prophecy:

> And the kings of the earth, and the great men, and the rich men, and the chief captains, and the mighty men, and every bondman, and every free man, hid themselves in the dens and in the rocks of the mountains, and said to the mountains and rocks, Fall on us, and hide us from the face of him that sitteth upon the throne and from the wrath of the Lamb [of God]: for the great day of his wrath is come, and who shall be able to stand? (Rev. 6:15–17).

Between World War III and Armageddon

For the period of almost seven years between World War III and the final battle of this era of world history, the battle of Armageddon, the United States and most of the rest of the world will be in a state of constant terror, turmoil, and warfare.

Those who claim to be striving for peace are, many of them, deceivers. The others who strive for peace are the ones being deceived. Either way, peace shall be but an illusion.

The Bible does not predict peace at any time during the Tribulation period (except for Israel which shall have a "covenant" for peace, and even that shall be broken). The following prophecy shall definitely come to pass:

> For when they shall say, Peace and safety, then sudden destruction cometh upon them, as [surely as] travail upon a woman with child; and they shall not escape (1 Thess. 5:3).

Washington's America – Disassociated

> . . . my ears listened to . . . the shouts and cries of millions in mortal combat . . .

The combat, be it with rioting mobs, marauders, or with invasion armies from abroad, will be long and arduous. It shall be so severe that only heavenly help shall allow this nation to "remain together." The call for help comes when, as stated in Washington's vision:

> I again heard the mysterious voice saying, "Son of the Republic, look and learn." When this voice had ceased, the dark shadowy angel placed his trumpet once more to his mouth, and blew a long and fearful blast.
> Instantly a light as of a thousand suns shone down from above me, and pierced and broke into fragments the dark cloud which enveloped America. At the same moment the angel upon whose head shown the word "Union," and who bore our national flag in one hand

369

and a sword in the other, descended from the heavens attended by legions of white spirits. These immediately joined the inhabitants of America, who I perceived were well-nigh overcome, but who immediately taking courage again, closed up their broken ranks and renewed the battle.

Who or what the "legion of white spirits" are, I cannot tell; but they are most likely the angelic "white calvary" such as was seen by so many surrounding a portion of the allied forces during a decisive battle in World War I. The horrified Germans ceased their barrage and the result was that the German army was put to flight.

Regardless of the exact manner, it is indicated that America shall receive help when it is "well-nigh overcome," and that the renewed courage will enable them to close up "their broken ranks" and to press on in the valiant struggle against all aggressors.

Biblical Clarification
of Washington's Vision Account

The next to the last declaration of Washington's "history in advance" is:

Again, amid the fearful noise of the conflict I heard the mysterious voice saying, "Son of the Republic, look and learn." As the voice ceased, the shadowy angel for the last time dipped water from the ocean and sprinkled it upon America. Instantly the dark cloud rolled back, together with the armies it had brought, leaving the inhabitants of the land victorious.

It has been previously stipulated that Washington had seen "vast armies devastate the whole country," and that the inhabitants of the U.S. were "well-nigh overcome." They were strengthened by the "legion of white spirits" from heaven and they "renewed the battle," but even so: Why the "instant" retreat of the "vast armies"?

Noting that the events in question are obviously very close to the end of the Tribulation period, look to the Bible to see what is recorded therein as being specific Bible prophecy pertaining unto the corresponding time. You will find a very remarkable correlation here. It is to be found in Revelation 16, as follows:

> And I saw three unclean spirits like frogs come out of the mouth of the dragon [Satan], and out of the mouth of the beast [the Satanic "king" of the end time], and out of the mouth of the false prophet [the wicked priest who officiated at the worship of Satan and of the Wicked one of 2 Thess. 2:8–10].
>
> For they are the spirits of devils, working miracles, which go forth unto the kings of the earth and of the whole world, to gather them to the battle of that great day of God Almighty (Rev. 16:13,14).

Satan's Last Stand in This Era

The dragon . . . that old serpent, called the devil, and Satan (so described in Rev. 12:7–9 and in Rev. 20:2) will be aware that his allocated time to rule upon this earth, and to seek for human worship thereon, is running out. That time period was to be his "equal time" with the ministry of Jesus Christ. The contest was really "no contest," but Satan (who has many followers) was to be given his "chance" nevertheless. Jesus' earthly ministry lasted for three and a half years; and whether it be considered coincidental or a planned "equal time," it all amounts to the same—and even you may choose whom you will worship.

Regardless, the Scriptures state that Satan and his cohorts shall send forth "spirits of devils, working miracles . . . unto the kings of the earth and of the whole world, to gather them to the battle of that great day of God Almighty. . . . And he gathered them together into a place called in the Hebrew tongue Armageddon" (Rev. 16:14–16).

Satan's Previous Rebellion

Isaiah and Ezekiel both record the account of the fall of Satan (Lucifer) from heaven. He was known there as "the anointed cherub that covereth." But he wanted to be "above the most High [Almighty God]."

Thou wast perfect in thy ways from the day that thou wast created, til iniquity was found in thee. [Note that Lucifer was created. One of his pretenses is that he always existed, which is not true.]

By the multitude of thy merchandise [Hebrew *rekullah*— traffic, trade] they have filled the midst of thee with violence, and thou hast sinned: therefore I [God] will cast thee as profane out of the mountain of God: and I will destroy thee, O covering cherub from the midst of the stones of fire.

Thine heart was lifted up because of thy beauty, thou hast corrupted thy wisdom by reason of thy brightness: I will cast thee to the ground, I will lay thee before kings, that they may behold thee (Ezek. 28:15–17).

How art thou fallen from heaven, O Lucifer, son of the morning! how art thou cut down to the ground, which didst weaken the nations!

For thou hast said in thine heart, I will ascend into heaven, I will exalt my throne above the stars of God . . . I will ascend above the heights . . . I will be like the most High.

Yet thou shalt be brought down to hell, to the sides of the pit.

They that see thee shall narrowly look upon thee, and consider thee, saying, Is this the man that made the earth to tremble, that did shake kingdoms; That made the world as a wilderness, and destroyed the cities thereof . . . (Isa. 14:12–17).

The Call to Armageddon

It seems to be quite apparent that it shall be in response to the call of Satan's messengers that the "vast armies" on America's soil will "instantly" turn back, "leaving the inhabitants of the land victorious." Their trials and tribulations will be almost over, for as soon as Satan gathers all of the armies of the world, which shall be under his power, to the place called Armageddon in the great valley of Megiddo, just a few miles north of Jerusalem, Christ will return to this earth with all of his saints; and He will defeat Satan and "the king" and their false prophet, and shall slay all of the ones who have followed them. The full account of the results, as stipulated, is recorded in Revelation 19:11–20:3.

After the Battle of Armageddon

With the end-time king-despot and his false prophet cast into the lake of fire and brimstone, and with one of God's angels having chained up "the dragon, that old serpent, which is the Devil and Satan," Christ shall establish his millennial (one-thousand year) reign of true peace on earth, and He shall rule over this world from Mount Zion in Jerusalem.

Washington's America – Delivered

The inhabitants of America—relatively few in number though they may be by that time—will greatly rejoice; and they shall recognize the righteous victory and the righteous worldwide rule of the Lord Jesus Christ, the Lord of hosts.

The closing statement of the "history in advance" portion of Washington's vision is his proclamation:

> Then once more, I beheld the villages, towns and cities springing up where I had seen them before, while the bright angel, planting the azure standard he had brought in the midst of them, cried with a loud voice: "While the stars remain, and the heavens send down dew upon the earth, so long shall the Union last." And taking from his brow the crown on which blazened the word "Union" he placed it upon the standard while the people kneeling down said, "Amen."

The placing of the crown of the "Union" upon the azure blue (heavenly) standard, and the American people kneeling down and saying, "Amen," are both certainly symbolic of the recognition by "the people" of America of their obeisance and their homage to the Lord. They will know the source of their deliverance.

Washington's vision correlates with the Bible prophecy account, evidenced by the quotation of the last two verses of Isaiah 18, as follows:

> They shall be left together unto the fowls of the mountains, and to the beasts of the earth: and the fowls shall summer upon them, and all the beasts of the earth shall winter upon them.
>
> In that time [after the tribulation is concluded] shall the present be brought unto the LORD of hosts by a people scattered and peeled, and from a people terrible from their beginning hitherto, a nation meted out and trodden under foot, whose land the rivers have spoiled, to the place of the name of the LORD of hosts, the mount Zion (Isa. 18:6,7).

Yes, this nation shall continue to live. And it shall bring its presents annually to the Lord of hosts in recognition of and in appreciation of His deliverance. It is not possible to separate the spiritual from the factual occurrences in regards to the destiny of America, for the spiritual is the factual, and very often the factual is the spiritual. This is true concerning the future destiny, as depicted in the closing statements of both the Bible and the secular prophecies just as it was true concerning the beginning of this nation's history. The Mayflower Compact, signed by forty-one of the adult male members of the Pilgrims aboard that ship as it lay at anchor alongside the present site of Provincetown, Massachusetts, in 1620, had as its first statement: "In the name of God, Amen."

27

A FINAL SUMMARY

Evidence has been documented and set before you throughout the pages of this book. Facts have been presented which have proven the absolute accuracy of Bible prophecies, and of others, as being "history written in advance." A brief summary of the nature of those facts, predictions, and admonitions will be given in this concluding chapter.

1. America Did Not Just "Happen"

Isaiah, a prophet of the living God, wrote a description of the United States during the 8th century B.C. His descriptive writing prophesied both the existence of and the destiny of this nation.

Washington's vision at Valley Forge in 1777 correlates with the Bible prophecy recorded by Isaiah and with other Bible prophecies.

The vision of the American evangelist gives additional information, Bible quotations, and evidences which are in harmony with the other accounts.

2. America Plays a Vital Role

We are living in the climaxing years of the history of mankind. That America plays a vital role in this era is greatly evidenced by the many correlations of the Bible and secular prophecies and the related documentary news items.

3. History, Science, and Geography

History, science and geography all attest to the truth in this book.

4. Proofs of Bible Truth

The total text of this book is a monumental verification of the truth of biblical prophecy. Many prophecies have been proven to be true by recorded history and by current news documentations. Known facts have been presented, not just to prove the truth of the prophecies of the Bible, but to show their application to events that now are happening on the world scene. International events occurring now were recorded as specific Bible prophecies many centuries ago. It is amazing to see the manner in which the ancient writers of Scripture described factors that fit recent developments in scientific fields; and it is equally amazing to see the way they portrayed the precise alignments of the nations of this generation in the terminologies of their times—2,500 years ago.

5. Future Prophecy Also True

Considering the fact that so many specific Bible prophecies have already come to pass, and considering the fact that documented news articles contained in this book reveal the great potential for the fulfillment of so many other of the Bible's prophecies (especially in relation to the soon-coming "Battle by Fire" which we term World War III), it is incongruous to even consider any possibility that the other prophecies should not also come to pass. Not one prophecy of the Bible has ever failed to happen exactly as declared therein.

TODAY IN BIBLE PROPHECY

To keep America informed of the fulfillment of specific Bible prophecies related to the return of Christ, I needed to work at it full time. I resigned my pastorate and began speaking inter-denominationally in 1960, started my radio program in 1965, and established Today In Bible Prophecy, Inc. in 1967 (the same year that Israel reconquered Jerusalem). The first "To-day In Bible Prophecy" news bulletin was published in March 1966.

Bible Prophecy News now is mailed monthly around the world. It carries documented news and pictures from many sources, gives the moment-by-moment progress toward the culmination of the latest Bible prophecy factors, and serves as a soul-winning tool that many use to convince their loved ones that prophecy is being fulfilled and that Jesus *is* coming soon.

Television

In 1974 I began producing a television program called *Today in Bible Prophecy*. This Bible-related news commentary is produced at KTBN channel 40, Santa Ana, California, and can be received anywhere in North America including Hawaii. A TV log is included in *Bible Prophecy News*.

Books

Many people wanted more information concerning the Rapture of the church. Since many more prophecies had been fulfilled, a new book was needed. In *Get All Excited—Jesus Is Coming Soon* I compiled exciting documentations showing specific fulfillments. I gave Bible explanations concerning the Rapture and the second coming of Christ. I gave unusual documentations about the soon-to-be-revealed Antichrist. And I gave vital information relative to the anticipated time for the Lord's return. (108 pages, $1.95)

Written primarily for those who are left after the Rapture and after the holocaust of World War III, *Those Who Remain* documents U.S. contingency plans for survival in a post-nuclear society. Many plans have been formulated. This book tells also of plans of the Antichrist as portrayed in the Bible. It contains a chronology of Middle East events from 1882 to the present and documents recent developments leading to the time of climax. It tells how to escape the coming holocaust. (*1980 edition*, 106 pages, $2.95)

These two books can be obtained direct from Today In Bible Prophecy, Inc. Address below.

Cassette Series on Revelation

The most comprehensive study I ever produced was a series of 215 radio broadcasts on the chronological order of the Book of Revelation. In this series, I correlated Old Testament prophecies, the words of Christ recorded in the Gospels, the prophecies of Paul and the apostles, and the entire Book of Revelation. I placed all the prophesied events in precise chronological order, verifying every listing with cross references. This very detailed study now is available on 43 cassettes, 5 programs per cassette, 215 broadcasts. For the entire series, send a tax deductible contribution of $120 or more to Today In Bible Prophecy, Inc. (address listed below).

To receive the highly documented *Bible Prophecy News* each month, send a contribution of any amount to

Dr. Charles R. Taylor
Today In Bible Prophecy, Inc.
P.O. Box 2500
Orange, CA 92669